INTERNATIONAL SOCIALISM ★

A quarterly journal of socialist theory

Spring

GW00722601

Cont

Issue 70 of INTERNATIONAL SOCIALISM, quarterly journal of the Socialist Workers Party (Britain)

Published March 1996
Copyright © International Socialism
Distribution/subscriptions: International Socialism,
PO Box 82, London E3.
American distribution: B de Boer, 113 East Center St, Nutley,
New Jersey 07110.
Subscriptions and back copies: PO Box 16085, Chicago,
Illinois 60616
Editorial and production: 0171 538 1626/0171 538 0538
Sales and subscriptions: 0171 538 5821
American sales: 312 665 7337

ISBN 189 8876 169

Printed by BPC Wheatons Ltd, Exeter, England
Typeset by East End Offset, London E3

Cover design by Mark Bell

For details of back copies see the end pages of this book

Subscription rates for one year (four issues) are:

Britain and overseas (surface):	individual	£14.00 ($30)
	institutional	£25.00
Air speeded supplement:	North America	nil
	Europe/South America	£2.00
	elsewhere	£4.00

Note to contributors
The deadline for articles intended for issue 73 of
International Socialism is 1 May 1996.

All contributions should be double spaced with wide margins.
Please submit two copies. If you write your contribution
using a computer, please also supply a disk, together with
details of the computer and programme used.

INTERNATIONAL SOCIALISM ★

A quarterly journal of socialist theory

SOUTH AFRICA has abolished white rule, but can Nelson Mandela meet the aspirations raised by the end of apartheid? Alex Callinicos analyses the forces that brought victory and shows how they are colliding with the ANC led government's endorsement of the capitalist system. He argues that Mandela has already abandoned some of the promises on which he fought his country's first free elections and goes on to outline a strategy for the workers' movement and the left.

STRIKES, DEMONSTRATIONS and protests shook French society late last year. Chris Harman looks at the origins of the revolt against French prime minister Juppé's plan, the role of rank and file activists and the politics of the official Communist and Socialist leaders of the movement. He examines the parallels with 1968 and the prospects for future struggles.

BLACK PANTHER Huey Newton's life is both an inspiration to socialists and a lesson that taking on the state without a clear strategy is a dangerous game, as Brian Richardson's review of Newton's autobiography shows. A more successful course is charted by Lenin's struggle to build a revolutionary party, as Adrian Budd's book review demonstrates.

KINGSLEY AMIS' very different life ended last year. Gareth Jenkins cuts through plaudits Amis' novels received and provides a critical view of his work.

CLASS STRUGGLE has never been far from the surface of British history and its full breadth is represented in our book reviews. Lee Humber reviews a new collection of essays on the English Revolution, Mark O'Brien reviews a classic history of the rise of the British working class, and Martin Smith's *Bookwatch* celebrates the 70th anniversary of the General Strike.

Editor: John Rees. Assistant Editors: Alex Callinicos, Chris Harman, John Molyneux, Lindsey German, Gill Hubbard, Colin Sparks, Mike Gonzalez, Peter Morgan, Ruth Brown, Mike Haynes, Judy Cox, Adrian Budd, Ian Goodyer, Mark O'Brien and Rob Hoveman.

South Africa after apartheid

ALEX CALLINICOS

Amid the cynicism and torpor that descended over the globe after it turned out that 1989 had not, after all, ushered in a new world order, South Africa's first democratic elections in April 1994 shone out like a beacon. In an era when politicians were generally held in profound contempt, the new State President, Nelson Mandela, towered like a colossus. Here at least there was a story that seemed to have a happy ending, as the new 'rainbow nation' stepped proudly into the future.

The sweeping victory secured by the African National Congress (ANC) in the elections after all marked the climax of a struggle that had been going on since before the movement's foundation in 1912. It was a struggle for which Mandela had spent 27 years in prison, a struggle that had been revived by the great Soweto school students' rising of 16 June 1976, a struggle that, above all, had been taken to even greater heights by the township insurrections and workers' strikes of 1984-1986. Around the world millions had identified with the cause of the black majority in South Africa, had supported it by taking part in demonstrations and consumer boycotts, and now felt the ANC's triumph as theirs as well. Apartheid, the barbarous system of racial domination that had made South Africa (in the words of one of its own diplomats) 'a polecat among nations', was finally gone.

It will soon be two years since that historic victory. How well has the ANC led Government of National Unity (GNU) fulfilled the hopes raised by its entry to office? Commentators typically approach this question by launching a sort of pre-emptive strike. They talk about the problem of 'expectations'. By this they mean that the black people who voted for the ANC in April 1994 did so in the belief that the political transformation represented by black majority rule would rapidly usher in a social and economic transformation as well. Having won the vote, they expected from an ANC dominated government jobs, houses, and schools as well. But—say the commentators—these expectations are 'unrealistic'. The GNU, like governments everywhere, has to worry about enhancing competitiveness and reducing public spending. The masses' hopes for a rapid improvement in their material conditions will have to be deferred, perhaps indefinitely.

If this argument is correct, it predicts a bleak future for South Africa. In 1990 42 percent of the population lived in poverty.[1] In 1991 South Africa had a Gini co-efficient, which measures the extent of income inequality, of 0.68, the highest in a group of 36 developing countries. That same year the poorest 40 percent of households earned 4 percent of national income, while the richest 10 percent received more than half.[2] In 1995 unemployment among Africans was calculated to be 37 percent— almost certainly an underestimate.[3]

The appalling economic plight of the black majority was summed up recently by the Socialist Workers Organisation of South Africa:

● *Only one out of five African households have running water BUT every white household has running water.*
● *One quarter of all African households get less than R300 a month. Two thirds get less than the breadline—R900 a month. BUT two thirds of white households get more than R2000 a month.*
● *Two thirds of African children and half of Coloured children live in overcrowded houses BUT only 1 out of 100 white children live in overcrowded conditions.*
● *Less than half of African kids live in a proper brick house. The rest live in shacks or huts BUT most white children live in a brick house.*[4]

Leaving in place such poverty and inequality would help to perpetuate the desperation and misery that have produced levels of violence, both political and criminal, making South Africa one of the most dangerous societies in the world. It would also, over time, undermine the political achievements of the ANC led mass movement. To see whether such a grim outcome is inevitable we need, in the first instance, to consider the process that brought about the triumph of April 1994 in the first place.

The path to power

The elections of 26-29 April 1994 were the outcome of a strategic compromise between the two main political actors in South Africa—on the one hand, the African National Congress as the dominant force among the black majority and the embodiment of their aspiration for national liberation; on the other hand, the National Party (NP), the historic party of Afrikaner nationalism, in power since 1948, responsible for turning apartheid into a system, but now pursuing 'reform' in close alliance with big business. [5]

That compromise was embodied in the Interim Constitution finally agreed on at the Multi-Party Negotiating Forum in November 1993. This provided the basis on which the country's first one person, one vote elections were held the following April. Under the settlement, South Africa was to become a non-racial liberal democracy, subject to certain limitations. The most important of these was that during the five year transition period in which the new National Assembly would draft a final constitution a coalition government representing all the parties that won at least 5 percent of the vote would hold office. It is by virtue of this provision that the GNU comprises not merely the ANC, but also the NP, and the Zulu tribalist Inkatha Freedom Party (IFP).

The rationale for this compromise settlement reflected both sides' assessment of the balance of forces, and in particular their shared belief that neither could decisively defeat the other. The risings of 1984-1986—and the persisting strength shown by the black organised working class during the State of Emergency which brought the insurgency to an end—convinced key figures in the regime that they would have to negotiate with the ANC. After becoming State President in August 1989, the new NP leader, F W de Klerk, made the decisive move in February 1990 of unbanning the ANC, the South African Communist Party (SACP) and the Pan-Africanist Congress (PAC), and freeing Mandela, as a prelude to full scale talks.

In the meantime, many township and union activists had concluded after the defeat of the mid-1980s rebellion that the regime could be removed, not by mass insurrection, but by a negotiated settlement. This had always been the long term objective of the exiled ANC leadership in the Zambian capital of Lusaka. Now the conditions were emerging in which this goal could realistically be pursued. But it is clear that the decisive initiative in making contact with the regime was undertaken independently by Mandela himself in Pollsmoor prison.

After an initial meeting with justice minister Kobie Coetsee during a spell in hospital in November 1985, Mandela was separated from his fellow ANC prisoners on his return to gaol. He later recalled:

Immediately in my mind I said: 'Well, this would be a good opportunity to start negotiations with the government and to maintain this element of secrecy.' If you are a member of an organisation and your comrades say: 'Don't do this,' whatever your views are, that you have to accept, and that is what I feared. I wanted to confront them [the ANC] *with a fait accompli.*[6]

While still nominally a prisoner of the South African state, and ignoring the initial objections of the ANC leadership, Mandela held a total of 47 meetings with a secret committee set up by Coetsee on the instructions of State President P W Botha. Despite the ground that had thus already been covered by February 1990, the path to a negotiated settlement proved tortuous and very bloody.[7]

The fundamental reason for this lay in the strategy pursued by de Klerk and the NP. It soon became clear that they were not negotiating in good faith. Their aim was, while conceding the formal principles of liberal democracy, to preserve the substance of white economic and political power. Initially, the regime harboured vain hopes of splitting Mandela off from what they believed to be the Communist dominated ANC in exile.

Then it sought to create an electoral alliance between the NP and conservative black organisations, above all Inkatha. All out warfare between ANC and IFP supporters, which had first developed in the townships and squatter settlements of Natal after the 1984-1986 risings, spread to the Pretoria-Witwatersrand-Vereeniging (PWV) region, the industrial and political heart of South Africa centred on Johannesburg, in July-August 1990. Overwhelming evidence rapidly accumulated of the role of a 'third force', backed by the security forces and allied to Inkatha, in stoking up the violence. The effect was to disorganise the ANC's popular base and force it onto the defensive.

To counter this attack the ANC leadership found itself compelled to turn to the masses. After a particularly revolting IFP massacre in the Vaal township of Boipatong in June 1992, the movement returned to the streets. The ANC and its allies in the Congress of South African Trade Unions (COSATU) had already launched a Mass Action Campaign after the collapse of the first attempt at formal all party talks, the Convention for a Democratic South Africa (CODESA), in May. Cyril Ramaphosa, secretary general of the ANC and the movement's chief negotiator, explained: 'We needed to put the entire struggle on a completely different plane, and that plane had to be resorting back to the major power that we had, which was our people.'[8] On 3-4 August some 4 million workers took part in a massive political general strike. After this demonstration of mass determination the NP could harbour no illusions about the extent and the depth of the ANC's popular support.

For Mandela and Ramaphosa, however, the Mass Action Campaign was only a brief detour from the negotiating table, a means of showing the regime how strong the ANC's hand was, and a way of allowing their increasingly angry and impatient supporters to let off a bit of steam. The 'Leipzig Option'—the strategy supported by some ANC and SACP leaders of using mass demonstrations to bring down de Klerk—was discredited after one of its main proponents, Ronnie Kasrils, was widely believed to have rashly led marchers into a massacre by soldiers of the Ciskei Bantustan at Bisho in September 1992.[9]

The same month saw a public resumption of contacts between the ANC and the NP (private discussions between Ramaphosa and his government counterpart Roelf Meyer continued throughout the Mass Action Campaign). But in order to secure a summit with Mandela that would agree the basis for carrying on with the negotiations, de Klerk had to make a symbolically crucial concession concerning the release of political prisoners. For Ramaphosa, that 'without a doubt was the turning point of the whole negotiating process.'[10] The ANC subsequently made its own major concession when Joe Slovo, chairperson of the SACP, persuaded it to accept the principle of 'sunset clauses', ie temporary departures from strict democratic principles such as a transitional coalition government that would help to overcome white fears of majority rule.[11]

The final settlement was, however, considerably more favourable to the ANC than de Klerk and his advisers had hoped. This outcome, however, did not derive chiefly from the negotiating skills of Mandela, Ramaphosa and Slovo. Once again it was a consequence of the intervention of the masses. In April 1993 a white fascist assassinated Chris Hani, general secretary of the SACP and one of the most popular ANC leaders. There followed a spontaneous explosion of popular anger. Two stayaways (political general strikes) and numerous demonstrations showed, not only that the black masses overwhelmingly backed the ANC, but that they might escape from anyone's control. The abyss was opening up before the regime. Mandela, not State President de Klerk, appeared on television to call for calm. Patti Waldmeir of the *Financial Times* argued that the assassination and the reaction had the effect of 'permanently tilting the balance in the ANC's favour and allowing them to extract the concession that elections would be held on April 27 [1994]'.[12]

There was, however, one final stage in the transition to democracy where the masses played a decisive role. The political realignment in 1992-1993 drew the ANC and the NP together, and left the IFP relatively isolated (although there is plenty of evidence of security force complicity in the violence that continued to rage in the townships and squatter camps of Natal and the East Rand almost up to election day itself). Inkatha's leader, Chief Mangosuthu Buthelezi, Chief Minister of the

KwaZulu Homeland, therefore threw his lot in with various other political forces threatened by the end of apartheid. These included principally the white far right. The angry black reaction to Hani's assassination terrified many whites, and rallied together right wing opponents of de Klerk's policy in the Afrikaner Volksfront (AVF), under the leadership of General Constand Viljoen, ex-Chief of the South African Defence Force (SADF).

The Freedom Alliance, a strange coalition of Afrikaner and African ultra-conservatives, now took shape. Aside from the AVF and the IFP, the principal backers of the Freedom Alliance were the rulers of two 'independent' Bantustans, the Ciskei and Bophuthatswana. Combined with Buthelezi's control of KwaZulu and of parts of Natal, this gave the opponents of the settlement an extensive territorial grip, and therefore the capacity substantially to disrupt the elections, which the Freedom Alliance threatened to boycott. Viljoen claimed to be training up a formidable military force, and could certainly count on plenty of sympathy in the ranks of the SADF.

The ANC responded to the far right threat, and the escalation of violence as the elections drew near, by offering Viljoen, Buthelezi and their cronies significant constitutional concessions. The Johannesburg *Weekly Mail and Guardian* argued that these actually worked to de Klerk's benefit. 'For the first time the NP will be able to claim some "victories" at the negotiating table', the newspaper commented.[13] It is hard to say how far this surrender to right wing blackmail would have gone had not the masses intervened.

At the beginning of March 1994 student demonstrations and workers' strikes paralysed Bophuthatswana. As his police started to mutiny and join the rising, the Homeland's president, Lucas Mangope, appealed to his Freedom Alliance partner, Viljoen, for help. The general responded by sending thousands of AVF 'farmers' to Bophuthatswana. What had been intended as a disciplined military operation disintegrated into chaos as the thugs of the fascist Afrikaner Weerstandsbeweging (AWB) joined the expedition, apparently against the wishes of Viljoen and Mangope. But they soon discovered they had chosen the wrong century. The glory days of the Boer republics were over, and their would be heirs were confronting blacks ready and able to fight and win.

Bophuthatswana soldiers refused to supply the AVF with the weapons Mangope had promised them, and threatened to attack the right wingers. The AWB were persuaded to pull out of the Homeland, and were followed slightly later by the AVF force. As they drove in convoys through its capital, Mmabatho, the fascists fired indiscriminately at people in the streets. At a roadblock three AWB men got involved in a shoot out with rebel soldiers and policemen. That night the world saw on television their last moments, as the fascists begged ineffectually for their lives. In a few minutes a giant shadow that hovered threateningly over South Africa's transition to democracy since the late 1980s—the white far right—was dispersed.

The effects of the Bophuthatswana rising were enormous. Mangope was toppled, and Bophuthatswana was reincorporated into South Africa.[14] Within a few days the Ciskei's military dictator, Oupa Gqozo, and his Bantustan had suffered the same fate. Viljoen, already uncomfortable with the more unsavoury or demented of his right wing allies—the Nazis of the AWB and the pro-apartheid no hopers of the Conservative Party—used the pretext of the debacle to break with the AVF and launch the Freedom Front to represent the cause of traditional Afrikaner nationalism in the elections. Buthelezi now found himself isolated. Outmanoeuvred by the ANC, who were able to draw into their camp the Zulu King Goodwill Zwelithini—long impatient with his uncle and prime minister's tutelage, Buthelezi grudgingly agreed to end his boycott only a week before the elections.

The historic achievement of the April 1994 elections was thus a consequence less of the skill and determination of the ANC leadership (though no one could deny that they had plenty of both), than of mass struggle. It was the risings of the mid-1980s, and what they represented—not merely the incredible courage and *elan* of the township youth, but the strength and endurance of organised black labour—that had forced de Klerk to the negotiating table in the first place. But even after the great breakthrough of February 1990, further mass action, sometimes orchestrated from the top, more often a result of initiatives from below, was necessary first to strengthen the ANC's bargaining hand and then to knock out the far right. Mandela's words to the people as voting began on 26 April were truer than he perhaps knew: 'This is your day.'

Talk of the 'problem of expectations' needs to be considered in this light. The oppressed and exploited—workers, students, unemployed, township and squatter camp dwellers—had won the great victory over apartheid. Whenever they were asked, they made it clear that they had been fighting for more than new laws and a new constitution. They had fought to change their lives dramatically for the better. Often they were prepared to put it in more theoretical terms by saying that they were fighting for socialism as well as national liberation. This was one reason why the red banners of the Communist Party had such a powerful attraction for the more militant workers and youth.

These aspirations deserve better than to be patronised by journalists and ex-Marxist academics who dismiss them as fantasies spun by those who fail to understand the 'realities' of the global market and of the kind of voodoo economics promoted by the International Monetary Fund and the World Bank. It was the black masses who put Mandela in his official residence at Tuynhuys, all his ministers in their offices and limousines, the members of parliament and of provincial assemblies in their seats. Their 'expectations' of a *total* liberation should serve as the benchmark by which the 'New South Africa' is judged.

From mass struggle to reformism

Yet even before the ANC took office in May 1994 it was already clear that it would introduce only limited changes in the social and economic structure of South Africa. The ANC and its close partner in the struggle, the SACP, had long been committed to what came to be known as the two stage strategy. Derived ultimately from Stalinist orthodoxy, this sharply separated the struggle against apartheid from that against capitalism. Its political conclusion was: first win national liberation by means of a broad democratic alliance of all classes of the oppressed population plus anti-apartheid whites; only once that has been achieved should the question of socialism come onto the agenda.[15]

The radicalisation produced by the risings of the mid-1980s and the development of a militant workers' movement made it harder in practice to keep the two stages separate from one another. Militant workers and youth were, as I have already pointed out, fighting for both national liberation and socialism. In the late 1980s the SACP tended to stress a 'left' version of the stages strategy which envisaged an 'uninterrupted' process in which the struggle against apartheid would imperceptibly merge into that for socialism.[16] The increasingly imminent prospect after February 1990 of a transfer of political power to the black majority should have made the question of what would happen once national liberation was achieved more pressing.

Yet in fact the closer the end of apartheid approached, the further the objective of socialism receded in the minds of the leaders of the Revolutionary Alliance uniting the ANC, SACP and COSATU. In part this was a consequence of the international political and ideological conjuncture. Stalinism in some form or other tended to form the horizons of the South African left, playing a crucial role in defining its conception of socialism, and offering a picture of the world divided into two blocs, the 'progressive' one united behind the Soviet Union and the imperialist one led by the United States.[17] The revolutions in Eastern Europe and the subsequent disintegration of the USSR therefore threw the left into disarray. Joe Slovo succeeded in skilfully distancing the SACP from the debacle in the East by issuing a celebrated pamphlet called *Has Socialism Failed?* in which he denounced the crimes of Stalinism, but this still left unanswered the question of what should replace the party's—and more generally the South African left's—now discredited model of socialism.[18]

The answer, nevertheless, soon became clear—social democracy. The SACP avoided explicitly embracing reformism (it preferred to call itself 'the Party of Democratic Socialism'), but Slovo in particular moved very quickly to reassure big business that the Revolutionary Alliance did not intend to introduce a planned economy. 'Socialism and the market are not, as its commonly supposed, opposed to each other in principle,' he told the Board of Directors of Woolworths. 'The market is a mechanism for the realisation of value, there is nothing inherently capitalistic about it.'[19]

Slovo's stance reflected a more general shift in the left's stance. Thus in response to right wing attacks on the clause in the ANC's Freedom Charter calling for 'nationalisation of monopoly industry', Alec Erwin, a leading COSATU intellectual and a key figure in the 'workerist' left wing of the South African labour movement, wrote: 'The issue is not one of state versus private ownership. It is whether we restructure our economy so as to minimise unemployment and poverty and maximise the supply of social consumption infrastructure.'[20]

This restructuring, it was generally agreed, would involve a mixed economy combining the market and planning, and would depend on winning the consent of big capital. The 'Great Economic Debate' launched by the left-liberal *Weekly Mail* carried, for example, a special supplement called 'Focus on Social Democracy', with articles such as one entitled 'Still Lots to Learn From Scandinavia'.[21] Bizarrely, the prosperous liberal democracies of northern Europe (themselves increasingly entering a serious crisis) thus became the model for a society with 40 percent unemployment.[22]

In the unions and the left there was increasing support for the concept of a social contract uniting the state, labour and capital around an agreed programme in which the unions would offer wage restraint in exchange for an economic strategy intended to reduce poverty and unemployment. To some extent this idea merely registered existing reality. The strength and militancy shown by the union movement during the Emergency of the late 1980s had even before February 1990 prompted both big business and the regime to move away from a merely repressive response towards one based on institutionalised bargaining between the government and the main forces in 'civil society', above all capital and labour.

The 'Laboria Minute' of September 1990, which laid out a framework for the reform of the trade union laws, represented the first fruit of this reorientation. COSATU followed this up by deciding to participate in the state's National Manpower Commission and, when mounting a general strike in November 1991 to protest at the de Klerk government's imposition of VAT, called for the establishment of a 'macro-economic negotiating forum'. Derek Keys, de Klerk's finance minister, responded to the extent of setting up, in November 1992, the National Economic Forum, on which both the unions and big business were represented. The development of West German style social bargaining was formalised with the establishment in February 1995 of the National Economic Development and Labour Council (NEDLAC), whose role was to be that of achieving a consensus between government, employers, unions, and community organisations over various economic and social issues.[23]

This shift towards social democracy was intended by its authors as a means of achieving some genuine social and economic change in favour of the black masses. COSATU's economic advisers contrasted two 'accumulation strategies'. The first, sometimes summed up by the slogan, 'Redistribution through growth', represented the liberal economic orthodoxy accepted by the NP and its big business allies. This involved a reduction in the economic role of the state (very substantial in South Africa) and extensive privatisation as part of a more general process of restructuring designed to make the country's manufacturing industries internationally competitive. The economic growth generated by more exports would benefit the black majority by increasing employment and therefore incomes.

To this approach—whose solution to the problem of black poverty was essentially a version of Ronald Reagan's notorious trickledown effect—the COSATU economists counterposed the alternative of 'Growth through Redistribution'. This would seek, in Stephen Gelb's words, 'to expand both employment creation and the production of basic consumer goods. In other words, rather than separating redistribution and economic growth, the aim would be to achieve growth through the more extensive and more rapid redistribution of incomes and wealth.' This objective would, however, be achieved not through 'a direct redistribution of incomes', but rather through 'the redistribution of *investment*'. Capital could, for example, be transferred from speculation in financial markets to the development of 'labour-intensive light industries' producing cheap consumer goods, or 'the expansion of infrastructural services, such as electricity and telephones, to the black townships in particular'.[24]

The result of implementing this strategy would not be a socialist economy, but rather a new 'accumulation regime'—a version of capitalism in which the black majority would have more jobs, better living standards, and therefore greater economic and political power.[25] There were, however, those who argued that 'Growth through Redistribution' and the broader approach of which it was part could act as a means of achieving socialism.

Thus the Canadian socialist John Saul defended against far left critics such as myself the strategy being pursued by the ANC and its allies as the pursuit of 'structural reforms'. The latter concept was devised in the 1960s by the well known French centrist André Gorz in order to identify an alternative to both social democratic reformism and what Saul calls 'any very precipitate plunge into full blown social revolution'. 'Structural' reforms are distinguished from ordinary reforms by being part of 'an emerging project of structural transformation' and basing themselves on 'popular initiatives in such a way as to leave a residue of further *empowerment*—in terms of growing enlightenment/class consciousness, in terms of organisational capacity—for the vast mass of the population, who thus strengthen themselves for further struggles and further victories'.[26]

Saul defended his position with a lot of noise and bluster, widening it into a 'revolutionary reformism' for which he claimed (rather unwisely in my view) the inspiration of the writings of the Russian socialist Boris Kagarlitsky.[27] Nevertheless, his argument does have the merit of providing a criterion, offered by one of the ANC's left supporters, by means of which to appraise its achievements to date in office. To what extent has South Africa's new government advanced a 'project of structural transformation' and led to greater mass 'empowerment'?

The test of office

The ANC finally crossed the portals of state power in May 1994. It could claim a popular mandate arising from its overwhelming electoral victory (see Table 1). Thanks to this triumph, it not only had a large majority in the National Assembly, but controlled seven of the nine provincial governments set up under the new constitution.

TABLE 1:
Results of the Elections of 26-29 April 1994

Party	Percentage of Vote	Seats
African National Congress	62.5	252
National Party	20.39	82
Inkatha Freedom Party	10.54	43
Freedom Front	2.17	9
Democratic Party	1.73	7
Pan-Africanist Congress	1.25	5
African Christian Democratic Party	0.45	2

[Source: A. Reynolds, (ed), **Elections '94 South Africa** (London, 1994)]

The ANC had campaigned on the Reconstruction and Development Programme (RDP), which set out a number of specific policy objectives intended to advance both 'social upliftment' and 'economic development' over the following five years. These included:

- building one million houses;
- creating 300,000 to 500,000 non-farm jobs a year;
- redistributing 30 percent of agricultural land;
- providing clean drinking water for the 12 million people currently denied access to it;
- introducing adequate sanitation for the 21 million people without it;
- supplying electricity to 19,000 black schools, 4,000 clinics, and two thirds of homes, all then without it;
- redressing the imbalance in access to telephone lines—one line for 100 blacks, 60 for 100 whites;
- a ten year transition to compulsory schooling;
- class sizes to be no more than 40 by the year 2000.

Here then was an ambitious programme of detailed demands that marked a definite commitment to 'Growth through Redistribution'. Yet the ANC did not have a free hand in implementing the RDP. The constraints to which it was subject in part were a consequence of the settlement it had negotiated with the representatives of the old order. Under the Interim Constitution, they sat in the new Government of National Unity.

The NP had been remarkably successful in winning one in five votes, and had managed to extend its constituency to include some blacks (notably in the Western Cape, where the Nationalists cynically played on Coloured fears of African domination to win control of the province). It was anyone's guess how people had really voted in strife torn KwaZulu/Natal, but in a post-election deal over the disputed returns the ANC conceded the IFP 50 percent of the vote there, thereby also giving it control of the provincial government and a substantial block of seats in the National Assembly.

And so F W de Klerk was appointed Second Deputy President, and Mangosuthu Buthelezi Minister of Home Affairs, while other members of their parties held cabinet posts.

But the ANC leadership were far more fundamentally constrained by the logic of the strategy they had adopted. The social democratic orientation adopted by the Revolutionary Alliance implied a commitment to working with, rather than confronting, let alone expropriating, capital. Mandela, Slovo and their comrades had worked hard to reassure big business that they could be trusted with political power. Their efforts were rewarded with success. A poll of 100 top business leaders published in December 1993 revealed that 68 percent wanted to see Mandela as president, 32 percent de Klerk, and none Buthelezi. [28]

This process of reassurance continued once the elections were over. The new government had to show its reliability in deeds as well as words. Only thus could local capitalists be encouraged to keep their money in the country, and foreign ones be persuaded to invest there. Mandela retained as his finance minister Derek Keys, the 'apolitical' businessman whom de Klerk had appointed to this post. The *Financial Times* reported that Mandela had made this decision 'despite opposition from within his own African National Congress', and that in doing so he had:

> *delighted investors, businessmen and white South Africans... Nothing else would have persuaded the outside world—not to mention sceptical South Africans—of his commitment to free-market economics and political moderation. Again and again, Mr Mandela has stressed the need to restore business confidence and attract foreign investment. Yesterday he took the most concrete steps possible towards achieving those goals.* [29]

Keys soon left the government for personal reasons, to be replaced by the equally conservative white banker Chris Liebenberg. It might seem as if these appointments were counterbalanced by those of two left wing ex-trade unionists to two other key economic ministerial positions. Jay Naidoo, former general secretary of COSATU, became Minister in the State President's Office with responsibility for the RDP, while Alec Erwin took the post of Keys's and later Liebenberg's deputy. It soon turned out, however, that they were not serving as red commissars keeping a watchful eye on the capitalist Minister of Finance.

Barely two months after the GNU took office, Patti Waldmeir of the *Financial Times* could write, 'With his well-cut suits and carefully tailored vocabulary, the new-look Mr Naidoo...is a figure of flawless economic orthodoxy. The firebrand trade unionist and militant socialist has become a persuasive advocate of fiscal and financial discipline.' As for Erwin:

> *to hear Mr Erwin...defend the need for discipline—with a fervour and passion few orthodox economists could equal—is to believe his conversion is genuine... 'Our commitment to fiscal discipline isn't just there because it looks good,' he told his first press briefing after entering public office. 'Fiscal discipline is fundamental to the strategy'... Once a doctrinaire socialist...he has made his peace with capitalism.* [30]

The GNU's commitment to 'fiscal discipline' was reflected in the fact that the R37.5 billion allocated to the RDP in 1994-1999 were to be found from savings in other government spending. But the government's first full budget, in March 1995, showed how far the ANC had gone in accepting free market economics. Accompanied by the abolition of various apartheid era restrictions of the export of capital, notably the financial rand, the budget was designed especially with foreign investors in mind. The *Weekly Mail* commented, 'That the focus of the Budget is the deficit before borrowing rather than a wealth tax, or some other unspeakable horror, speaks volumes about the the newfound conservatism of the ANC members of the government of national unity.'[31]

Liebenberg did make some effort to reallocate state spending towards 'social upliftment'. Defence's share of the budget was reduced from 8.7 percent to 7.2 percent, while housing's rose from just over 1 percent to nearly 3 percent. But at the same time, a change in the basis on which provincial governments' social expenditure was funded by Pretoria meant a shift in favour of the more sparsely populated, predominantly rural provinces to the disadvantage of the metropolitan regions. According to the *Weekly Mail*:

> *In both health and education, formulae were devised to move the money around—but in some areas, rigid application of the formulae may lead to hardship,* [sic] *such as Gauteng* [the PWV region] *and the Western Cape. In those two provinces, for instance, cutbacks in education spending mean that thousands of teachers may find themselves without jobs.*[32]

Moreover, the military—renamed the South African National Defence Force (SANDF)—found some rather surprising new patrons to defend their interests in bureaucratic infighting. The Minister and Deputy Minister of Defence in the new government had been leading figures in the ANC's military wing, Umkhonto weSizwe (MK)—respectively Joe Modise, former MK commander-in-chief, and Ronnie Kasrils, who had been MK's chief of intelligence. Kasrils was a romantic figure: when he found himself on the run from the security forces even after February 1990 he had become known as the 'Red Pimpernel'. He had been a leading figure among those in the ANC/SACP who were critical of the priority given to negotiations over mass struggle.[33]

Once bitter foes of the apartheid war machine, in office Modise and Kasrils became fervent defenders of the SANDF's demands for new equipment. The navy's plans to spend R1.69 billion on four corvettes caused particular controversy. Sounding like any NATO defence minister justifying his generals' and admirals' latest expensive toys, Kasrils argued:

*International crises can break out at amazing speed and every time they sur-
prise us... We're living in a world where there's greater competition for
scarce resources—and that's a major cause of war. Two weeks ago, Spain and
Canada had a flare-up over fish. We've got a billion-rand fishing industry
providing thousands of jobs and this will grow because our seas are rich.*[34]

While Kasrils was striving to make the seas safe for South African
fishing boats, how were the impoverished black majority faring?
Housing was in many ways the key issue. According to a report sub-
mitted by Mandela to the United Nations World Summit on Social
Development in March 1995, 15 percent of Africans lived in shacks, 17
percent in outbuildings, 14 percent in huts, 17 percent in hostels, and 45
percent in houses. Only 35 percent had flush lavatories.[35] Consistent with
his policy of placing representatives of the left in sensitive economic
posts, Mandela appointed Joe Slovo Minister of Housing. Soon after he
had taken office the *Financial Times* reported:

*Mr Slovo believes that 50,000 houses can be erected this year, rising to
125,000 in 1995, 175,000 in the following year and 225,000 in 1997.*
   *How close Mr Slovo comes to reaching these targets will be one of the yard-
sticks by which black South Africans will judge the ANC at the next election.*[36]

The desperate shortage of housing in the PWV region was indi-
cated by the fact that some 200,000 people had established new
squatter settlements in the years before the 1994 election. The ANC's
victory encouraged more to occupy empty land. In early June 1994
Johannesburg City Council destroyed a shack settlement at Liefde en
Vrede, leaving several hundred without shelter on one of the coldest
nights of the harsh Highveld winter. The PWV premier, Tokyo
Sexwale, condemned the evictions, but Slovo said that some of the
land invasions had been orchestrated 'by outsiders who do not have
the best interests of [the squatters] at heart', and the provincial land
ministry claimed that the occupations could 'create a climate con-
ducive to "Third Force" exploitation'.[37]
   This hostility to initiatives from below was also reflected in the deal
Slovo struck with the Association of Mortgage Lenders in October 1994.
The banks and building societies agreeing to make up to R2 billion available in loans for low cost housing and to end their racist practice of
'red-lining', ie refusing to lend to anyone wishing to live in certain black
areas. In exchange, Slovo undertook to break the 'culture of non-
payment'—the boycotts of payments on rents, services, and mortgage
bonds that had developed in the townships during the mid-1980s and had
continued after February 1990 and indeed April 1994. 'We cannot allow

the spirit of populism to dominate our practice,' he declared, promising 'to restore the rule of law'.

Banks would be given full government backing in their efforts to repossess the houses of bond defaulters, and would be indemnified where 'abnormal township conditions' made it impossible for them to foreclose. Moreover, the *Weekly Mail* reported, 'the state will effectively take over the red-lining function by witholding mortgage indemnities in unstable, violent and crime-ridden areas—like Katlehong on the East Rand—where the commercial risk is unacceptable.'[38] The emergence of what the same paper called 'Slovo, the Boycott Buster,' won him the praise, after his death in January 1995, of Adriaan Vlok, brutal NP Minister of Law and Order for much of the 1980s:

> *He very soon realised that to develop our country and to start building houses, you need money—and to get this, economic development is a prerequisite.*
>
> *He also realised that it was impossible for the state to care for all the needs of everybody. Therefore he was one of the first ANC members to point out—clearly and directly—that people must pay their rent and service charges and plead for greater private-sector involvement.*[39]

These compromises might have been acceptable if they actually delivered new houses. A crash public house building programme would have been a real step towards achieving the Revolutionary Alliance's ostensible objective of Growth through Redistribution. This would not only have begun to meet the popular demand for housing (estimated at 1 million in PWV alone) but would have created new jobs in the construction sector, in turn increasing demand and employment in consumer industries. Instead Slovo and his successor concentrated on drawing up blueprints and negotiating with the private sector. According to Anton Harber, editor of the *Weekly Mail*:

> *Asked in February* [1995] *how many houses had been built since the ANC came to power, the new Minister of Housing, Sankie Nkondo, had to say it was only about 800. (It would take 550 houses a day—including weekends, public holidays and builders' holidays—for the ANC to meet its promises of 1 million houses within five years.)*[40]

By October 1995 10,600 state funded houses had been built that year, compared to Slovo's target of 125,000.[41] The failure to deliver on the ANC's housing promises was symptomatic of a more general malaise. The RDP Ministry—supposedly the powerhouse of change—became a watchword for slow moving bureaucratic procedures justified by incomprehensible gobbledegook. One critical economist pointed to the snail's pace at which the R2.5 billion RDP Fund was being spent:

[C]onsidering the fact that only 55 percent of the 1994/5 RDP Fund was allocated (of which only a small fraction was actually spent), indications are that the RDP Fund process has become snarled up in red tape.

Some analysts are even suggesting that the net effects of the RDP has been to slow social spending. [42]

Reviewing the GNU's record from a generally sympathetic viewpoint in April 1995, Harber wrote:

After a year in office, South Africa's political leaders are talking defensively. Minister Jay Naidoo speaks, in the language of South Africa's new bureaucrats, about the lack of capacity, the need for rigorous business plans, the demands of fiscal discipline, the absence of effective local government, and other factors that have slowed down implementation of the Reconstruction and Development Programme...

They have become defensive because if you measure the success of the Government of National Unity in purely numerical terms—the number of houses built, the number of people who have access to free health care or potable water—then it scores disturbingly low.

Apart from a few showy (and important) presidential projects, such as the provision of a daily peanut butter sandwich to schoolkids and free health care for infants, all the key ministries such as housing, health and education will tell you that they are still at the stage of policy formulation and structural planning, prior to the actual implementation of the RDP. [43]

Elsewhere than on the critical social and economic front the picture was the same—the GNU has failed to impose a radical change of direction. One of the most striking examples was in the area of foreign policy. Under the feeble guidance of Alfred Nzo, one of the many mediocrities from the ANC's bureaucracy in exile placed in senior ministerial positions thanks to the patronage of the ambitious First Deputy President, Thabo Mbeki, the Department of Foreign Affairs became a symbol of conservative inertia.

Mbeki was personally responsible for cultivating friendly relations with the Nigerian military regime (even though the day Mbeki met its head, General Sani Abacha, during a visit to Nigeria, 43 people were publicly executed by firing squad). When, at the end of October 1995, a military tribunal in Nigeria sentenced Ken Saro-Wiwa and eight other pro-democracy activists to death, Mandela opposed any attempt to isolate Nigeria, arguing instead for a policy of 'quiet diplomacy'. The

execution of the activists ten days later was thus, among other things, a
public slap in the face for the South African president.

'Quiet diplomacy' had strong echoes of the policy of 'constructive
engagement' with the apartheid regime pursued by Ronald Reagan and
Margaret Thatcher in the 1980s. One of Saro-Wiwa's lawyers told
Mandela in a letter, 'Were quiet diplomacy pursued in South Africa...I
doubt you would be alive today.' The hapless Deputy Foreign Minister,
Aziz Pahad, was left to defend the GNU's policy, explaining, 'We do not
see anything wrong in principle with constructive engagement, but that
does not mean weak constructive engagement.'[44]

In other areas as well the GNU pursued policies which could hardly
be described as designed to achieve 'structural transformation'. Using
wildly inflated police figures, home affairs minister Mangosuthu
Buthelezi enthusiastically launched a campaign against 'illegal immigrants' from other parts of Africa, mostly neighbouring countries
devastated by the apartheid regime's policies of destabilisation in the
1980s. When local and foreign capitalists complained about the undeniably appalling levels of crime in South Africa, the government did not
respond that these were an inevitable consequence of the massive
inequalities that had, for example, set the impoverished townships and
squatter settlements of Gauteng alongside the plush white suburbs of
Northern Johannesburg. Instead the ANC took a leaf from Tony Blair's
book and campaigned on the slogan, 'Tough on crime, tough on the
causes of crime', in the November 1995 local government elections. One
ANC leader, Gauteng premier Tokyo Sexwale, went much further,
calling for a referendum on the restoration of the death penalty.

The gravy train

And then there was the matter of the 'gravy train'. As in former
colonies on attaining independence, the installation of an ANC led government was accompanied by an influx into well paid positions in the
state apparatus of supporters of the liberation movement—both as conventional civil servants and in the form of the mass of consultants and
'change operatives' that surrounded the new ministers. One admittedly
cynical and unsympathetic observer, the South African born Oxford don
R W Johnson, declared that 'the fact is that power in South Africa is
being transferred to the same bureaucratic bourgeoisie that took power
elsewhere in Africa'.[45]

Parliament accepted a report recommending that MPs should be paid
'market related' salaries—R16,000 a month, compared to the R900 basic
minimum for public sector workers. When Desmond Tutu, the Anglican
Archbishop of Cape Town, attacked the 'gravy train', the ANC parlia-

mentary caucus declared that criticism of MPs' salaries was 'racist'. Tutu responded by asking, 'Have you noticed my complexion?'[46]

The most embarrassing single scandal to affect the GNU in its first year concerned Allan Boesak, the best known Coloured politician in the ANC. After Boesak had fronted the ANC's unsuccessful election campaign in the Western Cape, Mandela nominated him as South African ambassador to the United Nations in Geneva. It then emerged that Boesak had secretly diverted over R400,000 donated by Scandinavian charities from the Children's Trust, over which he presided, to his separate Foundation for Peace and Justice, where it was used, for example, to help pay off his mortgage.

Like John Major hanging on to one of his sleazy ministers, Mandela insisted on defending Boesak to the bitter end. Even after Boesak had been forced to resign as ambassador designate in February 1995, the president seized on an incompetent official report exonerating him to declare, 'Allan Boesak is one of the most gifted young men in the country…he deserves a very high diplomatic post.'[47] The ANC was, however, compelled to respond to the scandals by seeking to tighten up its own ethics code and the rules governing MPs' extra-parliamentary earnings.

Big business also helped to power the gravy train. As Anton Harber put it, '[t]he role of the private sector has been to try to create a few extremely wealthy and powerful black individuals who would provide a bulwark against accusations that South Africa's most powerful companies are all-white. So white business is financing and advising a line-up of instant millionaires.'[48]

Other motives were at work as well—for example, the ancient one of removing opposition to important projects by greasing the right palms. Sol Kerzner controls Sun International (SI), the leisure empire whose most famous asset is Sun City in Bophuthatswana. Despite being wanted by the police on charges of bribing former Transkei president George Mantanzima, he was able to stay out of gaol and cultivate a very catholic range of political contacts. According to the *Weekly Mail*:

> *Kerzner has retained high-level connections in both the previous and current governments. He was a friend of former Bophuthatswana president Lucas Mangope, in whose territory he made the foundations of his fortune, the Matanzima brothers in the Transkei, and the late Ciskei ruler, Lennox Sebe. He attended Deputy President Thabo Mbeki's 50th birthday party and was an honoured guest at Mandela's inauguration…*
>
> *Last month [ie October 1995] it emerged in KwaZulu-Natal that a new gambling consortium, African Sun International, in which SI is involved, is linked to people close to the provincial government. They include Mangosuthu Buthelezi's son 'Zuzi', Finance MEC [Member of the Executive Council]*

Snezele Mhulungu, ANC stalwart Walter Sisulu and former aide to F W de Klerk, Richard Carter.[49]

Much of the proved corruption of ANC politicians was petty stuff. It paled by comparison with that of the old NP regime and its Bantustan hangers on, let alone with that inherent in the capitalist system itself.[50] Nevertheless, the gravy train was a symptom of the ANC leadership's alienation from those who had elected it, and who were waiting impatiently for real improvements in their lives.

Managing capitalism

'Structural reforms' in South Africa would, John Saul argued, be part of 'an emerging project of structural transformation'. But the longer the ANC held office the harder it became to deny that it was, in effect, pursuing a free market policy of Redistribution through Growth. One leading left intellectual, Eddie Webster, conceded that 'the Government of National Unity has accepted the macro-economic constraints of the liberal international economic order'.[51]

This was evident not simply in what the GNU failed to do—the snail's pace at which the RDP was implemented—but also in what it did do. Thus the March 1995 budget provided for public sector pay to rise by 3.25 percent, implying a 6 percent cut in real wages for most workers. Mandela defended the wage cut, saying, 'Without tightening our belts it will be difficult to resolve our economic problems.'[52] Meanwhile, in June 1995 Trade and Industry Minister Trevor Manuel announced, as part of South Africa's implementation of the latest round of the General Agreement on Tariffs and Trade, substantial cuts in tariffs likely to lead to massive job cuts in the textile, clothing and motor industries.

One symptom of the drift of policy was the government's U-turn on privatisation. Before April 1994 the Revolutionary Alliance had opposed the NP government's efforts to privatise some of the large number of parastatals (or nationalised industries). The RDP promised to 'reverse privatisation programmes that are contrary to the public interest'. But, after an extensive campaign mounted by big business, Thabo Mbeki announced in December 1995 that he was to preside over a new cabinet committee designed to speed up the 'restructuring' of the state sector. This would involve inviting 'strategic equity partners to join our public corporations'—ie minority private shareholdings in such plum parastatals as Telkom and South African Airways.[53] The *Financial Times* reported that '[t]he cabinet has already decided that the proceeds from any sales would be used to reduce official debt... The private sector has warmly welcomed the government's announcement.'[54]

This shift represented a marked victory for big business. While broadly supporting the GNU, business leaders pushed for faster moves in a free market direction. Thus they criticised finance minister Liebenberg's target for the budget deficit—5.8 percent of Gross Domestic Product in 1995-1996—as too high. 'There is a strong view within the business community that attempts to reduce the budget deficit should be accelerated,' claimed the South African Chamber of Business (SACOB) in December 1995. This would require deep cuts in public spending. Yet at the same time Ray Parsons, SACOB's director-general, admitted that the upturn in the economy—which grew by 3 percent in 1995 and was forecast to expand by 4 percent in 1996—represented 'jobless growth'. Only 50,000 of the 350,000 new job seekers to enter the labour market in 1995 had found work. 'A key characteristic of the current economic upturn is that the benefit of the growth that has been experienced so far has been confined to a relatively small proportion of the population,' Parsons said.[55]

The logic of Redistribution through Growth was that a flourishing free market economy would generate jobs and prosperity for the poor. But, nearly two years after Mandela's inauguration, there were no signs of any such trickledown in South Africa. The growth rates delivered by Liebenberg's and Erwin's pursuit of economic orthodoxy were far below the 8 to 10 percent annual increase in GNP which labour minister Tito Mboweni estimated was necessary to reduce unemployment substantially and to provide jobs for new labour market entrants.[56] Meanwhile big business was demanding from the GNU policies—in particular spending cuts—that would instead increase unemployment.

And what of the foreign investment that free market policies were meant to attract? One economist estimated capital inflows in 1995 at 2.5 percent of gross domestic product. But much of this was speculative money used to buy bonds and shares that could leave the country as quickly as it had entered it. Moreover, although R2.5 billion worth of foreign direct investment was made in the first half of 1995, Alan Hirsch of the Department of Trade and Industry admitted that 'there is almost a total lack of foreign investment in outward-oriented manufacturing', the key sector in any strategy for improving South Africa's long term competitiveness.[57]

The Left in disarray

Here, one would have thought, was a situation ripe for a challenge from the left. And, in a country with the most powerful trade union movement in Africa, closely allied with one of the last mass Communist Parties in the world, one could see the political forces capable of mounting such a challenge. Yet—astonishingly, disgracefully—no such challenge emerged.

In part, this was a reflection of the close links binding the SACP to the ANC. Often NP propagandists and liberal journalists had demonised the party, seeing it as a sinister demiurge controlling Congress from behind the scenes.[58] But, whatever might have been true in the past, by the 1990s the SACP was no longer a tight Stalinist organisation. The lines of political division within the broader movement cut through the party as well. Thus, when one SACP leader, Ronnie Kasrils, advocated the 'Leipzig Option'—mass action to bring down the NP—after the collapse of CODESA and the Boipatong massacre, he was challenged by another, Jeremy Cronin. It was the party chair, Joe Slovo, who persuaded the ANC to accept 'sunset clauses' acknowledging white claims, while its general secretary, Chris Hani, was taking a much more radical stance. Though strongly supported by the best organised workers and the left intelligentsia, the SACP had become a relatively loose social democratic organisation.

There were some efforts to raise the SACP's distinct political profile. Thus a Socialist Conference for Reconstruction and Development met in Johannesburg in mid-November 1994. It had been convened by the SACP and COSATU, and, as the title suggests, was intended to operate within the framework of the RDP. 'What we need now is the deepening and consolidation of April,' Cronin told the conference.[59] Though this approach was strongly contested by representatives of the far left present, the most striking feature of the whole affair was its low key character. The organisers restricted the attendance to a mere 150. This hardly suggested that the mass organisations behind the conference were giving much priority to hammering out an independent socialist strategy.[60]

More than the SACP's commitment to the Revolutionary Alliance was involved here. The bulk of the left no longer had any conception of what their alternative was to the existing capitalist society. This ideological disarray was summed up by a throwaway remark by Joe Slovo—in many ways the key socialist intellectual in South Africa, central leader of the SACP, ex-Chief of Staff of MK, the ANC's chief strategic thinker and one of its main negotiators with the NP—reported after his death in January 1995: 'Socialism can come later...when I have discovered what it is.'[61]

There were, however, organisations to the left of the SACP still willing to fight for socialism. The South African far left was, however, crippled both by its negligible numbers and influence and by, in the main, a highly sectarian attitude towards the ANC and the SACP. This latter attitude was well expressed by the decision of the Workers

Organisation for Socialist Action (WOSA) to stand candidates in the April 1994 elections. At a time when the main line of political polarisation was between, on the one hand, the ANC as the embodiment of the masses' hopes of liberation, and, on the other, the representatives of the old order—the NP and Inkatha—this was an act of sectarian folly, for which WOSA (in the shape of its electoral front, the Workers List Party) was justly punished by receiving a miserable 4,169 votes.[62] The Socialist Workers Organisation (formerly the International Socialists of South Africa), sister organisation of the Socialist Workers Party in Britain, was careful not to cut itself off from ANC and SACP supporters, but it was far too small to present itself as a credible alternative to the Revolutionary Alliance.

In the absence of any powerful socialist challenge to the GNU's free market policies, popular impatience found expression chiefly in the unlikely person of Winnie Mandela. Disgraced for her role in the 1989 murder by her bodyguards of a young boy, separated from her husband and compelled to give up her ANC posts in 1992, she nonetheless bounced back, and was appointed Deputy Minister of Arts and Culture, Science and Technology in May 1994. She also recaptured her position as president of the ANC's Women's League. This comeback reflected her success in cultivating a popular base among the most impoverished of the ANC's supporters. Thus squatters in the East Rand shack settlement of Phola Park called Mandela 'Mother' on her regular visits to offer desperately needed material assistance provided through her Coordinated Anti-Poverty Programme.

Winnie Mandela was, moreover, a leading figure in an ANC faction that came to be known as the 'populists'. These included Peter Mokaba, ex-president of the ANC Youth League, and Bantu Holomisa, who, after being pro-ANC military ruler of the Transkei, was appointed Deputy Minister of Environmental Affairs in the GNU. They had links with elements in the SACP—notably Chris Hani, until his assassination, and Harry Gwala, the tough Stalinist who, before his death in June 1995, was one of the main ANC leaders in the killing fields of KwaZulu/Natal.

While none actually opposed the negotiating process, they expressed impatience at its slow progress, and backed popular demands for rapid change. They were also more willing to indulge in anti-white rhetoric. While such language was out of keeping with the ANC's traditions of non-racialism, it was popular with the rank and file. During the bloody and protracted transition to democracy in the early 1990s, PAC slogans— of which the most famous was 'One Settler, One Bullet'—were taken up by angry ANC supporters. Peter Mokaba made himself notorious when, at Hani's funeral in April 1993, he terrified whites by leading the chant, 'Kill the Boer, Kill the Farmer'. (Embarrassed ANC spin doctors subsequently explained what Mokaba wanted to kill was 'the system', not individual whites, but somehow this didn't ring quite true.)

Populists such as Winnie Mandela and Holomisa nevertheless received ministerial posts in part because it was too dangerous to exclude them from the new government. As President Lyndon Johnson said of J Edgar Hoover: 'Better to have him in the tent pissing out than outside pissing in.' Moreover, they enjoyed a powerful backer in the shape of Thabo Mbeki. The *Weekly Mail* explained: 'While he is usually associated with the more conservative wing of the party, he has at crucial times relied on the support of Winnie Mandela and some of her more militant associates'.[63] Thus, at the ANC's December 1994 congress, the Youth League and the Women's League had backed Mbeki against his chief rival, Cyril Ramaphosa, even though he belonged to 'much the same pragmatic ideological camp as Ramaphosa', in his successful bid for the post of National Chairman, and—in effect—heir apparent to Nelson Mandela.[64] Despite an attempt by Mandela to impose his own nominees on the congress, the populists did very well in the elections to the ANC National Executive Committee.

Nevertheless, in the early months of 1995 a crisis developed around Winnie Mandela's role in the government. A series of factors were involved—rows involving her high handed behaviour in the Women's League and another ANC affiliate, the Congress of Traditional Leaders of South Africa, allegations of corruption (which were used to justify an illegal police raid on her home), and a speech she made attacking the slow pace of change. Nelson Mandela made two unsuccessful attempts to sack her. The first time, in February, Mbeki talked him out of it. The second time, in April, the unlikely figure of Buthelezi came to Winnie Mandela's rescue, arguing that, as a leader of one of the governing parties, he had not, as the constitution required, been consulted over her dismissal. Despite these fiascos, she was finally removed.

The *Weekly Mail* welcomed the prospect of Winnie Mandela's dismissal as the 'Fall of a Greedy Elite'.[65] Undoubtedly there were serious allegations of corruption against not only her, but also against Mokaba over the National Tourism Foundation he had set up with donor funds but which subsequently went bust. Indeed Winnie Mandela was no socialist. She lived a luxurious lifestyle, and her politics were based on no serious class analysis of South African society. She encouraged her supporters to look to her for improvements of their lot, rather than to organise for themselves. Her unholy alliance with Buthelezi over her dismissal, moreover, probably discredited her with many who had previously looked to her.

None of this, however, can alter the fact that Winnie Mandela was the *only* prominent figure in the Revolutionary Alliance to give sharp and clear expression to the masses' demands for rapid and dramatic change. To their everlasting shame, the socialist intellectuals and trade union and community activists who had emerged in the 1970s and 1980s to create a powerful left in South Africa had, by contrast, stayed silent. For all her many faults, Winnie Mandela had acted as a lightning conductor for popular aspirations. Yet she offered no coherent alternative to the GNU, merely a more radical version of the ANC's nationalism. From where could a real alternative come?

The Mandela government and the workers' movement

From the long historical view, the ANC's victory represented the culmination of the great wave of national liberation movements whose rebellion against colonial domination is one of the grand themes of the 20th century. At the same time, however, the ANC is set apart from other nationalist movements by its close alliance with a powerful and independent working class movement. This distinctive feature is itself a reflection of the peculiarities of South African historical development, and in particular of the way in which industrial capitalism established itself from the late 19th century onwards through promoting institutions of racial domination that after 1948 were elaborated into the apartheid system. By a happy historical irony, the very success of segregation and apartheid in promoting the development of modern capitalism in South Africa gave rise to a black working class whose growing economic power underlay the popular insurgencies of the 1970s and 1980s.[66]

The principal organisational expression of this power was the trade union movement which emerged after the Durban strikes of January-February 1973. Its strongest wing was COSATU, closely allied to the ANC from its inception in 1985. The importance of the unions to the nationalist movement was demonstrated after the emergency imposed in June 1986 caused the collapse of the various community based organisations—civic associations, youth and student congresses, etc—that had flourished during the township risings of the mid-1980s. The civics in particular never fully recovered from this setback.

Thereafter COSATU served as the backbone of the ANC led mass movement, for example, mobilising for the stayaways of 1992-3, and, in the Witwatersrand at least, providing the cadre of shop stewards who formed teams of canvassers during the 1994 elections. The presence of ex-trade union leaders such as Naidoo and Erwin in important ministerial posts, and the important role played by the former mine workers' leader Ramaphosa as ANC secretary general provided some indication of COSATU's contribution to the nationalist movement. (Indeed, no less than 50 COSATU leaders, many of them very senior officials, took up political office after April 1994.[67])

Following the elections, the *Financial Times* acknowledged the strength of the organised working class: 'With 3.5 million members, or 26 percent of the economically active population, the unions are a leading force in society.'[68] The development even under de Klerk of institutionalised social bargaining was an acknowledgement of this fact. To that extent Eddie Webster is right to highlight what he calls 'the multi-layered institutionalised bargaining process between classes' as a distinctive feature of post-apartheid South Africa. He goes on to argue that '[t]his unique combination in the Third World of a powerful and strategic labour movement in alliance with a left-centre government allows one to envisage the emergence of a social-democratic programme' that, while not challenging 'the fact of capitalist economic ownership', would promote 'equity-led growth' based on 'tripartite agreements between labour, management and government'.[69]

The main evidence Webster could offer in support of this hope was the new Labour Relations Bill announced by the Labour Minister, Tito Mboweni, in February 1995. Certainly this sought to take South Africa further along the road of corporatist bargaining. In addition to industry wide negotiations between employers and unions through Bargaining Councils (a new name for the Industrial Councils set up by General Smuts in 1923), every workplace with more than 100 employees would be required to set up a Workplace Forum to promote the sharing of information and decisions; moreover, the details of the new labour law were to be hammered out by the concerned parties at the main social-bargaining body, NEDLAC.

The bill, however, had a number of negative features. Unlike the old apartheid era legislation, it did not place employers under a duty to bargain. Though the right to strike was recognised, it was denied to workers providing 'essential services' and 'maintenance services': the latter was a new category, covering the potentially very broad range of activities whose interruption would lead to the 'physical destruction of plant, machinery or the working area'. Employers were given the right to lock out, and to hire scab labour. Moreover, the existence of a Workplace Forum would impose restrictions on industrial action. Unorganised workers and those in small workplaces were left out in the cold. Only a registered union could organise a picket, and employees in workplaces with less than ten trade union members were denied the right to a shop steward.[70]

In any case, the GNU's willingness to institutionalise social bargaining came with a price tag—what Derek Keys, Mandela's first finance minister, called 'a tacit, never expressed understanding' under which the unions would restrain their wage demands in exchange for the social reforms promised in the RDP.[71] In fact, the new government made its demands for pay restraint up front. After the March 1995 budget called for a 6 percent cut in the real wages of public sector workers, the *Financial Times* praised the GNU for 'the combative attitude it is taking towards pay demands', and went on:

> One of the most serious concerns about the country's long-term ability to compete internationally was that the government which took office last May would prove too sympathetic to the demands of organised labour.
>
> It is slowly dawning on the unions that this supposition might not be entirely correct.[72]

Neither the GNU's tough line on pay nor COSATU's commitment to a social contract prevented workers from going on strike. On the contrary, as Brian Fowlis put it, 'the "New South Africa" was faced with a massive strike-wave only weeks after the election...the action showed the labour movement to be less in awe of the ANC-led government than might have been expected: the sheer size and its widespread nature, as well as its timing...can leave no other explanation'.[73]

Some 3.9 million strike days were 'lost' in South Africa in 1994—up from the previous year, but below the 4.2 million in 1992.[74] Given both the effective disappearance of the political stayaways that were so characteristic of the 'struggle years' of the 1980s and the coming to office of a government strongly supported by the organised working class and stuffed with its former leaders, this figure represented a formidable degree of militancy. Workers showed in practice their vision of a transformation that went well beyond winning the rights of political citizenship.

At the centre of their immediate preoccupations was pay. In the first nine months of 1995 wage disputes were responsible for 93 percent of all strikes. In fact 1995 saw quite a sharp fall in the level of the industrial struggle. There were only 870,000 strike days 'lost' in the first three quarters of the year, compared to a five year average of 2.6 million. But beneath these figures was a marked shift in the pattern of the economic class struggle. Strikes were concentrated for the first time in the public sector and the parastatals. This reflected to some degree the fact that the new government had lifted the old regime's ban on public sector strikes. But, more importantly, it was a consequence of the fact that state workers' wage increases were being held below the rate of inflation, while workers in the private sector, where union organisation was strongest, were able to win settlements of around 10 to 12 percent, which kept their pay in line with prices. The third quarter of 1995 saw a sharp rise in strike activity compared to the very low levels recorded in the first half of the year (775,000 strike days between July and September) with two especially bitter disputes involving nurses and municipal workers in Gauteng province (formerly PWV).[75]

Its attitude towards strikes was a key test of whether the ANC in office was pursuing a strategy of 'structural reform' involving what John Saul calls the 'empowerment' of the masses. As André Gortz, the theorist of this strategy, put it, '[t]he emancipation of the working class can become a total objective for the workers, warranting total risk, only if in the course of the struggle they have learned something about self-management, initiative and collective decision—in a word, if they have a foretaste of what emancipation means'.[76]

Far, however, from seeing in the strikes an opportunity for workers to get a 'foretaste' of their 'emancipation', the government bitterly attacked any manifestation of direct action on the ground. The police, armed with all the brutal apparatus familiar from the apartheid era of guns, batons, dogs, and teargas, were regularly mobilised against strikers.

Opening parliament in February 1995, Mandela made a point of attacking violence by striking workers. In April 1995 he denounced workers' and students' protests at the University of the Witwatersrand (Wits): 'Where we have put our foot down is where people use the right of protest to commit crimes, to destroy property, to take hostages, to interfere with the rights of other students.' And when policemen in the Transkei mutinied, he ordered the SANDF in to crush them. 'I told them, if you have to use live bullets, use them,' he recalled in a subsequent interview.[77] (This threat was not an idle one: when black policemen at Orlando East station in Soweto went on strike in January 1995 in protest against their racist treatment, the all white riot squad from Krugersdorp was called in; it opened fire on the strikers, killing one and injuring others, and then arrested them, beating up and insulting some.[78])

ANC leaders more junior than Mandela displayed the same hostility towards strikes. Thus Philip Dexter, an MP and former official of the National Education, Health and Allied Workers Union (NEHAWU), attacked the Gauteng nurses' strike. 'Previous industrial action including in the public sector, took place in the context of apartheid,' he explained, under 'a government openly hostile to black workers and their aspirations. The ANC is the complete opposite of this.' Admittedly, 'public service workers do have legitimate grievances', but these should wait upon the creation of a 'Public Service Forum' pursuing 'a strategy of co-determination between the government as employer and representative of the people's will and the public service workers, together with other directly affected interest groups'.[79]

Once again workers were being told to wait for a rosier tomorrow. In fact, the striking nurses had already had an experience of 'co-determination' when the health unions accepted a pay deal at the Public Service Bargaining Council which gave the lowest paid workers a 22 percent increase, but better paid workers (ie those earning R2,000 a month or more) only 5 percent. So the professional nurses, who belonged to this latter group, went on strike rather than accept a pay cut. The *Weekly Mail* commented: 'The placatory tone usually present when ANC cabinet ministers face similar issues has been noticeably absent. Instead, the nurses have been ordered back to work, with threats of legal action if they stay out'.[80]

Tokyo Sexwale, ANC premier of Gauteng province, claimed that the NP was behind the nurses' and municipal workers' strikes. He complained that the municipal workers' tactic of littering the streets of Johannesburg—which helped win them wage increases ranging between 11 percent (for middle grades) and 20 percent for the low paid in October 1995—gave white business a bad impression of black people. 'Johannesburg is my city, the capital of Gauteng, and I won't let people say: look what happens under a black government.' Paul Mashatile, Gauteng ANC secretary, claimed that workers' demands were 'just a smokescreen', and that the municipal strike 'can only serve the interests of people who are bent on undermining the ANC government'.[81]

Interestingly the SACP distanced itself from these attacks, calling them 'deeply insulting to nurses and municipal workers', and acknowledging that the strikes 'brought real...energies out onto the streets...The great majority of municipal workers and nurses marched with ANC posters and portraits of President Mandela.' But the party also warned against 'a working class romanticism. Not all workers strikes are necessarily justified or even progressive,' it argued, citing the irrelevant example of racist strikes by white workers, while 'some tactics (like trashing a city centre) are ill advised'.[82]

In fact, the strikes reflected above all the economic pressures on workers, especially in the public sector. To concern about the cost of living and impatience over the slow pace of change was added also anger at the fact that the bosses weren't exactly following Mandela's call for tighter belts. Thus a *Weekly Mail* survey of 26 of the top 150 companies revealed in August 1995 that, for example, directors of Rainbow had awarded themselves a 40.7 percent pay increase, those of Tongaat Hullett 40 percent, and those of South African Breweries 24 percent; these handouts to rich executives reflected higher profits—in the case of these three companies respectively over 100 percent, 55.4 percent, and 30 percent.[83] 'Keep the last carriage on the gravy train for us', said a poster during the Gauteng nurses' strike.

The strikes inevitably put some strain on the relationship between the ANC and COSATU, partners though they were in the Revolutionary

Alliance. In fact, Fowlis argues that 'the ANC and trade unions [had] to some extent drifted apart' even before the GNU took office in May 1994. He identifies three factors as responsible. In the first place, 'a degree of disillusionment with the ANC' gradually set in after February 1990, in particular because of their concessions to the NP and big business over economic policy. Secondly, there was a 'growing clamour [in the unions] for greater independence within the alliance'. Indeed, in 1993-1994, in the immediate run up to the elections, two major unions, the metal workers (NUMSA) and the clothing and textile workers (SACTWU), both strongly workerist in the 1980s, passed resolutions highly critical of what the latter called 'alliance politics'; there was even (though Fowlis does not mention this) a revival of the old idea of a union based workers' party separate from the ANC. Thirdly, the influx of ex-union officials into government and parliament was likely to weaken both COSATU by depriving it of 'many of their best intellectual[s] and most effective leaders' and its alliance with the ANC, since the elections had severed the 'visible link' of union officials holding ANC (and often also SACP) positions and 'left today's union leaders with more freedom to concentrate on the concerns with [sic] their members, even if those concerns mean taking action which might embarrass the government'.[84]

Fowlis somewhat overstates the degree of alienation between the ANC and COSATU. The pre-election talk of launching a new workers' party soon blew itself out. Two prominent workerists of the 1980s, and former general secretaries of the unions most critical of the ANC, NUMSA and SACTWU, respectively Moses Mayekiso and Johnny Copelyn, were soon sitting on the government benches in the National Assembly. (There Copelyn hardly did much credit to the cause of independent unionism when it emerged that he had been paid a sum estimated at R1 million as a result of business deals he had made while managing SACTWU's investments.[85])

The new generation of union officials loyally defended the Revolutionary Alliance and sought to restrain their members from going on strike. For example, in the case of the Gauteng nurses' strike, the Socialist Workers Organisation pointed out: 'Every union, including SANA [the conservative South African Nurses Association], the right wing HOSPERSA and the left wing NEHAWU, accepted the argument that nurses should, as the SACP acknowledged, not strike, whatever their grievances'.[86] It is, moreover, certain that the overwhelming majority of those involved in the strikes were loyal supporters of the ANC and President Mandela.

What may be true, however, is that the new officials, lacking the authority that came from leading struggles against the bosses and the state in the 1970s and 1980s, were less effective in restraining their members than their predecessors would have been. The *Financial Times* went so far as to talk of 'a crisis of leadership' caused by the departure of 100 COSATU officials, 'not only to high offices of state, but to the private sector and academia'. It predicted that 'the unions' clout within ...corporatist structures will inevitably diminish—at least until a new crop of articulate and forceful unionists can emerge to take the place of those lost. And perhaps more importantly, the leaders' ability to deliver the co-operation of the union rank and file may also be jeopardised.'[87]

Old or new, the union leaders had in any case to balance between two sources of pressure—one from the government and big business to preserve industrial stability, the other from their members to fight for pay increases and for social reforms. Both to demonstrate to the ANC and the bosses that they were too powerful to be ignored as a social partner, and to retain the loyalty of their rank and file, the COSATU leadership were compelled themselves to initiate strike action.

Thus, impatient at the employers' obstructionism during the negotiations in NEDLAC over the new Labour Relations Bill, COSATU called two weeks of protests culminating in a stayaway on 19 June 1995. A million workers came out in support of the federation's demands, which included centralised wage bargaining, the right to strike without dismissal, a ban on lockouts and scab labour, and the legalisation of union shops.[88] A compromise falling well short of COSATU's demands was eventually reached after the employers had threatened to sit out a six month strike rather than accept the imposition of centralised bargaining. The labour consultant Frans Rautenberg told the *Weekly Mail* that:

> '*the conflict is a sign of a profound and basic disagreement between labour and business, and the beginning of a crack in the alliance between the ANC* [sic: COSATU?] *and the government.'*
> *He sees the clash, which ultimately the government will be faced with handling, as part of a worldwide trend as economic pressures force governments to seek labour market flexibility.*[89]

Rautenburg's words proved to be prophetic. In December 1995 the GNU capitulated to the 'worldwide trend' towards, not merely 'flexibility', but also privatisation, and decided to sell off minority shareholdings in some parastatals. COSATU reacted with fury, accusing the government of breaching an agreement made only a week earlier that no changes in the state sector would be made without full consultation and until an overall policy on 'restructuring' had been agreed. Instead, COSATU was being asked 'to rubber stamp someone else's agenda'.[90] Significantly it was the South African Railways and Harbour Workers

Union (SARHWU), traditionally one of the COSATU affiliates most loyal to the ANC, that called protest strikes on 13 December.

At a rally that day SARHWU president Nelson Ndisina accused the GNU of behaving like 'the previous National Party governments which took decisions on our behalf'. And he declared, 'As workers of South Africa, we will not allow anybody, I repeat anybody, to privatise.' The speech by Sam Shilowa, general secretary of COSATU, at the same rally dramatised the balancing act in which the union leaders found themselves engaging. On the one hand, he declared, 'There is no debate on whether COSATU supports transformation, reorganisation and restructuring, because we want an efficient system and to root out corruption.' On the other hand, he used much more militant rhetoric: 'As workers your rights are sacrificed on the altar of profits... You must remain in a state of readiness, so that when we say *Kubo! Ningene kubo*—Hit them! You must hit them'.[91]

By the time of the strikes an agreement had been cobbled up to smooth COSATU's ruffled feathers—a joint committee was established to review the future of the state sector, and a moratorium placed on future government statements on the issue.[92] It was a sign of the pressures from below on COSATU leaders, and of their own anger, that they nevertheless organised further protests and called a one day general strike on 16 January. This strike was then called off at the last moment, after yet more government promises and rumours that the powerful National Union of Mineworkers was opposed to the action. The affair illustrated the contradictory position in which the union leaders were placed. Like trade union bureaucrats everywhere they were seeking to reconcile the inherently antagonistic interests of capital and labour—but in a society with appalling levels of mass poverty and powerful traditions of working class militancy. They—and South Africa itself—were likely to have a rough ride.[93]

Future prospects

There were indeed formidable problems confronting the ANC led Government of National Unity. Some reflected the political inheritance of apartheid. Of these the most serious was Inkatha. The IFP entered the New South Africa controlling KwaZulu/Natal, the second most important province, and with substantial parliamentary and ministerial representation at the centre. Despite the ANC's successful courting of the Zulu King, Goodwill Zwelithini, Buthelezi was able, thanks to his long established control of the sources of both patronage and repression in KwaZulu, to retain the loyalty of most chiefs. In the GNU he behaved like a semi-detached cabinet minister, often distancing himself from government decisions.

More dangerously, the IFP pressed for a constitutional status for KwaZulu/Natal that would make it effectively autonomous. The Inkatha dominated provincial government threatened unilaterally to implement a constitution to this effect, defying the popularly elected National Assembly's right to settle the political future of South Africa as a whole. In fact, however, the IFP was seriously divided, with KwaZulu/Natal premier Frank Mdlalose and other members of the provincial leadership in favour of more cautious policies than Buthelezi and his personal advisers, predominantly white right wingers. This helped create a condition of political paralysis in the province. Mandela responded to the IFP's secessionist threats with tough talk, but held back from any decisive action. The ANC's leadership in KwaZulu/Natal, which had failed to mobilise effectively for the April 1994 elections, was weak and divided. The IFP was able to force a delay in local government elections in the province, held in the rest of the country in November 1995, until the following March.

Against this background, the dreadful war between the 'spoos' and 'sdus', respectively armed supporters of the IFP and the ANC, continued in the townships, squatter camps, and villages of KwaZulu/Natal. In the first ten months of 1995 over 2,000 people died in political violence in the province, which the Human Rights Commission described as being in 'a situation of near anarchy'.[94] Half a million refugees fled from their homes to escape the killing. The worst bloodshed seemed to be concentrated in the Port Shepstone area, on Natal's south coast. Kipha Nyawosa, ANC chairman in the village of Shobashobane, which he described as 'an island of ANC surrounded by a sea of IFP areas', lost 14 members of his family between October 1994 and June 1995. 'Before the elections, my family was alive. Now they are dead', he told the *Weekly Mail* in September 1995. 'I don't feel this new South Africa we got last April'.[95]

On Christmas Day 1995 some 600 well armed IFP supporters attacked Shobashobane. They disembowelled Nyawosa, cut out his heart and mutilated his genitals, and butchered 18 other people. Before the raid independent monitors and ANC officials had begged the local police commander for help. According to the *Independent on Sunday*, '[t]he police response was to raid ANC houses and confiscate weapons, a move which left Shobashobane defenceless.' Political violence in KwaZulu/Natal over Christmas left a total of 189 people dead over seven days. Violence monitor Mary Haas claimed that responsibility lay with 'an old boy network still involved in destabilisation', embracing white right wingers and elements in the police. 'It is driven by a right-wing ideology that likes Buthelezi because it sees him as its creation. It believes that if you control KwaZulu/Natal, with its ports and harbours, then you control South Africa'.[96] In what the *Weekly Mail* called 'a political defeat for the African National Congress', the IFP was able to prevent a central government police team from investigating the Shobashobane massacre and others like it.[97]

The carnage in KwaZulu/Natal raised the more general question of the extent to which the ANC could rely on the loyalty of the security forces it had inherited from the old NP regime. The reality of the third force behind the escalating violence of the 1990s was made clear when in October 1995 the former Minister of Defence, General Magnus Malan, and several senior military officers were charged with the massacre of 13 people in 1987. This was one of the many atrocities committed by a group known as the 'Caprivi 200', IFP supporters trained by the SADF in the Caprivi strip. The aim behind this operation, according to a secret Military Intelligence document attached to the indictment, was 'to set up a group of well-trained troops that can be used offensively against the ANC, UDF [United Democratic Front] and related organisations'. Buthelezi, the home affairs minister, was nearly arrested along with Malan and his generals.[98]

But, though the most senior personnel associated with the apartheid terror had been removed, and some were even being called to account, the repressive apparatuses of the South African state remained largely unchanged. They represented a formidable threat to any elected government that sought seriously to change society.

The basic problem facing South Africa, however, was that, as we have seen, the ANC led government was *not* seeking seriously to change society. Unless, through some miracle, free market economics produced a real trickle down effect, the prospect was one of growing mass impoverishment and, in all likelihood, political disillusionment. What would these produce?

Developments in neighbouring Zimbabwe help to define one possible scenario. There too the final attainment of national liberation in 1980 led to the transfer of political power to the black majority, but left economic power in the hands of white settler and foreign capital.[99] At the end of the 1980s popular discontent found a focus in a huge scandal ('Willowgate') which engulfed the ruling Zimbabwe African National Union-Patriotic Front (ZANU-PF). An alliance of students and trade unionists was able to scupper President Robert Mugabe's plans to set up a one party state, but, thanks to the weakness of the political opposition, he hung onto power.

By the early 1990s ZANU-PF had abandoned its earlier economic nationalism, and was pursuing an Economic Structural Adjustment

Programme (ESAP) of free market policies demanded by the World Bank. ESAP had a predictably devastating effect on jobs and living standards. Yet Mugabe found a way of deflecting the mass hunger for change—black empowerment. This slogan was initially raised by a black middle class lobby called the Affirmative Action Group. It argued that the source of Zimbabwe's problems lay in the continued economic domination of whites; the solution lay in systematic state promotion of the interests of black capitalists. This analysis found a resonance among black bosses who, in the main owning small businesses, were harder hit by ESAP than the bigger firms, which were controlled by local whites or foreign multinationals. The government itself took up the slogan (and even used it to justify its 1994 attempt to hand over farms expropriated from whites to individual black 'entrepreneurs', including various ministers and other state officials). ZANU-PF overwhelmingly won a general election in April 1995 amid massive popular apathy.[100]

'Black empowerment' was already a buzzword in South Africa before the ANC came to office. Inasmuch as it concerned what Meshack Mabogoane describes as 'the significant advancement of blacks in the corridors of corporate power', it took two forms. One was the promotion of blacks to senior positions, including directorships, in established companies. Beginning in the early 1990s, this took off under the GNU, especially in the parastatals. The other was the establishment of powerful black controlled enterprises. Here probably the most important development was the emergence of New Africa Investments, which Mabogoane calls 'a black economic empowerment flagship', headed by Dr Nthato Motlana, a long standing ANC figure in Soweto. Motlana saw African capitalism growing as Afrikaner business had developed from the 1940s, through a pyramid of shareholdings giving control over a large number of companies. But, if we take the analogy seriously, the advancement of Afrikaner private enterprise was greatly aided by the established English speaking capitalists, above all the great Anglo-American Corporation, which saw it as a way of defusing pressures from the NP regime, and which still dominate the South African economy. Indeed, Mabogoane observes, black economic empowerment:

> *has been perceived as both co-option of a black elite and its enrichment with very little real control by the very same. Whenever a black economic empowerment venture is announced the black directors would either be non-executive or chairmen while the whites take on the top operational roles. This is construed as tokenism and window dressing, carried out by major companies in response to pressures from both government and organised black groups. It is seen as a subtle means of legitimising continued white control of corporations.*[101]

Whether or not black empowerment represented any real change in the structure of South African society, it was increasingly taken up in ANC circles. Minister of Public Services and Administration Zola Skweyiya accepted the description of him as an 'Africanist', and said: 'The ANC shouldn't shy away from blacks becoming capitalists. The only question is—how do we achieve it?'[102] Professor William Makgopa, headhunted by Wits University to serve as deputy vice-chancellor and symbol of black empowerment, horrified white academics with pronouncements like: 'The primary principle of a South African university should be to capture and encapsulate the essence of Africa.'[103] (A group of them, including the supposedly left wing historian Charles van Onselen, who had also been a bitter foe of student and worker protests at Wits, challenged his academic credentials, and forced his suspension.)

Despite the ANC's traditions of non-racialism, and the important role played by whites and Indians in the liberation struggle, Africanist attitudes could be found near the very top of the government. Thus the *Weekly Mail* wrote of Deputy President Thabo Mbeki:

> *He is also prone to playing an Africanist ticket when it suits him. It is seldom public, but people around him have said that he knows exactly when and with whom he can successfully play on the sense of an African—rather than a black or a South African—identity.*[104]

It is therefore easy to imagine the ANC in the future, faced with mass discontent because of the absence of real social and economic change, playing on the rhetoric of black empowerment, and presenting mass impoverishment as essentially a racial issue to which the solution would be the replacement of white by African capitalists. Should it not do so, then there are other political organisations rooted in the traditions of black exclusivism, above all the PAC, who would be quick to play this card.

Observers often argue that the pressures on the ANC will cause it to split at some stage. There are various versions of this prediction—for example, a breakaway by Winnie Mandela and the populists, or a decision by the SACP to operate as an independent organisation. Such scenarios need to be treated with some scepticism. 'Never underestimate the ANC,' is one of the great lessons of South African politics. It has survived terrible defeats, and seen off a succession of political challenges—from the PAC in the late 1950s and early 1960s, from Black Consciousness in the 1970s, from the workerists in the 1980s.

An essential ingredient in the ANC's success has been its ability to contain often quite diverse tendencies within the same movement. This has allowed it to tack and turn as the political wind changes. This is likely to continue to be the case in office. Thus, despite the general moderation of the GNU's economic policies, ANC general secretary Cyril Ramaphosa made a well publicised attack in July 1995 on 'monopolies' like Anglo-American, declaring, 'The ANC is committed to breaking the stranglehold these companies have, and ultimately the government will have to act'.[105] Nelson Mandela actually took part in a COSATU march in Johannesburg during the federation's campaign over the Labour Relations Bill the previous month. The government, moreover, did in effect respond to the Gauteng strikes by promising to find an extra R9 billion for public sector wages.

So far there has been no significant decline in the ANC's popularity. It won two thirds of the popular vote in the November 1995 local government elections, and even made inroads among the NP's Coloured supporters in the Western Cape (though Cape Town, along with KwaZulu/Natal, was excluded from the poll). Should, however, the ANC begin to lose support, some sort of at least apparent shift to the left—whether in the shape of a greater stress on black empowerment or in the pursuit of more substantial reforms than have yet appeared—cannot be ruled out, perhaps in the run up to the next elections, due in 1999. What is highly unlikely, however, is that any such turn would mark an abandonment by the ANC of its commitment to managing South African capitalism.

Conclusion

In 1985, long before he had (as the *Financial Times* put it) 'made his peace with capitalism', and become Deputy Minister of Finance in the GNU, Alec Erwin wrote a perceptive analysis of the limits of what he called the 'liberation politics' of the ANC and movements like it. This politics depended for success on mobilising a cross-class coalition against the regime. 'To have raised different class interests during such a struggle would have been divisive and divisive forces take on some of the stigma attached to apartheid.' The NP's reform policies, however, created a situation where 'liberation politics [is] no longer liberation politics but rather a process of negotiating'. At the same time the structural crisis of the South African economy put a fundamental social transformation onto the agenda. But 'the nature of the unity forged in liberation politics...suppress[es] class interests and transformation. In the South African situation—and elsewhere—a change of regime in circumstances where transformation has not been addressed leaves intact the structure and interests that are so minimal to the mass of workers and rural population'.[106]

Such a change of regime indeed took place in South Africa in May 1994. And, as Erwin predicted, 'the mass of workers and rural population' have yet to see any significant change to their lives. It is important to understand that this failure is not a matter of personal betrayal or backsliding (though the abandonment by core elements of the South African left of any attempt to pursue a socialist alternative is indeed shameful). There can be few groups of individuals in the world with finer personal records of political courage and sacrifice than Mandela and his ANC ministers.

Rather, the failure of the ANC in office to pursue any real attempt to transform society is a consequence of the strategy it has pursued. Like reformists at other places and times, the Revolutionary Alliance has made its genuine desire to achieve the 'social upliftment' of the black majority conditional on the revival of the fortunes of capitalism in its country. But it has done so at a time when capitalism on a global scale is experiencing profound turbulence and instability. A consequence is to place immense competitive pressures on individual economies.

In this context, the plight of South African capitalism is particularly serious. The chronic low productivity of manufacturing industry that is part of the inheritance of apartheid does pose severe tests on South African firms' ability to negotiate world markets.[107] A recent study of the South African car industry suggested that, though wages are low by international standards, low productivity eliminates much of the competitive advantage this might offer (see Table 2).

TABLE 2: *Labour costs in vehicle assembly*

Plant	Labour cost per hour ($)	Labour hours per car	Labour cost per car ($)
South Africa	5.6	63.5	355
Mexico	6.0	24.3	145
United States	38.0	18.56	705

[*Source: Survey on Investing in South Africa, **Financial Times**, 2 May 1995*]

The difficulty is that addressing this crisis of competitiveness requires an assault on the improvements in wages and working conditions that black workers made in the 1980s thanks to the development of the independent unions. In other words, reviving South African capitalism depends on the ANC in government taking on the powerful workers' movement that played a central role in its victory over apartheid. John Saul rightly celebrates 'the vibrancy and radical push at the base of South African society'.[108] He does not see, however, that the pursuit of reform within a capitalist context will make the vitality of grassroots working class and community organisation increasingly an embarrassment to the Mandela government. The conflicts between the GNU and organised workers chronicled in this article are merely the opening skirmishes in a much larger struggle.

Moreover, the choice Saul presents between 'structural reform' and 'barbarism' does not counterpose genuine alternatives. The reformist strategy adopted by the Revolutionary Alliance in the early 1990s has so far produced no substantial socio-economic reforms. This is no paradox, but rather an instance of a familiar pattern. Again and again, social democratic governments in the developed capitalist countries that set out to reform capitalism have ended up as its managers, and consequently have found themselves attacking their own working class supporters.

It is precisely the absence of reform, and the resulting misery and disillusionment that this is likely to create in the black masses, that will feed the forces of barbarism in South African society. The slaughter in KwaZulu/Natal is not merely a hangover from the apartheid past, or a symptom of the persisting alliance between the IFP and forces in the state apparatus. The less the movement assembled around the ANC is able to offer a convincing and effective strategy for improving the material situation of the black masses, the more many of the most wretched and impoverished members of the population are likely to look to alternative ethnic solutions, which, however retrograde, offer both psychological comforts, and, often, immediate economic benefits.[109] The ANC's failure substantially to change South African society is likely to strengthen Inkatha. The choice is thus, not between barbarism and reform, but between socialism and barbarism.

It follows that, while it proved possible in the end to remove the political institutions of apartheid within a capitalist framework, the social and economic inheritance of the malign South African partnership between capitalism and racial domination cannot be removed without a socialist revolution. It is plain that the main organisation of the South African left, the Communist Party, is politically incapable of assuming such a task. The workers' movement in South Africa therefore needs a new socialist party—though undoubtedly the most important recruits to its ranks will come from the militant workers and youth who today still look towards the SACP and the ANC (one of the chief disabilities of the bulk of the Trotskyist left in South Africa has been its sectarian hostility towards these organisations). Building such a party will, no doubt, be a difficult and arduous task. It is no less urgent, however, if the great hopes raised by the final defeat of apartheid are not to be followed by a terrible reckoning.

Notes

I am grateful to Paul Allen, Tony Cliff, Charlie Kimber, John Rees and Julie Waterson for their help in writing this article.

1   *Weekly Mail*, 15 May 1992.
2   *Weekly Mail and Guardian* (hereinafter *WMG*), 11 March 1994.
3   Ibid, 17 March 1995.
4   *Socialist Worker* (Johannesburg), 11 October 1995. In November 1995 £1=R5.669, $1=R3.635. Under the apartheid system the population of South Africa—estimated in 1995 at 41.24 million—was divided into four main racial groups: Africans (71.5 percent of the population), Coloureds (9 percent), Indians (2.9 percent) and whites (16.6 percent). The first three groups, disenfranchised and discriminated against under apartheid, are all referred to in this article as 'black', though sometimes this term is restricted solely to Africans.
5   For further information about, and analysis of, the process sketched out in the following paragraphs, see A Callinicos, *South Africa between Reform and Revolution* (London, 1988), 'Can South Africa be Reformed?' *International Socialism*, (1990), and 'Introduction' to Callinicos (ed) *Between Apartheid and Capitalism* (London, 1992). M Murray, *The Revolution Deferred* (London, 1994), paints a powerful portrait of South African society on the eve of majority rule. It is particularly good at bringing out what Murray calls 'the inner connection between the rise of post-apartheid parliamentary democracy and the "dead weight" of embedded structural continuities left over from the past' (p viii). Unfortunately, apparently under the influence of the great French historian Fernand Braudel, he tends so strongly to stress the 'structural underpinnings', and to treat political events as mere 'surface appearances' (p ix), that he often fails to grasp the dynamics of the struggles that unfolded during South Africa's democratic transition.
6   Interview in *Death of Apartheid* (BBC-TV, 1995), Part 1. This series, presented by the veteran South African journalist Allister Sparks, is an invaluable source of information on the transition to democracy. See also Mandela's own account in his memoirs, *Long Walk to Freedom* (London, 1994), pp 624-627.
7   Accounts of the negotiating process can be found in A Sparks, *Tomorrow is Another Country* (London, 1995), in S Friedman (ed) *The Long Journey* (Johannesburg, 1993) and *The Small Miracle* (Johannesburg, 1995), and in A Callinicos, 'The End of Apartheid and After', *Economic and Political Weekly*, 3 September 1994.
8   Interview, *Death of Apartheid*, op cit, Part 2.
9   For a contemporary discussion (highly critical of the 'Leipzig Option') of the strategic options facing the Revolutionary Alliance, see J Cronin, 'The Boat, the Tap and the Leipzig Way', *African Communist*, 3rd Quarter, 1992.
10 Interview, *Death of Apartheid*, op cit, Part 2
11 J. Slovo, 'Negotiations: What Room for Compromise?', *African Communist*, 3rd Quarter, 1992.
12 *Financial Times* (hereinafter *FT*), 4 December 1993.
13 *WMG*, 25 February 1994.
14 This process could, however, easily have gone awry. Mac Maharaj, the ANC leader sent as part of a team representing the Transitional Executive Council to Bophuthatswana, has described how he had personally to intervene to block efforts by General Georg Meiring, chief of the SADF, in collaboration with Viljoen and de Klerk, to keep Mangope in office: see A Sparks, *Tomorrow*, op cit, pp 214-219.

15   The classic statement of the two stage strategy is the SACP's 1962 programme, *The Road to South African Freedom*, in *South African Communists Speak* (London, 1981). It was reaffirmed in the party's 1989 programme, *The Path to Power*, published in *African Communist*, 3rd Quarter, 1989. For a critique, see A Callinicos, *South Africa*, op cit, pp 65-72.

16   See the discussion of this shift in my interview with the SACP leader Jeremy Cronin, 'The Communist Party and the Left', in Callinicos (ed), *Between Apartheid and Capitalism*, op cit, pp 83-6.

17   This was true, not only of the SACP, but of the bulk of the orthodox Trotskyist tendencies. The Unity Movement, historically the most important influence on the South African far left, had long taken up an extremely uncritical attitude towards the Stalinist bureaucracy in the USSR, for example, defending its suppression of the Hungarian Revolution of 1956: see B Hirson, *Revolutions in My Life* (Johannesburg, 1995), pp 256-64. This attitude tended to influence even those who had broken with the Unity Movement. I vividly remember visiting South Africa shortly after the defeat of the August 1991 conservative coup in Moscow to discover that most of those calling themselves Trotskyists regarded this as a defeat for the left as well.

18   J Slovo, *Has Socialism Failed?* (London, 1990). Slovo discusses the SACP's Stalinist past in his posthumously published autobiography: for a relevant extract, see 'Restoring Socialist Morality after Stalin', *WMG*, 1 December 1995.

19   *Business Day*, 12 December 1990. See also J Slovo, 'Nudging the Balance from "Free" to "Plan" ', *Weekly Mail*, 30 March 1990.

20   A Erwin, 'Capital Need Not Bridle at the Label "Socialist" ', *Weekly Mail*, 30 March 1990. The workerists were a group initially of mainly white socialist intellectuals who played a key role in building the independent unions in the 1970s and 1980s. Critical of the ANC-SACP stages strategy and of the subordination of the workers' movement to the broader anti-apartheid alliance that it implied, they sought to defend the autonomy of the unions. Beyond some vague speculations about the possibility of building a Brazilian style 'workers' party', they failed, however, to address the question of socialist political organisation. As 'populists' supporting the ANC and SACP became increasingly dominant inside COSATU in the late 1980s, the workerists increasingly abandoned their distinctive stance. Many, including Erwin, joined the SACP when it was publicly relaunched after February 1990. See A Callinicos, *South Africa*, op cit, chps 4 and 5, and, for a view more sympathetic towards the eventual merger of workerists and populists, J Baskin, *Striking Back* (Johannesburg, 1991).

21   *Weekly Mail*, 12 July 1991.

22   The difficulties facing the European model of 'Rhenish capitalism' are analysed in A Callinicos, 'Crisis and Class Struggle in Europe Today', *International Socialism*, (1994).

23   For a critique of the shift towards social democracy, see A Callinicos, 'Social Contract or Socialism?', in Callinicos (ed), op cit, *Between Apartheid and Capitalism*.

24   S Gelb, 'Democratising Economic Growth', *Transformation*, 12 (1990), pp 35-36. This entire issue of *Transformation* is devoted to the 'Recommendations on Post-Apartheid Economic Policy' embodying the Growth through Redistribution strategy drawn up at a workshop in Harare. The analysis underlying this approach is developed much further in S. Gelb (ed), *South Africa's Economic Crisis* (Cape Town, 1991).

25   The pursuit of a more 'progressive' version of capitalism has also become a major preoccupation of the west European left. Will Hutton's *The State We're In* (London, 1995) is a forceful argument for what has come to be known as 'stakeholder capitalism'. Two critiques of this intellectual shift are A Callinicos,

'Backward to Liberalism', *International Socialism*, (1995), and C Harman, 'From Bernstein to Blair', *International Socialism 67* (1995).

26   J Saul, 'South Africa: Between "Barbarism" and Structural Reform', *New Left Review*, 188 (1991), pp 5-6. See, for a critique, A Callinicos, 'Reform and Revolution in South Africa', *New Left Review* 195 (1992), and Saul's reply, in the same issue.

27   J Saul, 'Structural Reform: A Model for the Revolutionary *Transformation* of South Africa?', *Transformation*, 20 (1992). Kagarlitsky develops the idea of 'revolutionary reformism' in *The Dialectic of Change* (London, 1990); see my review, 'A Third Road?', *Socialist Worker Review*, February 1990.

28   *WMG*, 3 December 1993.

29   *FT*, 7 May 1994.

30   Survey on South Africa, *FT*, 18 July 1994.

31   *WMG*, 17 March 1995.

32   Ibid, 17 March 1995.

33   R Kasrils and Khuzwayo, 'Mass Struggle is the Key', *Work in Progress*, 72, January/February 1991. Kasrils' autobiography, *Armed and Dangerous* (London, 1993), gives a rather *Boys Own* account of his exploits in MK.

34   *WMG*, 7 April 1995.

35   Ibid, 15 March 1995.

36   Survey on South Africa, *FT*, 18 July 1994.

37   *WMG*, 10 June 1994.

38   Ibid, 21 October 1994.

39   Ibid, 13 January 1995.

40   Ibid, 31 March 1995.

41   Survey on South Africa, *FT*, 21 November 1995.

42   N Nattrass, 'The Two Faces of the RDP', *WMG*, 15 September 1995.

43   Ibid, 21 April 1995.

44   Ibid, 17 November 1995.

45   RW Johnson, 'Enrichissez-Vous!', *London Review of Books*, 20 October 1994, p 17.

46   Ibid.

47   *WMG*, 28 April 1995.

48   Ibid, 21 April 1995.

49   Ibid, 17 November 1995.

50   See 'Where is the Real Corruption?', *Socialist Worker* (Johannesburg), 22 February 1995.

51   E Webster, 'Speak Out, Social Democrats!', *WMG*, 18 August 1995.

52   *FT*, 21 March 1995.

53   Ibid, 8 December 1995.

54   Ibid, 9 December 1995.

55   Ibid., 7 December 1995. .

56   Survey on Investing in South Africa, *FT*, 2 May 1995.

57   *WMG*, 22 December 1995.

58   For a well informed and relatively mild example of this literature, see S Ellis and T Sechaba, *Comrades against Apartheid* (London, 1992).

59   *WMG*, 11 November 1994.

60   Two discussion documents presented to the conference, 'Challenging the Neo-Liberal Agenda in South Africa', and 'The Present Situation and the Challenges to the South African Left', were published in *South Asia Bulletin*, XV:1 (1995). Allison Drew's editorial introduction to this special issue on South Africa, 'Building Democracy in Post-Apartheid South Africa', contains a brief account of the conference along with some more general reflections.

61   *FT*, 7 January 1995.

62 In the future it may well be necessary for revolutionary socialists to present an alternative to the ANC electorally, as well as on other more important terrains. To attempt to do so in the circumstances of April 1994 with the forces then available was, however, a serious error.

63 *WMG*, 3 March 1995.

64 Ibid, 28 April 1995.

65 Ibid, 3 March 1995.

66 The interdependence of apartheid and capitalism and, consequently, the political centrality of the black working class, were demonstrated by the work of the so called 'Revisionist' school of Marxist historians in the 1970s, but the basic idea had been anticipated by critics of the Communist Party's stages strategy in the early Trotskyist groups from the mid-1930s onwards. See, for example, the documents edited by Baruch Hirson in *Revolutionary History* 4:4 (1993). W Beinart and S Dubow (eds) *Segregation and Apartheid in Twentieth-Century South Africa* (London, 1995) is a useful selection of historical essays more or less influenced by 'Revisionism'.

67 *WMG*, 13 May 1994.

68 Survey on South Africa, *FT*, 18 July 1994.

69 Webster, 'Speak Out, Social Democrats!', *WMG*, 18 August 1995.

70 Critiques of the Labour Relations Bill include 'Defend the Right to Strike for All!', *Socialist Worker* (Johannesburg), 8 February 1995, and D Bosch and D du Toit, 'Size Does Count', *WMG*, 24 February 1995.

71 Survey on South Africa, *FT*, 18 July 1994.

72 *FT*, 21 March 1995.

73 B Fowlis, 'The Post Election Strikewave in South Africa', *Leicester University Discussion Papers in Politics*, P95/1 (1995), pp 1, 9. See also Z Mtshelwane, '"Struggle as Usual" in the New South Africa?', *South African Labour Bulletin* 18:3, July 1994.

74 *FT*, 21 March 1995.

75 M Mabogoane, 'Wages Whip Workers into Strike Action', *WMG*, 6 October 1995.

76 Quoted in J Saul, "Barbarism", op cit, p 6.

77 *Socialist Worker* (Johannesburg), 25 April 1995.

78 *WMG*, 10 February 1995.

79 P Dexter, 'Nurses' Conduct is Unacceptable', *WMG*, 15 September 1995.

80 *WMG*, 8 September 1995.

81 *Socialist Worker* (Johannesburg), 11 October 1995.

82 'The RDP Needs Class Struggle', *African Communist*, 3rd Quarter,1995, p1

83 *WMG*, 25 August. 1995.

84 Fowlis, 'Post Election Strikewave', op cit, pp 9-17.

85 *WMG*, 13 and 28 April 1995.

86 *Socialist Worker* (Johannesburg), 20 September 1995.

87 Survey on South Africa, *FT*, 18 July 1994.

88 *Socialist Worker* (London), 24 June 1995.

89 *WMG*, 23 June 1995.

90 *FT*, 9 December 1995.

91 *WMG*, 15 December 1995.

92 *FT*, 15 December 1995.

93 For a brief summary of the Marxist theory of the trade union bureaucracy, see A Callinicos, *Socialists in the Trade Unions* (London, 1995), ch 2.

94 Survey on South Africa, *FT*, 21 November 1995.

95 *WMG*, 22 September 1995.

96 *Independent on Sunday*, 31 December 1995.

97 *WMG*, 5 January 1996.

98 *WMG*, 8 December 1995.

99   For a contemporary account, see A Callinicos, *Southern Africa after Zimbabwe* (London, 1981). A useful, and more recent, survey is C Stoneman and L Cliffe, *Zimbabwe* (London, 1989)—though it appeared, absurdly, in a series called 'Marxist Regimes'.

100   There is a helpful discussion of black empowerment in B L Zano, 'Racism in Zimbabwe', *Socialist Worker* (Harare), May/June 1995.

101   M Mabogoane, 'The Genesis of Black Empowerment', *WMG*, 15 December 1995. The astonishing story of Anglo-American is told in D Innes, *Anglo-American and the Rise of Modern South Africa* (London, 1984).

102   *WMG*, 15 December 1995.

103   Ibid, 7 July 1995.

104   Ibid, 28 April 1995.

105   *FT*, 28 July 1995.

106   A Erwin, 'The Question of Unity in the Struggle', *South African Labour Bulletin*, 11:1, September 1985, pp 60-1, 70.

107   See, for example, D Kaplan, 'The South African Capital Goods Sector and the Economic Crisis', in Gelb (ed), *Economic Crisis*, op cit.

108   J Saul, "Barbarism", op cit, p 7.

109   C Charney, 'Vigilantes, Clientelism and the South African State', *Transformation* 16 (1991), stresses the role of patronage in creating and sustaining movements like Inkatha.

France's hot December

CHRIS HARMAN

December 1995 saw the biggest eruption of class struggle in France for a quarter of a century. Some 2 million public sector workers took strike action over a three and a half week period. The strikes reached a crescendo each week with one or two days of action, when demonstrations in both Paris and the provincial towns involving from 1 to 2 million people drew in not merely workers on all out industrial action, but many other groups from the public sector and substantial numbers of delegations from the private sector.

This was not a general strike, insofar as it was confined to key parts of the public sector. But it virtually paralysed communications in cities right across France. And it thrust the class struggle to the centre of political life. For a month newspapers, television and radio programmes were dominated by discussion of 'the social conflicts'. All this happened barely eight months after the celebration by the right wing parties of the victory of their candidate, Chirac, in the presidential election, coming on top of their massive 390 seat majority in parliament. Disillusionment with 14 years of Mitterrand as Socialist Party president had led many workers to break with their traditional allegiance to the left parties—with around a quarter voting for the fascist National Front—at the same time as union membership had suffered a very big fall.

The strikes and demonstrations inevitably evoked comparisons with two great previous upsurges of working class struggle in France—that of 1936, which led to the first introduction of paid holidays and the 40 hour week and the first spread of mass trade unionism in France, and that of 1968. But they also raise questions which go far beyond French politics. At the international level they have already helped put in question a central strategy of key sections of European capital, Economic and Monetary Union. They have also raised, right across Europe, the questions of how far ruling classes dare to go in their attempts to cut back on welfare provision. They have constituted a challenge to all those, everywhere, who want to pretend the class struggle is a thing of the past.

For these reasons, the question of the character of December's strikes is central for socialists. Were they merely defensive or did they raise wider issues? Will they quickly be forgotten, or are they potentially a prelude to events of immense significance? And, if they are, what implications does this have for the political activity of socialists?

Causes

The immediate cause of the French strikes was prime minister Juppé's 'plan' for the social security system—the '*Sécu*'. It involved a series of measures which hit all workers, but especially those in the public sector:

●An increase in the number of years public sector employers had to work before they were entitled to their retirement pensions from 37.5 to 40—a measure already imposed on private sector workers in 1993;
●Increased hospital charges and restrictions on prescriptions;
●The freezing and taxing of family benefit paid to low income families with children and increased health insurance contributions for pensioners and the unemployed;
●A new tax of 0.5p in the pound, including on the lowest wages;
●Taking control of the health insurance system away from joint union-management bodies and putting it directly in the hands of the state, which would restrict payouts on a yearly basis.

Juppé boasted that this was the reform his predecessors had been afraid to carry through 'for 30 years'.

Alongside the Juppé plan proper were other 'reforms', announced in the same few days. One was a '*contrat de plan*' (draft agreement) providing for a radical rationalisation of the French railway system, with a widespread cutting of services and closing of stations and lines, similar in many respects to the Beeching Plan implemented in Britain in the 1960s. Another raised the prospect of a partial privatisation of the telephone service—and, by implication, other public sector industries. A third proposed an overhauling of the tax system to increase the burden on wage earners while reducing that on top incomes.

The immediate motive behind these measures—as well as for a public sector wage freeze announced a month earlier—was to cut back the French state's budgetary deficit, with the aim of reducing it to the 3 percent 1999 Maastricht criteria for European Economic and Monetary Union. This led some people to see Maastricht as the only factor behind

Juppé's move. Thus the French Communist Party leader denounced President Chirac's call to clamp down on the deficit as a 'lining up with Chancellor Kohl' of Germany and a 'raising of the white flag' in the face of the financial markets which 'raised decisive questions for France and its sovereignty'.[1]

The pressure for Economic and Monetary Union clearly played a role in the timing of Juppé's measures. He belongs to the wing of the French ruling class which sees such a union, involving French, German, Belgian and Dutch capitalisms, as central to building up the position of the French ruling class internationally. But, interestingly, much of the pressure for the cutbacks in the deficit comes from rival groups inside the ruling class and the conservative parties, who are resistant to Economic and Monetary Union. For them, the issue of the budget deficit is not an issue which arises out of one or other foreign policy strategy, but rather from the pressing needs of French capitalism regardless of the strategy it pursues.

Large budget deficits have been a characteristic feature of almost all capitalist economies in the crises of the last two decades. As the *Financial Times* has put it:

> The US has one. The Europeans have one, and now even Japan has one. What do they all have? A serious fiscal problem. This is the theme of the decade, one that will shape the rhythm of financial life and form the cacophonic background sound to political debate in almost every industrial country.[2]

The deficits are a product of the wider crisis of the system. Growth rates substantially lower than those of the 1950s, 1960s and early 1970s mean that government revenues do not rise fast enough to meet levels of spending, even if these rise more slowly than in the past. Indeed, such revenues can stagnate, or even fall, as governments slash taxation on profits to compensate big business for the decline in long term profit rates and reduce taxation on higher range incomes. As the *Financial Times* notes:

> The overall ratio of government spending to GNP in industrial countries stabilised in the early 1980s. It did so, however, at levels that individual governments were unable, or unwilling, to cover by taxation... The resulting fiscal deficits...increased the ratio of gross public debt to GNP from 41 percent in 1980 to 72 percent in 1995. Unfunded pension promises ensure that there is worse to come almost everywhere.[3]

The result is what is sometimes called 'the first world debt crisis'—
the fear that, at some point, government debt for one or other major
industrial country will reach a level which the international money
markets are no longer prepared to finance, resulting in enormous
domestic instability and 'a major shock to the world's financial system'.[4]
The result is that all the great industrial powers are under pressure to deal
with the deficits, but do not know how to do so:

> *Governments will be punished if they inflate their way out of their*
> *quandary—they will not be permitted to tax their way out—and their*
> *economies will probably not grow out of it either. What is left is just to whittle*
> *away unceasingly at the promises made in an earlier, happier era.*[5]

The situation is particularly serious for the European capitalist states,
whether or not they implement the Maastricht proposals. In the 1950s,
1960s and 1970s they were all able to enjoy high rates of profits and
rapidly growing economies while making substantial concessions to
workers over wages, hours of work and welfare legislation—either as a
response to high levels of industrial struggle (Belgium 1960-1961,
France 1968, Italy 1969-1975) or in order to pre-empt any such struggles
disrupting social stability (Scandinavia under a succession of Social
Democrat governments, West Germany under both Christian Democrat
and Social Democrat governments).

In the 1980s and early 1990s they have attempted to cut back on
certain of these concessions, with a widespread 'rationalisation' of
private industry leading to growing unemployment, increases in taxation
at the expense of workers (under the Mitterrand governments in France
and with the 'unity tax' imposed by Kohl in Germany), attempts to keep
wage increases below that of the cost of living (the dismantling of the
scale mobile in Italy), direct attacks on welfare provision (under both
Social Democrat and right wing governments in Scandinavia, the
pension reform in Italy). But this has still left the European capitalisms at
a disadvantage when it comes to competition with Japanese and
American capitalisms. Its productivity levels in industry are lower than
in either Japan or the US, the real wages it pays are higher than in the US
(although not Japan), and its employees work far fewer hours:

AVERAGE HOURS WORKED (per full time employee per year 1994)[6]

Japan	1,964
US	1,994
Canada	1,898
Britain	1,826

Italy	1,803
Sweden	1,620
Holland	1,615
France	1,607
Denmark	1,581
Belgium	1,581
West Germany	1,527

'Today a German works three months each year less than a Japanese and 13 weeks less than an American'.[7] Nor is that all. The average number of hours worked per year has been rising in the US, so that the average worker now works three weeks a year longer than in 1980, while average French and German employees work, respectively, two weeks and three weeks less than in 1980. No wonder spokespeople for sections of European capitalism increasingly complain about 'Eurosclerosis', saying that they are paying too great a price for the social component of the so called 'social market' economy, with Chancellor Kohl insisting West Germany must 'adapt to profound changes in its way of life with longer working hours'.

Capitalists right across Europe are putting on pressure for 'more flexible' working practices, a longer working year, longer qualification periods for pensions and a lower level of payments, a 'rationalisation' of health provision and increased indirect taxation. All are pushing 'anti-inflationary' and deregulatory policies designed to prevent firms giving in to pressure from workers for wage increases to maintain living standards. Everywhere the trend is for them to adopt the language of 'neo-liberalism'—of a Thatcherite attitude to welfare and public services. The Juppé plan fitted perfectly with this approach.

Juppé's tactics

Juppé's strategy, then, was at one with those of the other sections of European capitalism, whether pro or anti-Maastricht. But there were peculiarities to his tactics, resulting from the political situation.

First there was the sudden, unprepared way in which he introduced the plan. During the 14 years of the Mitterrand presidency, there was a long, drip drip series of attacks on the conditions and benefits of French workers. Two attempts to speed up these attacks, during periods with Mitterrand as president and a right winger as prime minister, led to a sudden rise of sharp struggles, unpopularity for the government and a quick return to the long drawn out approach. This is what happened late in 1986 when premier Chirac retreated in the face of a series of huge student protests and a very effective rail strike, leading to a loss of momentum for his government and electoral victories for the Socialist

Party a couple of years later. It happened again in 1993-1994 when, despite an enormous parliamentary majority, conservative premier Balladur had to retreat in the face of huge protests over his attempts to cut the minimum wage for young workers and a very militant strike at Air France. Chirac himself seemed to learn the lesson of these experiences when campaigning for president in the spring of 1995: he stole the election from his right wing rival, Balladur, with populist promises to tackle unemployment, to keep the welfare system intact and to raise wages. This stance won Chirac the votes of many workers who were disillusioned by the experience of the Socialist Party in office, and even gained him a near endorsement from Blondel, the leader of France's third most important union federation, *Force Ouvrière.*

Once the conservative majority was entrenched, with Chirac replacing Mitterrand as president and Juppé taking over the premiership, there was growing pressure from business interests to forget such talk. At first Juppé seemed to resist these pressures and sacked a key minister who pushed for harder action. But this created unease in business circles who began to feel they had a government in no fit state to push through their policies. The franc came under pressure on international money markets, Juppé was subject to repeated attacks from within the conservative parliamentary majority, and opinion poll support for both Juppé and Chirac among the small business section of the population dropped by about half.[8]

Juppé and Chirac tried, desperately, to ease the big business and political pressures on them. Juppé announced a public sector wage freeze in October, even though this led to a highly successful one day protest strike by public sector unions. Chirac made a television address in which he admitted he had 'underestimated the seriousness of the problem' of the budget deficit.[9] But still big business and the right wing parliamentarians were uneasy until, a fortnight later, he suddenly presented his 'reform' package to the National Assembly.

The attitude of big business and the parliamentary right towards the government was transformed. Suddenly it seemed to have a powerful sense of direction. This was 'the second birth of the prime minister', *Le Monde* reported.

> *For the first time in six months Alain Juppé has refound his breath. In one go he has enlarged his room for manoeuvre... He has carried through a political salvage operation.*[10]

'Financial markets saluted the plan',[11] it was reported. It even seemed he would get support from sections of the socialist opposition. 'Juppé has hit home', admitted the one time Socialist Party prime minister,

Michel Rocard, while his colleague, the former health minister, was ready 'to support the government'.[12]

Yet there was more panic than forethought to Juppé's 'coup'. In his desire to win such plaudits he failed to learn the lessons of the most successful government attacks on workers' conditions in Europe over the last two decades. They have always depended on carefully thought out strategies designed to divide workers one against another. The key to Thatcher's success in her first two terms in office was the 'Ridley plan'— a detailed strategy, drawn up while the Tories were still in opposition in the late 1970s, for taking on strong groups of workers one at a time, leaving others temporarily untouched. So when, for instance, in 1981 she faced growing unofficial strikes against pit closures, she retreated, not taking on the miners until another three years of building up coal stocks and preparing the power stations had passed. And during the course of the great miners' strike she had no hesitation in conceding wage increases to other groups like rail and postal workers so as to isolate the miners, or in holding back her appointee as coal industry boss, MacGregor, when he wanted drastic action which might lead to other sections of workers coming out in support of the miners. It was not until her third term of office that she made the fatal mistake of pushing through a measure—the poll tax—that hit virtually all workers simultaneously.

By contrast, Juppé opted for measures which hit directly at the pension rights of all groups of public sector employees, reduced health care for everyone and increase taxes—and did so at the same time as pushing a scheme which meant a massive attack on rail workers' jobs. It was as if he was trying to do in a few weeks what it had taken Britain's Tories a decade to achieve—and this only six months after promising the opposite in an election.

He also made one other very serious error. He upset what had, historically, been the big trade union federation most amenable to the schemes of French capitalism, *Force Ouvrière*. The union arose from a split engineered in the Communist-led CGT union at the onset of the Cold War in 1948-1949, and in many sections of the economy FO survived because of support from the government and employers. This enabled it to be the dominant union among traditionally non-militant groups of civil servants. It also led to it being granted key positions of influence in the joint employer-union committees that administered the 300 billion franc welfare insurance system. As an article in *Le Monde* has told, the French employers' federation, the CNPF, had had an alliance 'which allowed the FO to direct the National Office of Sickness Insurance for 28 years'.

As a result of the friendly attitude shown to it by employers and the government for most of the last 48 years the FO leadership had tended to stand aside from protests organised by the other big union federations, the CGT and the CFDT, helping to ensure most strikes were minority strikes of one union or the other.

FO's secretary general, Marc Blondel—elected to office with the support of the pro-Chiracians in the unions (as well as a group of would be Trotskyists[13]) was certainly not intent on breaking this alliance. He had taken a benevolent attitude to Chirac in the presidential elections in the spring, held two or three private meetings with him in the autumn and said in public that he had 'the ear of Chirac'. At the beginning of November he signed an agreement with the employers' federation over 'annualisation of working hours'—a measure that he had previously denounced.[14] And he sought to silence speculation about government threats to the social security system by boasting, after a meeting with the labour minister Jacques Barrot on 11 November, that 'the social security system is safe'.[15]

Yet part of Juppé's coup was to pull the rug from under this tradition-ally close ally in the union bureaucracy. His 'reforms' involved not merely an attack on the welfare benefits of FO's members, but also threatened the domination by the bureaucracy of that union over the health insurance adminstration—and the well paid appointments that went with it. Hardly surprisingly, the poodle turned bitterly on its master. 'This is the end of the social security system, the biggest act of rape in the history of the republic,' declared Blondel. 'The social security system is the property of the workers and the government is stealing it.'[16] He was soon calling for protests, including strikes, against his former friends in government.

There was just one consolation for Juppé. The leader of the second most important union federation, the CFDT[17], Nicole Notat who has been very close to the Socialist Party leadership, welcomed his 'reform', although saying certain apsects of it needed negotiation. A substantial minority of unions affiliated to the FO and some of the smaller union federations took a similar attitude. This led Juppé to hope that the union protests would never be more than tokens and his proposals would survive unscathed.

The reaction

He was soon proved wrong. The first day of protests on Friday 24 November involved more than half a million people—more than in the protest against the public sector wage freeze on 10 October—despite the fact that it was not formally endorsed by the *Force Ouvrière* leadership. As *Le Monde* told, 'the country was virtually paralysed'.

What was to have been a day of protest against the increase in the number of years necessary to qualify for pensions in the public sector turned into a gigantic cry of discontent against the prime minister and his plan for social security... Rarely has a demonstration in Paris been more impressive. Behind the civil servants and local government employees there was a river of workers from the engineering and chemical industries, from textiles and the print. They came from Thomson, from Alcatel, Sextant Aviation, Dassault, Renault, Peugeot, RVI or Ford. The teachers were also there in large numbers... Although Marc Blondel of the FO had boycotted the day, a number of FO militants were present behind a coffin symbolising 'the death sentence for pensions'.

And in the provinces the demonstrations were relatively larger even than in Paris. In Marseilles, for instance, 'not since 1968 had such a demonstration taken place'. Tens of thousands more marched in a score of cities, from Toulouse and Lyons in the south to Lille in the north.[18] And the anger was not merely against the government, but also against any union leader who tried to justify its actions. Nicole Notat of the CFDT was forced to leave the demonstration in Paris after being subjected to violent abuse by her own members.[19]

Most significantly it soon became clear that the protests were not going to be like most days of action and 'general strikes' called by the unions over the last quarter of a century—one day affairs designed merely to force governments and employers to pay heed to the union bureaucrats. Not only was the railway network and public transport in the Paris region paralysed for the day, but general assemblies of workers in the big rail depots decided to continue their action, meeting each morning to decide to stay out longer. By Monday the railway network was virtually at a standstill and only 40 percent of metro trains and buses were running in Paris. On top of this, agitation in the colleges, which had begun in Rouen more than a month before, began to increase with a day of demonstrations on the Wednesday 22 November leading to a growing wave of student strikes across the country.

The ground was ready for an even more powerful day of protests the following Tuesday, 28 November. And this time, the *Force Ouvrière* leadership decided their interests lay in making the protest as large as possible. As *Le Monde* put it the evening before, 'for the first time since the split of 1947, the general secretaries of the CGT and the FO will march side by side in Paris.' Against the background of another massive wave of demonstrations across the country, Paris experienced 'one of its most spectacular traffic jams.'[20]

Yet, even now, the government could hope that the strike movement would subside. The talk among many union leaders was not of spreading strike action but of putting the emphasis on a national demonstration to be called in three weeks time, on Sunday 17 December. Juppé had said in a newspaper interview in mid-November, that he would 'be forced to resign if 2 million people demonstrated' against him, and this seemed to some 'moderate' leaders an easier way to fight than launching a wider strike movement. 'You cannot make the strike of the century every month,' said Jean Paul Roux of the independent union UNSA, 'many civil servants cannot lose two days of wages at six week intervals in the run up to Christmas'.[21] The leaders of FO and the CGT had shaken hands but it was by no means clear that they would collaborate on further strikes. What is more, a substantial chunk of the Socialist Party was still offering more direct help to Juppé. More than a hundred 'experts' and 'intellectuals' associated with the party signed a statement of support for the principles of 'reform in social security', saluting Nicole Notat for her 'courage and independent spirit' in opposing the protests.[22] And while the party's recently chosen leadership under Jospin claimed they were in 'solidarity' with the protests, they refused to take part in them, claiming they would not 'play with fire'.

But the strikes of the railway and transport workers were increasingly solid and began to spread to the postal sorting offices, which were usually located near the railway stations. A report in *Le Monde* told what happened in Paris:

> *Tuesday evening, some postal workers brought together some striking railway workers they had met on the demonstration of that day. At 8pm delegates from the CGT and the* [independent union] *SUD called ,'To throw the Juppé plan into the dustbin of history'. The railway workers have called for solidarity. 'The railway and the Parisian transport workers are not enough. There is need for the post and the electricity and gas workers. We can win, but it needs everybody. We are going to paralyse the economy.'*
>
> *Within quarter of an hour the strike was voted for. The group went out and visited the different offices. There was an improvised general assembly. The same speakers took up the same arguments. 'Already ten centres in the provinces are on strike. It is necessary to do the same everywhere.' So it was, they voted to strike and then, led by railway workers, walked along the rail track to the Austerlitz sorting office on the other side of the Seine which they also pulled out.[23]*

Such scenes seem to have been repeated in many other places. Thus in the sorting office at Sotteville near Rouen:

> *A hundred people assembled in a semicircle under the sorting office's neon lights. Three speakers represented the two main unions—the CGT, from which a circular told of the state of the movement in the post throughout*

France, and SUD, whose leaflet told, 'The rail workers and the students are the example we must follow. We must not let such a chance go'. According to everybody, the strike had to extend through all of France in all sectors. You only needed to have had a visit from the Sotteville railway workers to grasp the power of the movement. 'Their general assembly,' explained a union activist, 'was a true meeting in a huge locomotive repair shop. There were a good thousand people there, solid, united, discussing with ardour, impatient to have a go and ready to go all the way. It was extraordinary. It was such a pleasure to see.' The meeting decided to send delegations to all the big postal offices in the region, to the railway workers, to the nearby Renault factories. One activist told, 'It's necessary to mobilise, to have general assemblies everywhere, to convince the people at France Télécom to take action now rather than find themselves isolated when they face the threat of privatisation. That's how to construct a genuine national strike'.[24]

Another report from Rouen tells:

On Wednesday 29 November about 400 rail workers went to Renault-Cleon for the shift change at midday. At the main gate the mood was very dynamic. The CGT delegates at the works called on the workers to join the rail workers in struggle by stopping the next day. At the gates of the factory cordial discussions took place between the rail workers and the Cleon workers, but some recalled with bitterness that they had been isolated and let down by the union leaders during their strike in 1991.

After the demonstration of Thursday 30 November which involved the student and workers, including 1,600 rail workers, morale improved somewhat.

*On Monday 4 December several hundred rail workers took part in meetings with workers at the gate or inside a number of firms: Ralston, Alsthom, CPAM, CHU, Grande Paroisse, etc. The visit to Sernam led to this centre going completely on strike. Following the example of the rail workers, 200 employees of **Chèques Postaux** visited the employees of CPAM who voted for the strike.*

The demonstration of Tuesday 5 December broke all records, with journalists talking of 20,000 demonstrators. About 3,000 rail workers were at the head of it along with 500 Cleon workers. In many private firms stoppages took place that Tuesday with considerable participation in the demonstration, especially from Legrand, Rhone Poulenc and Grand Paroisse factories.[25]

A similar pattern was followed throughout much of the country, in large and small towns alike.[26] In Lyons rail workers went to the postal sorting offices and then the bus garages to get them out.[27] In Limoges, rail workers visited the social security office and the telecom workers before holding a joint meeting with striking electricity and gas workers.[28] In Bayonne the striking rail workers were joined by the electricity and gas workers on 28 November and the postal workers on the following day, and were soon meeting daily in front of the municipal hall to decide on actions for the day (such as cutting off electricity to the luxury hotels).[29]

By the end of November the railways, the Paris metro and buses, all the country's major sorting offices, and substantial numbers of telecom and electricity and gas workers were on strike, and were to stay out for the next three weeks. As the strike went on they were joined by growing numbers of teachers, until the majority were on strike. Even in sectors where management claimed only a minority were actually striking—as in the post, the telecom, electricity and gas—the strike was made effective by, for instance, the occupation of premises. In certain regions, electricity workers who were unable to close down much generating capacity, seized control of offices and put the mass of consumers onto the reduced night time tariffs during the day.

In other parts of the public sector a pattern emerged in which people would work nominally for part of the week, but then vote at general assemblies for a total stoppage on the twice a week days of action. On such days the core sectors on strike would be joined by much wider numbers of civil servants, dockers, airport workers, hospital workers and delegations from the private sector—even enjoying support from traffic police who refused to hand out parking tickets. On some of the days the newspapers were shut down by strikes of the CGT in the print. Sit-ins in local government buildings, the blockading of the channel tunnel rail route, demonstrations across airport runways, occupations of motorway pay booths (with collections from motorists for strike funds)—all highly 'illegal' actions which the police did not dare resist—added to the effectiveness of the strikes.

No one knows exactly how many strikers there were at any point in time. The occupation and blocking of premises in the core striking sectors meant that neither the management nor the union knew for certain whether those not working were on strike or simply not able to get to work. The paralysis of the transport system and the huge traffic jams further complicated the picture. So too did fluctuating numbers on strike on 'normal' days and demonstration days. All that is certain is that the strikes did paralyse key parts of the country's infrastructure and that as the days passed growing numbers of workers were involved in the strikes. And all the way through well over half the population expressed sympathy with the strikes in opinion poll surveys.

The strike was never a general strike, in that it never involved more than delegations on demonstrations from the great part of the private sector. But it did paralyse much of the economic life of the country and create a situation which the government could not resolve without making important concessions.

This was shown by what happened to the government's own strike breaking plans. It announced it was going to break the transport strike in Paris by putting on a fleet of scab buses. In reality it could never provide transport for more than a small minority of commuters and the traffic jams meant that journeys which might have taken 40 minutes now took three or four hours. The ruling RPR party issued a call to its activists on Friday 1 December to form 'transport users committees to organise a demonstration against the strike, probably next Thursday'.[30] Its model was supposed to be the half million strong demonstration De Gaulle's supporters had been able to mobilise in the last week of May 1968. In fact, the most it could achieve was a couple of hundred people marching in Paris and local RPR deputies were soon abandoning any attempt to get committees off the ground. Similarly, 'threats' by government deputies to 'resolve the crisis' through a referendum or general election came to nothing as it became clear the government would lose either—by-elections in December led to large swings to the left. In the end, Juppé had to abandon his talk of 'standing firm', give notice that he was prepared to negotiate with the unions, 'put on ice' the plan to rationalise the railway system, drop his insistence on increasing the number of years public sector employees had to work to earn their pensions, and announce a 'social summit' with the union leaders for 22 December.

Different sorts of mass strikes

Rosa Luxemburg's classic work *The Mass Strike, the Political Party and the Trade Unions*, which was based on the experience of the events of 1905 in the Russian empire (including her native Poland), told how a spontaneous strike movement can erupt, moving from economic to political and back to economic demands. She emphasised the spontaneity of the process, which escaped any attempt to control it by labour movement bureaucrats and which even revolutionary socialists could have problems keeping abreast of. She showed how what began as a movement in one sector could spread until it presented a general political challenge to the state and, in doing so, could raise the most despondent and unorganised sections of workers to begin to present their own economic and then political demands.

But not all great mass strikes of the last century have moved in the way described by Rosa Luxemburg. We have also had repeated experiences of what has been called 'the bureaucratic mass strike'—a strike movement carefully organised from above by trade union officialdom so as to assert its bargaining power with the employers and government and to maintain its influence over the mass of workers. Tony Cliff, for instance, described some 35 years ago how Belgian labour leaders organised strikes on these lines at the beginning of the century in the battle for the suffrage—and to gain access for themselves to the Belgian parliament. He tells how they nominated from above strike leaders in each industry and locality to make sure not only that strikes started as instructed, but were also brought to an end the moment the bureaucrats wanted them to.[31] Tony Cliff and Donny Gluckstein pointed out ten years ago how a great defensive struggle, the British General Strike of 1926, fell into very much the same pattern:

> *It had very little in common with the sort of mass strike described by Rosa Luxemburg. From the very beginning the TUC leaders made it clear they intended to keep a tight grip on the strike. They took it upon themselves to decide who would stop work and who would not.[32]*

The ability of the union leadership to keep control in this way (aided by terrible mistakes made by the British Communist Party under the influence of the Stalinised Communist International) meant that, although the strikers showed enormous unity and solidarity, the return to work on TUC instructions nine days later resulted in a devastating defeat for the movement.

Such 'bureaucratic mass strikes' became a feature of the working class movement in a number of advanced industrial countries in the 1980s. Employers and governments were determined to take back from workers some of the things they had conceded in the 1950s, 1960s and 1970s. Union leaders felt they had no choice but to show governments they mattered as 'negotiating partners' and allow the anger among the workers they represented some expression. They did so by calling for widespread industrial action, but attempting to make sure they kept control over its tempo, its militancy and its duration. As I wrote nine years ago:

> *There have been a succession of big public sector strikes on this model in recent years in: Holland, Belgium, Sweden, Finland and Denmark. In each case a right wing social democrat trade union bureaucracy suddenly felt compelled to call for a short lived spell of industrial action from a working class movement that had been previously relatively passive. The weakness of traditions of struggle has usually allowed the union bureaucracies to keep control of these strikes. For a few days an industry or a country is virtually paralysed then the union leaders reach a deal, everything returns to normal and stability returns.[33]*

But even in the 1980s, I noted, 'there have been cases of bureaucratic strikes partially escaping the control of the union bureaucracy'. For instance, in Denmark in 1985 a million workers out of a population of five million voted at thousands of meetings to prolong a mass strike after the union leaders advised them to go back to work. They did return to work a couple of days later, but their action was enough to force the Schluter government to abandon its attempts to emulate what Thatcher had done in Britain.

It is very important for socialists faced with mass strikes to be clear into which category they fall. A strike which spontaneously unleashes the militancy, combativity and growing class consciousness of the mass of workers opens up enormous prospects of both a challenge to existing society and the building of socialist organisation. By contrast, a mass strike which remains tightly in the hands of the trade union bureaucracy arouses enormous hopes among the mass of workers, only to dash them in way that can lead to years of demoralisation.

Most living struggles escape any watertight compartmentalisation. Trade union bureaucrats may initiate action from above, with the clear intention of keeping it under their own control and ending it on their own terms. But this does not mean they are always able to impose their own will on the mass of workers who respond to their call. Once workers move into action they begin to discover their own capacity to fight and to control things—and there is always at least the beginnings of a threat to the trade union bureaucracy in this. Indeed, this is one powerful reason why trade union leaders call off struggles just as the employers begin to fear the power displayed by the working class movement.

The unions, rank and file activism and the dynamic of the French strikes

The French strikes began in a way very similar to the 'bureaucratic' mass strikes typical of the 1980s. The trade union bureaucracy pushed the struggle forward because it wanted to prove itself to be the essential 'mediator' between the government and the working class. All the unions opted for a return to work once the government had shown it was prepared to negotiate with them and had made concessions short of the complete repeal of the Juppé plan. And although many rank and file activists were unhappy about this, nowhere were they confident enough either in their own views or in their own strength to continue the struggle despite the bureaucracy.

But from a very early point on the movement began to break out of the usual bureaucratic confines. It displayed the spontaneous militancy, combativity and growing class consciousness which Rosa Luxemburg emphasised. It did so because it gave expression to the enormous bitterness towards existing rulers, bosses and institutions that is characteristic of the popular mood in the 1990s right across the advanced countries. In a very real sense it was a product of those features that differentiate the 1990s from the 1980s.

Typically, in the 1980s, some sections of workers displayed enormous bitterness which exploded into very angry struggles—as with the steel workers, the miners and then the national newspaper workers in Britain. But other sections felt that, somehow, provided they made limited concessions to the employers, they would be protected from the worst aspects of the crisis—and, indeed, with the boom of the late 1980s even felt they might be able to benefit individually from 'people's capitalism'. By contrast, the effect of the recession of the early 1990s has been to destroy such illusions and to create a very widespread feeling that the system offers people little, even if there seems to be no alternative to it.

This has found expression in deep disillusionment with existing political systems and politicians, and in sudden swings of opinion. So in France, very large numbers of workers who had voted for the left in the two presidential elections of the 1980s voted for the right in the parliamentary elections of 1993. This did not stop them expressing support for the struggles against the new prime minister, Balladur, by Air France workers and by young people resisting a reduction in the minimum wage. Nor did it stop many who abstained or voted with the right wing parties in the first round of last spring's presidential election (an exit poll suggests that manual workers ['*ouvriers*'] gave only 42 percent of their votes to the parties of the left[35] and as many as 27 percent to the fascist Le Pen) swinging back behind the Socialist Party candidate, Jospin, who got an unexpected 47.4 percent in the second round.

Such bitterness and volatility meant that the moment serious action began in defence of working class interests, very large numbers of people identified with it, seeing it as offering a solution to their own problems.

A second important feature of the French events was that although they came after a long period of defeats and retreats by organised workers—especially during the years in which the Socialist Party controlled both the presidency and the parliamentary majority and in which the union bureaucracy held struggles back in the hope of maintaining influence with ministers—this was interspersed with certain spectacular victories or near victories, like the 1986 students' and rail workers' actions and the 1993 Air France strikes.

Finally, the French union bureaucracy entered the struggle in a particularly fragmented condition, only able to exert a direct influence over workers insofar as it could persuade rank and file activists to follow its lead.

As we have seen, the French trade unions have been divided into rival federations since the beginning of the Cold War, nearly half a century ago. This has had great advantages for French capitalism. It has meant that militant strikes, even when successful, have rarely given birth to the sort of powerful shop floor organisation that existed, for instance, in Britain in the 1960s and early 1970s. The union federations all too often ended up putting more stress on poaching members and influence from each other than on fighting the employers. The result was that even after the general strike of 1968 union membership only grew a little, and then went into decline in the 1980s, with the CGT membership in 1994 only a third of the 1977 figure[36] and combined union membership less than 10 percent of the workforce.

The influence of the unions over the workforce is much greater than the figures for union membership alone suggest. France has long had a state organised system of works councils. Under this different unions compete in annual elections in each workplace to determine who will be paid part of the time to represent the workers and run facilities such as factory canteens. And even if, say, the CGT only has 6 percent of the workers in a workplace as members, it might still win 60 percent of the places in such elections. Hence the paradox, inconceivable in Britain, that non-union members in a unionised workplace can show a high degree of support for the principles of trade unionism and even, on occasions, be the most militant when strikes break out. Hence also, however, an often ferocious level of competition between militants belonging to different unions as each tries to oust the other from works council positions. When it comes to such competitive situations, not only the FO and the CFDT, but also the CGT will disown militancy to win votes.

Historically the CGT has never hesitated to expel those who are too militant for the confederation's line. This was one of the factors that allowed the CFDT to pick up many people who regarded themselves as on 'the left' in 1968 and after. It has also, on occasions, allowed sections of FO to give themselves a left cover by accepting those who were too radical for the CGT. More recently, the CFDT has also expelled those it sees as too militant, leading to the creation of the SUD union by its expelled ex-postal service members.

The decline in union membership in the 1980s and 1990s has accentuated the fragmentation of the union structure still more, leading to fighting within as well as between union federations. Both the FO and the CFDT leaderships face internal opposition—in FO from those who believe it must not at any cost give up its old strategy of boosting its influence by doing favours for the employers, in the CFDT from those who believe it is losing influence because it has abandoned militancy for the policies of the right wing of the Socialist Party.

There are also less clear cut splits inside the CGT, to some extent reflecting divisions inside the Communist Party leadership on how to adapt to the situation since the collapse of the USSR and the failure of the Socialist Party governments (brought to power in the first place by the 'Union of the Left' between the Socialist Party and the CP). In the case of the CGT, the central argument is how it can break out of its 'marginalisation'—of a situation where its weakness and the influence of rival federations means it has little influence over the behaviour of either the employers or the government. The arguments over this issue have forced it to abandon the monolithic rigidity that characterised it in the past, with the union's leader Viannet now admitting it made mistakes in 1968—not, of course, by failing to follow a revolutionary path, but by cutting itself off from forces that could have built the union's membership and influence and instead, to some extent, driving those forces in the direction of the CFDT.

The announcement of the Juppé plan was both a challenge to and an opportunity for the fragmented union bureaucracies. Juppé was, in fact, saying that he did not take them seriously, yet the anger he was creating provided them with a chance to enormously increase their support among workers. They could only do so, however, if they encouraged their activists in the workplaces to agitate in a way that were bound to go well beyond the normal bureaucratic channels.

The challenge, as we have seen, was very serious for FO, with the majority of its members in the public sector and its privileged position in the social security administration. At the same time, when Nicole Notat of the CFDT came out in support of the Juppé plan, the FO leadership also saw an opportunity—that of detaching those CFDT members who were in the public sector away from Notat's union. Meanwhile, the CGT leadership saw a massive opportunity for itself. The anger produced by the Juppé plan among the mass of workers provided it with an opportunity to show how important it was as, historically, the union to which the most militant activists looked. Its mobilisations, it believed, could put the other union federations in the shade: something it showed clearly on Friday 24 November, when it turned what was meant by other unions as simply a protest over particular demands into a much more general revolt against the Juppé plan—for instance, using coaches provided by Communist Party-run municipalities to bus very large numbers of people from the suburbs to the central Paris demonstration. And its opportunities were even greater when Blondel was forced to embrace the CGT leaders on 28 November. In every workplace, FO activists who for decades had been resistant to CGT mobilisations now had no argument against taking part in protests in which the CGT activists were the driving force.

The radicalisation of workers

There is no doubt that a key role in getting the strikes off the ground was played by union activists from the CGT. Nor is there any doubt that these activists were encouraged to move in the first days of the strike by the union's full time officials. It was CGT militants in the railways who took the initiative in calling for general assemblies and strike votes, and then in arguing to pull out postal, telephone, electricity and gas workers. And they were not doing so just as individuals, but in accord with the desires of their union leaders. However, once the movement took off the CGT leaders began to lose direct control over events. At the general assemblies workers from all unions, and from none, expressed their views. And these views often became increasingly radical as the movement grew.[37]

The unions all refused to raise the demand for the resignation of the Juppé government, but when individuals started chanting the slogan on demonstrations, thousands of others would take it up. Placards would declare, '2 million and one'—meaning Juppé should keep his promise to resign if the demonstrations were more than 2 million strong. Typically, nurses in Paris sang, 'Juppé we're going to kick your arse',[38] while in Clermont Ferrand the 15,000 to 20,000 workers who paraded for hours through the centre of the town chanted, 'Down with the Juppé plan, Juppé must resign'.[39]

Along with the radicalisation of the demands went a radicalisation in political attitudes—often from workers who would say they were 'non-political'. A report about the central bus and tube workshop in Paris could tell:

A red flag flies over the front wall. A young non-union worker put it there as a symbol for the workplaces occupied since 28 November. He said to himself, 'there, the Paris Commune, that's French enough'. The union delegate of the CGT, somewhat annoyed, rushed to surround it with tricolours.'[40]

One report of interviews with strikers says:

They no longer believe in politics, in 'the left and the right'. They no longer believe in journalists either. 'They're like the politicians, distant from us, and their papers are not reality. They never let us speak on the TV.' And when the machinists talk about democracy in France, they say it is 'totalitarian', like in the RATP. It's a false consensus, they go through the form of having a dialogue, and after that the employers do what they want.[41]

A senior official of the FO metal workers' federation—which did not call for an all out strike—told journalists that he was worried about a social crisis which he judged to be 'very grave'.

Wage earners no longer believe in the ballot box. The strike is the only way left to them to change things.[42]

The demand for a wider generalisation of the struggle even found expression at the Congress of the CGT which took place in the second week of the strike. In the past such congresses had always been sewn up in advance by the federation's leadership. But its central leadership was divided over the long term strategy to increase the union's influence, between 'traditionalists' and 'renovators'. That split allowed other voices, not falling into either camp, to get a hearing.

Already on Monday [the first day of the congress] *some delegates protested at the general secretary's appeal for negotiations, demanding he insist on the immediate withdrawal of the Juppé plan and call for a general strike. This issue, which was not on the agenda of the congress, caused lively exchanges between delegates. Half the interventions called for the general strike, some saying that the absence of this slogan blurred and made ambiguous the position of the CGT. 'The general strike is the only way to make the government give in', a rail worker thought. ' Congress must show the determination of the CGT to go right to the end.'*

The level of generalisation of these struggles is shown by the way in which workers from one industry went to pull out workers from other industries. It is shown too by the way workers intermingled with each other on demonstrations, without any concern for which union or which sector people were from.[43]

The symbols of the struggle were, everywhere, from France's revolutionary traditions, even though many of the strikers and demonstrators had clearly not voted for the left in last spring's elections and a substantial minority of workers had voted for the National Front. The strike was often strongest in towns and cities in the south of the country where the Front does particularly well electorally. In Toulon, where the Front runs the council, 25,000 demonstrated in support of the strike in a city of 100,000; in Marseilles, where the Front has long had a strong base, there were three demonstrations in less than a fortnight of 160,000 to 200,000 people in a city whose population is around 800,000. Everywhere there were red flags, and a marked feature of all the demonstrations was the singing by thousands of people of the *Internationale*—something that has taken place so rarely in the last 25 years that most workers did not know the words!

Embryos of rank and file control

The level of involvement of the mass of workers in the strikes was much greater than has usually been the case in French strikes. Even in the general strike of 1968, the usual pattern was for the minority of active union members to get the other workers out on strike, send them home, and then occupy the workplaces by themselves for the duration of the struggle. And even the occupying minority were often not very actively involved in the movement, playing cards or table tennis to pass the time, rather than debating and demonstrating. In contrast, the December strikes were characterised by a very high level of activity, with the union activists calling daily 'general assemblies' where members and non-members alike voted on whether to keep the strike going for another 24 hours and, in many cases, discussed what to do to draw new sectors of workers into the struggle.

This meant there was an enormous potential for the development of new forms of organisation from below, based upon workers' democracy rather than bureaucratic manoeuvring. Workers were on strike together, with some groups pulling others out and helping to sustain their struggle. It was only a small step further to turn general assemblies of one sector into joint general assemblies of the whole class in a locality, and to fuse individual strike committees into co-ordinating committees for a whole town or a whole locality's workers.

This certainly began to happen in a number of cases. Thus a teacher from the 20th *arrondissement* of Paris tells how, after his school voted to strike:

> We went down to the local postal depot which was out on strike. There were about 100 of them having a meeting in the canteen. It was amazing, everyone was applauding us, just a little school! They proposed a local demonstration on Thursday morning, before the national march, to go around local work-places. Everyone thought that was a great idea and it was decided straight away to contact other local strikers. Armed with leaflets we set off on a tour of local workplaces—the office of the Paris water company, where a delegation walked straight in while the rest chanted outside, a large residential nursing home, where a group of the home's workers comes to the door— nearly all low paid, women and black—the big Monoprix supermarket, into which about 20 striking teachers, postal workers, bus workers and school students marched straight.

The fruits of this kind of local contact and initiative were seen a few days later. Some 500 strikers from workplaces across the district met together to plan joint activity across the *arrondissement*, agreeing to establish a regular co-ordinating committee between the striking workplaces in the *arrondissement*. Similar moves were reported from several other Paris districts. And in some places outside Paris, the level of co-ordinated organisation seems to have gone further. A CGT militant has told how they created a strike organising committee in Rouen:

> *First we put forward the appeal at a general assembly of the SNCF workers. The text proposed the withdrawal of the Juppé plan as the axis around which to build for a general strike. Once the general assembly had approved the text, we worked on it in a committee that had representatives from all the trade unions present among the workers. We were unanimous in our conviction that we had to spread the movement across all the categories of railway workers. So we visited the SNCF repair workshops at Quatre Mares (with 800 workers, one of the region's largest workplaces).*
>
> *When we explain the SNCF rationalisation plan, the workers got very excited. All this at 5 o'clock in the morning. Some of the Quatre Mares workers came to strengthen the picket lines...*
>
> *That afternoon we found ourselves in an all-plant general assembly. The atmosphere was crazy. People were drumming, trumpeting, whistling. Nothing had been organised apart from speeches by representatives of the trade union federations. We tried to 'regularise' the situation by creating a strike committee...with five or six representatives mandated by the general assembly of each sector, plus the regular representatives of each union.*
>
> *And so it was from day three of the strike onwards. Each morning the unitary organising committee in each sector, together with the shop stewards, organised the general assembly. At the beginning of the afternoon, the central committee planned that afternoon's joint meeting...*
>
> *The afternoon meeting was held in a yard where we normally park trains awaiting repairs. The atmosphere was incredible. The big assemblies were like rallies. But they did represent the heart of the strike, the heart of working class democracy.*
>
> *It was through this daily meeting that all the workplaces and all the trade union bodies were gradually infected with the spirit of the strike. At the beginning you had two or three workers coming from a particular firm or depot. Then they started bringing their workmates! And for three weeks this railway yard was THE meeting place for all the sectors in struggle. The Rouen post sorting centre was the first to join the strike, Then there was **Électricité de France**. The Renault auto plant at Cleon decided to join us after 800 of us went to talk to them...*

You can't say it became a general strike committee. It wasn't thought of in that way. But it certainly did represent a meeting place, a forum for initiatives for all the sections involved in the struggle.

Together we drafted a leaflet which we distributed on 11 December when we blocked all the roads into Rouen. More than 1,000 workers from all sectors met at the SNCF depot at 4am—teachers, postal workers, Renault workers, we blocked the town that day. The next day we organised a 'forum of struggle' just in front of the town hall. An experience like that changes your way of thinking.[44]

There is a very similar report about the organisation of the strike in Dreux—the town of 35,000 people some 60 miles from Paris where the National Front made its first electoral breakthrough:

The rail workers pushed forward a new, open form of struggle against the Juppé plan and the rationalisation of the railways by making their general assemblies wide open to all the other sections in struggle, to the press and to democratic organisations. Discussions took place in front of comrades from other parts of the public and private sector.

The small premises by the railway line, close to the workshops, became a humming beehive where everything was debated—how to carry the movement forward, the preparation of the demonstrations, providing daily meals, the organisation of the creche for strikers' children...and making links with other sectors. The railways workers went to meet the postal workers, the hospital workers, the gasworkers, the teachers, the council workers. And then everyone often found themselves together in front of private factories with loudhailers, songs, red flags, leaflets with the call for the general strike in the public and private sectors.

The movement allowed the strikers—railway workers, public sector and private, to come together. This was no longer a movement of 'everyone for themselves', but one of 'all together'.[45]

In bringing together 'native' French, Turkish, North African and other workers from the rail, the post and the manufacturing plants in the region, together with unemployed youth from the high rise estates, the movement must have had a huge political impact on a town where the growth of the National Front has been described as 'irresistible'[46] and where the fear of the Front winning control of the council led all the Communist and Socialist candidates in the local elections last year to withdraw in favour of the non-fascist right, leaving what was once a left wing council without a single left wing member!

The union leaders apply the brakes

The radicalisation and politicisation of the movement was bound, eventually, to clash with the conservatism of the union bureaucracies. This did not merely apply to the union leaders like Notat who opposed the movement from its inception. It also applied to the CGT and FO leaders who had initially pushed their activists to initiate strikes.

They wanted to increase the prestige and negotiating power of the union they controlled, not to unleash some general confrontation with the government, still less with the capitalist class as a whole. And they certainly did not want to see co-ordinating committees which were not under the control of the union take command of the struggle. They turned their attention from pressing down on the accelerator to making sure they controlled the steering wheel and then, a few days later, to applying the brakes.

What mattered to them was asserting their power to mediate between the government and the working class. For Blondel that meant putting on pressure for a restoration of the FO's privileged position in the public sector and, if possible, in the adminstration of the social insurance funds. For the CGT it meant reasserting its traditional position as the most powerful union, the key organisation that any government that wanted to restore 'social peace' had to take into account. For both federations that meant spreading the movement within the public sector and getting token action in the private sector, but then ending the movement through negotiations. A perceptive article in *Le Monde* spelt out the CGT's position:

> *The CGT has the advantage over the other federations of being everywhere at the head of the movement, playing a determining role in the SNCF* [rail], *the EDF-GDF* [electricity and gas], *the post and the RATP* [Parisian metro and buses]. *It does not face any competition in the rail, unlike in the strike at the end of 1986, when it was pushed aside, like the other unions, by two* [unofficial] *rail workers' co-ordinations. It multiplies its calls for strikes so as not to be overtaken by more or less spontaneous movements. It thus seems to control the majority of the strikes and appears indispensable, especially on the rail, when it comes to finding a way out of the conflict.'*[47]

Viannet spelt his aims out in a newspaper interview. The concessions the government were making over public sector pensions, he said, 'are the result of the strong mobilisation'. He continued, in the

> *days to come, we will obtain other concessions, but for that we need to maintain the mobilisation... The accusation of a 'political strike' makes no sense. Recently I was demonstrating in front a small group of lads—I don't know*

who they were—who were shouting, 'Juppé, Get Out!' I turned to them and said, 'Who do you intend to put in his place?' They were silent after that, because the question is not whether its Juppé, Tom, Dick or Harry, but what politics they put forward and how they respond to the issues raised by the social movement.[49]

At the CGT Congress the leadership could not prevent calls from the floor for a general strike. But it could ensure they came to nothing. One speaker described them as 'schemes from the past'. Others made great play of the difficulty of extending the strike from the public sector to private industry workers, 'not directly affected by the Juppé plan'. And, in the end, the leadership pushed through a resolution calling for a 'generalisation' of the struggle, with a view to achieving 'genuine negotiations based on the demands of the strikers'.[49]

The private sector

One proof of the 'prudence' of the CGT leadership is shown by what happened in the private sector. The failure of significant sections of the private sector to join in the strike wave was, people recognised at its conclusion, its weakest feature. The union leaders put forward an argument to the effect that there was no real possibility of the private sector joining in the strikes. The private sector workers, it was said, did not have the same immediate interest in the defeat of the Juppé reforms as the public sector, where the eligibility for pensions was under attack. The years of large scale redundancies had created an atmosphere in the private sector, people added, which made its workers frightened to strike. Finally, the anti-strike laws made it difficult to get legal strikes at short notice.

These arguments were not only heard from union leaders. They were also repeated at the daily general assemblies of strikers, where people who wanted the private sector to come out would explain how difficult it was. And, as a French revolutionary explains, 'much of the left accepted the same argument'.[50] But there is some evidence that the arguments were wrong.

There was the same general feeling in the private sector as in the public sector—that the strike wave was necessary. This is shown by opinion polls, by the way in which private sector workers would crowd the pavements to clap and cheer the demonstrations, and by the huge private as well as public sector participation on the last great day of demonstrations, Saturday 16 December. The bitterness was certainly there among private sector workers, waiting to be tapped.

What is more, fear of victimisation certainly did not prevent a few parts of the private sector joining the struggle. In some parts of France lorry drivers took action of their own around their unions' demand for retirement at the age of 55, blocking the roads.[51] At Caen 'wage earners participated on mass in the demonstrations, with several thousand workers from Renault Vehicles from the Blainvile-sur-Orne factory, from the Moulinex works, from Citroen, from Crédit Lyonnais, Crédit Agricole and Kodak.[52] In Clermont Ferrand, thousands of Michelin workers regularly joined in the twice a week demonstrations, taking time off work to do so. And miners in Lorraine and the south fought a bitter battle for wages, including running battles with police.

There was certainly a hesitancy among private sector workers about throwing themselves into the struggle. But the same hesitancy was also there, at first, among some of the public sector workers who eventually struck and held out to the end. What was needed, a French revolutionary argues, 'was not a question of the union leaders just issuing a General Strike call and doing nothing else. It was a question of laying the ground for such action with appropriate demands.'[55] The most appropriate demand was the one which some groups of workers and some local union federations began to raise anyway—to return to private sector workers the pension entitlement after 37.5 years which the government was now threatening to take away from public sector workers. In fact, although the CGT and FO leaders engaged in rhetoric about 'generalising' the struggle to the private sector, they made virtually no practical efforts to get more than token support for demonstrations.[56]

At Renault, the CGT's strongest single base in the engineering and motor industry, the federation did start discussions on pushing the demand for pension rights after 37.5 years. But, a report tells,

> Daniel Sanchez, the central delegate of the CGT for the Renault group, put forward this objective without making it into a real slogan. 'We are ready to go all the way', he said, 'even up to a general strike'. But Renault could not simply dissolve itself in a movement with themes that were too general. 'We must conserve our own dynamic'.[57]

In practice, this meant the union behaved 'prudently'.[58] Only at Cleon, where as we have seen the initiative of the Rouen rail workers was decisive, does it seem that substantial numbers of Renault workers threw themselves into the movement. Elsewhere the CGT leadership seem to have been happy for relatively small groups of workers to join demonstrations, with no action at all occurring in some plants.

As an FO delegate at the Gare Saint Lazare confided to a newspaper reporter at the end of the strike:

> The leaderships of the CGT and FO never wanted to go to a general strike. Viannet and Blondel would shit in their pants at the idea. The movement was

becoming too spontaneous, too autonomous. You could see it on the ground. They applied all the brakes to prevent the organising of general strike committees in the localities.[59]

The paper *Socialisme Internationale* spelt out the lessons of the strike:

All the potential that found expression in the December strikes remained in an embryonic state. The union leaders never called for a general strike nor sought to build it. Viannet and Blondel said often enough that they wanted negotiations for one to accept their word for it.

What the workers themselves wanted more and more and what could have been won was the fall of the government... The attempts to create structures linking up different section of workers remained isolated and localised. These initiatives were not encouraged by the union leaders. These had too great a fear that they would give rise to co-ordinations controlled by the workers themselves and which could begin to elect their own representatives raised up by the struggle and not professional negotiators like Viannet and Blondel...

The initiatives which were taken depended in general on whether there was one or more militants ready to organise the movement and enlarge the mobilisation. It is this which explains the enormous heterogeneity of situations. Where militants were present to propose initiatives and establish connections between workers from different sections, the dynamic developed very quickly. In other cases, the strike lost a lot of its dynamism and left the strikers isolated...

To organise that required a political leadership determined to bring down the government. Neither the Communist Party nor, even less, the Socialist Party, wanted to give such leadership. Hiding behind the excuse of not 'taking over' the movement, they left their militants without leadership and did not offer any way forward for the workers in struggle.[60]

The student movement

One feature of the December movement that seemed reminiscent of 1968 was the involvement of students. While public sector workers were paralysing the transport system, France experienced its biggest wave of student struggles since 1986—a wave which began several weeks before the public sector strikes. The involvement of the students proved how wrong are those journalists and others that repeat, year after year, that students have changed since the 1960s and can never be involved in struggle again or show a widespread interest in politics.

At the same time, however, the dynamic of the student struggle and its relationship to the workers' movement was different in a number of important respects to 1968. In 1968 the student movement began in humanities faculties in Paris and grew within the space of a few days into a huge confrontation with the French state involving many tens of thousands of students, raising demands about not merely their own conditions but the nature of society. The students were very quickly talking about 'revolution' and trying to win workers to the same notion.

In 1995, the movement began with the particular demands raised by certain groups of students in provincial towns over conditions, only slowly spreading to the rest of the country. It never reached the level of political generalisation of 1968. It was thousands of railway workers who led the demonstrations singing the *Internationale*, not thousands of students.

The first struggle began when science and technology students in Rouen went on strike on 9 October in protest at cutbacks in funding which meant an acute shortage of teachers and equipment. They demonstrated through the streets of the city, raising the demand for an increase of 12 million francs (about £1.75 million) in the university budget and staged a spectacular occupation of the rectorate. After police threw them out the struggle escalated to involve the humanities students and, by the first week in November the government felt under enough pressure to concede three-quarters of their demands, promising the creation of 188 new teaching posts.

The government clearly hoped to contain the student revolt within the one university by its concession. It was probably encouraged in this by press reports of students' attitudes, which seemed to show them far from the revolutionary ideas of 1968. Many expressed complete indifference to official politics, saying that the 'socialism' of the 14 years with Mitterrand as president had done nothing for them. But, at the same time, their anger was about more than particular questions of university teaching and resources. They expressed deep resentment at what society offered them: they spoke of a future of low salaries and job insecurity. And this discontent existed in many other places besides Rouen.

Far from ending the movement the government's concession to Rouen encouraged its spread. In the fortnight that followed the Rouen settlement, Metz, Toulouse, Tours, Orleans, Caen, Nice, Montpellier, Perpignan and many other universities staged strikes and demonstrations, each raising its own demands for additional funding, and the first universities in the Paris area finally joined in the struggle on 16 November. Demonstrations across the country on Tuesday 21 November involved more than a 100,000 students. When the first big protests against the Juppé plan took place three days later, a contingent of some 3,000 students behind a banner calling for 'student/worker unity' received massive applause from other participants. When a further national student demonstration was called for 30 November, it turned in many provincial cities into a joint demonstration of rail workers, students and others against the government—in Marseilles, 'two thousand students and rail workers marched behind a common banner,'[61] while, as we have seen, students were among those who joined the rail and postal workers in the delegations to the factories in places like Rouen.

But although the feeling that the students were in struggle alongside them gave an impetus to the spread of the public sector strikes over the following week, the students never played anything like the central role of 1968. And there are indications that the student moment began to subside just as the workers' movement was reaching its peak. By the first week in December, with demonstrations bigger than in 1968 in many provincial cities, the role of the students in them declined, while in Paris students usually went on the demonstrations as individuals, not in university contingents.

A national co-ordination was set up for striking students from across the country and it played a role in calling the demonstration on 30 November. But reports suggest that it was much more representative of wide numbers of students in some of the provincial centres than it was in Paris, where it was very much dominated by old established activists from one of the rival national student unions, UNEF. As a French revolutionary tells:

The student movement was big in Toulouse and perhaps a few other places. Elsewhere there were three days of mass mobilisation, which were bigger than anything since 1986, but in reality not that huge. So in Nanterre, in the Paris suburbs (the epicentre of the 1968 revolt) 3,000 were involved out of 30,000. And after the three days, the movement began to go into decline. The rival student unions, one led by the Socialist Party and one by the CP, who only organise 1 percent of the students between them, fought with each other, and in addition there were groups of anarchists and so on involved. This could give the false impression the whole movement was more radical than it was.[62]

The revolutionary paper *Socialisme Internationale* reports:

This infighting considerably harmed the student movement, so that even where it had not yet attained much support on the ground the fighting between the two principal unions and the tendencies within them still went on. To gain control of the national student co-ordination, the delegates, who were often union activists, outbid each other in immediately putting forward national demands without trying to root their movement in each college by raising concrete issues. This led the student strikers to marginalise themselves rather than involve the students not yet on strike in the movement.

This led the students' movement to decline very quickly, leaving isolated the universities, such as Toulouse, where the struggle was more solidly organised.[63]

This picture seems to be confirmed by a report in *Le Monde*, which explains that: 'The student co-ordination seems virtually to have disintegrated before it was born after 21 November. While some students are representative, others have not been chosen by general assemblies at all...'[64]

These weaknesses did not stop the student movement increasing the disarray of the government. Nor did it stop many, many thousands of students getting involved in demonstrations and actions in support of the public sector strike. And, in all likelihood, it will not stop many students from learning very important lessons in practice about their ability to struggle alongside workers in future. But it did mean the students could not play the role they played, to some extent, in 1968 of injecting a ferment of revolutionary ideas, however inchoate, into the workers' movement.

Negotiations

In the very week Viannet was arguing vehemently at the CGT congress against calls for a general strike and the bringing down of the government, he was also, in private, doing something else. 'Viannet's telephone was working a great deal on Thursday—between Viannet and Blondel of the *Force Ouvrière* in order to prepare a day of action, but also between Viannet and Jean-Pierre Denis, the assistant secretary general at the Elysée [ie to Chirac]...'[65] On that day Juppé had told his ministers to open negotiations, especially over the issues in dispute on the railways. That Sunday (10 December), 'contacts of a discreet and secret nature multiplied between the government and the unions.'[66]

The following Tuesday and Thursday saw the biggest demonstrations yet—in many provincial cities up to twice the size of those the week before—despite continual predictions from the government and a section of the media that the movement would enter into decline. The question now facing the union leaders was whether to keep the movement going—in particular by keeping the rail workers on strike—until the whole Juppé plan was withdrawn and so deal the government a mortal blow, or to accept piecemeal concessions that put the railway rationalisation plan 'on ice' and withdrew the increase in the qualification period for public sector pensions.

The CGT faxed a circular to all its railway branches on the Friday morning after the biggest demonstration and the most widespread strike action yet, as workers were boasting they had topped the 2 million figure which Juppé had said would cause him to resign. It urged them to call off the strikes and 'continue the struggle by other means'. It claimed it wanted the movement to keep going, so as to put pressure on the government to make more concessions—calling a very large demonstration in Paris on Saturday 16 December and a smaller day of action the following week. But effectively it was winding down the movement.

Very large numbers of individual strikers were not happy when they received the rail union's fax. At first, one report tells, 'many CGT branch officials were convinced it was a forgery'.[67] At the Gare du Nord in Paris the general assembly decided by 200 votes to one, with a few abstentions, to remain on strike[68]. The South West Paris rail depot voted by 102 votes to one, with 12 abstentions, to stay out. In Lyon the vote to continue was 637 to 190. In Rouen, the CGT officials were careful not to take the initiative in suggesting a return to work, leaving that to a CFDT official; on the Sunday the vote was still 138 to 2 to continue the strike.[69] Newspaper reports of general assemblies in the post, the electricity and gas and, especially, in the large rail depots told of furious discussions, with workers saying that more was involved in the struggle than just a strike over particular demands. The return to work on the railways was not complete for two or three days, and some of the Paris transport workers held out even longer. Some groups, like the Caen postal workers and the Marseilles transport workers were still on strike over their own specific demands a fortnight later. But the movement as a whole was at an end by the time Juppé's 'social summit' took place.

Politics

The behaviour of the unions in winding down a movement they had previously encouraged should not, really, surprise anyone. Unions are bureaucratic structures that balance between the organised workers and the employing class, seeking to use their influence over one in order to be accepted as 'partners' by the other. And French unions are no different. The CGT was quite happy in 1968 to negotiate the Grenelle agreement with the Gaullist prime minister Pompidou. The leaders attempted to bring the strike to an end on terms which were much worse than large sections of workers wanted—and paid the price when a huge mass meeting at Renault Billancourt broke out into chants of 'Don't sign, don't sign'.[70]

Union bureaucracies always try to end mass strike movements when they go beyond a certain point. For they begin to go beyond the issue of this or that negotiation with the powers that be to a complete challenge to their authority. Political issues are raised—and that requires the sort of political response that the trade union bureaucracy is incapable of making. Even those in the bureaucratic structure who personally would identify with a political response are constrained from providing it by the requirements of operating through the structure. What matters then is political organisation, not simply trade union organisation. A CGT activist at the Gare du Nord told one newspaper reporter:

> *The union federations followed their old reflexes about the need to end a strike. But this movement was more than just an industrial conflict. It became a critique of the elites, of the neoliberalism imposed by truncheons and cutbacks, of wealth kept in a few hands, of a society that no longer concerns itself with people. The movement arrived at a point where it had to become political. It created a new consciousness, and no one has the right to betray it.*[71]

The main political organisations of the left were as incapable of rising to the level of the movement as the union leaders. The party that gets most electoral support from French workers is the Socialist Party. It was completely incapable of offering a political alternative in December 1995. During the 14 years of Mitterrand's presidency its leaders had accepted exactly the same economic logic that led Juppé to push his 'reforms'. So it was hardly surprising that about half the Socialist Party leadership agreed with those reforms while the other half refused to turn verbal opposition to those reforms into any practical agitation.

The second major political organisation of the left in France is the Communist Party, which historically has had more influence with militant sections of workers. It took a stance which, on the face of it, was much more outspoken than that of the Socialist Party. On 20 November, before the strikes had even begun, its national secretary, Robert Hue, judged anger against the Juppé plan to be 'legitimate'. And, as we have seen, the CGT, over which the party exercises a great deal of influence, played an active role in initiating the strikes. But it soon became clear that the party was no more prepared to agitate in the workplaces and streets than was the Socialist Party. The party leadership insisted that the question of bringing down the government was not on the agenda since 'the Communist Party was not ready for the dissolution of the National Assembly'.[72] Hue insisted the rest of the left was 'not ready for the progressive alternative'[73] and that 'you must not say to the movement what it's not saying itself. The movement today is not ready for a political change'.[74] Not only did this mean that Hue insisted, 'the idea of a general strike is not on the order of the day',[75] it even meant that the CP leadership hesitated before supporting a Socialist Party motion of censure on the Juppé government in the national assembly![76] No wonder there was considerable criticism at a meeting of the party's national committee in the first week in December:

> *There were several questions about and criticisms of the party's prudent*
> *conduct. Several federation secretaries brought up the feeble 'visibility' of the*
> *Communists in the actions and demonstrations, some wanting more common*
> *actions with the CGT, some wanting the party to act in another way.*[77]

The main aim of the party's leadership in the last few years has been to regain some of the strength in lost in the 1970s and 1980s. Until then, not only did it attract many of the most militant French workers, it was also the biggest voting force on the left, receiving 5 million votes. This enabled it to combine a Stalinist dedication to the foreign policy of the USSR with an essentially parliamentary approach at home. What this meant was shown in May 1968, when it played a key role in persuading workers to end their strikes in return for wage increases and the calling of a general election by president De Gaulle. But both its Stalinism and its parliamentarianism backfired on it from then on.

Support for the USSR became increasingly unpopular and risked isolating the party both from many militant workers and from other parliamentary forces. At the same time its electoralism led it into an uncritical alliance with Francois Mitterrand's refounded Socialist Party, which carefully manoeuvred to win over millions of former Communist voters. Yet the party stuck to the alliance, with ministers inside Mitterrand's first government even as that government turned against the workers who had voted for it—until Mitterrand booted them out. The result was that after losing votes to the Socialist Party, it suffered in the mid-1980s from a further loss of support as disillusionment with the Socialist Party governments set in. Then the party leader, Marchais, reacted with an increasingly sectarian, Stalinist response, seeking to hold on to the party's diminishing membership by driving out anyone trying to open up a debate on what had gone wrong. The only result was to make things go from bad to worse for the party, until it risked electoral annihilation, getting considerably fewer votes than the fascist NF and only twice those of the Trotskyist candidate, Arlette Laguiller.

Hue, who took over as party leader in 1994, has sought to escape from this increasing marginalisation by a double strategy. On the one hand he has called for the final jettisoning of Stalinism, saying that this led to missed opportunities, especially in 1968 when it 'viewed the movement with the eyes of the 1950s', and opening up discussion with others on the left—even going so far as to send a representative to the funeral of the Belgian Trotskyist Ernest Mandel and organising an official meeting between representatives of the Communist Party and the Trotskyist LCR as the strike wave was rising on 29 November.[78] On the other, Hue has made it clear that the key to overcoming the 'marginalisation' of his party is by making an opening to the right. He talks of basing the party on 'the great French traditions of humanism' and he has followed a strategy since the victory of the right in last spring's elections of 'constructive' opposition. This has involved attacking the government for forgetting its electoral promises as it subordinates 'French' interests to it search for European unity, with the Communist Party issuing a call for a referendum on European Economic and Monetary Union on the 25th anniversary of De Gaulle's death—a clear attempt to appeal to sections of the nationalist right.

From this perspective, the movement against the Juppé plan provided the party with an opportunity to pick up support. It could only rejoice at the embarrassing situation in which a Socialist Party which had won so many votes from it in the past now found itself. But the CP was also desperate to avoid the movement making more difficult the alliances it sought with 'anti-European' forces to the right of it. Hence its insistence that building the movement was the task of the CGT and not of the party, and its opposition to calls for a general strike and its resistance to any notion of overthrowing the Juppé government.

There have been two significant Trotskyist organisations to the left of the Communist Party since 1968—*Lutte Ouvrière* and the *Ligue Communiste Revolutionaire* (LCR). *Lutte Ouvrière* combines a stress on the production of regular bulletins around workplaces with relatively successful electoral interventions—especially the repeated presidential campaigns of Arlette Laguiller. In the 1970s *Lutte Ouvrière* was both smaller and less visible than the LCR. But it picked up support in the early and mid-1980s as the only left organisation to insist, from the beginning, that Mitterrand and the Socialist Party would betray their supporters. Some of its members played a key role in one of the co-ordinations that led the 1986 railway strike, and Arlette Laguiller made a considerable impact in last year's presidential elections, getting 1.5 million votes, including those of one in 14 manual workers.[79]

But these successes have been accompanied by enormous weaknesses in theory and practice. The theory has always been mechanical and dogmatic—repeating over and over again a few basic points. Some of these points have been correct, like its stress on the cental role of the working class and workplace struggles. Others have been wrong, like its contention that the USSR remained a degenerated workers' state to the end, while oddly, China, Cuba and the Eastern Europe were said always to have been capitalist, or its belief that Islamic fundamentalism is qualitatively worse than any other form of petty bourgeois politics. In neither case has it been able to use its theory to develop 'a concrete analysis of concrete situations', as Lenin once put it. And parallel with this mechanical theory has gone a similarly mechanical view of revolutionary politics. For *Lutte Ouvrière* there are only two tasks—to raise concrete economic questions in particular workplaces, and to make general propaganda through election campaigns and workplace bulletins. It has lacked any notion of using a revolutionary paper as an 'organiser', drawing people around it as its takes up particular agitational issues and generalises from them. Nor has it had any notion that politicisation does not *only* take place in the workplace, but also in struggles outside the workplace, particularly against oppression. So, for instance, it has repeatedly refused to agitate against the growing influence of the Nazi National Front on the grounds that 'the NF does not exist in the workplaces'.[80]

All these faults came together during the December strike wave to stop *Lutte Ouvrière* in any way meeting the need for revolutionary leadership. Individual members of *Lutte Ouvrière* clearly played a leading role in particular workplaces—just as particular members of the Communist Party did. But the organisation as a whole made no concerted attempt to provide a political lead. Its members put little effort into selling its paper during the demonstrations, there was no attempt to put up posters or to put out leaflets attempting to give some direction to the movement, and Arlette Laguiller did little to provide any guidance to the people who had voted for her in the spring.

These were not accidental failings. They rested on a complete inability to understand the potential of the movement, which in turn was a product of mechanical theory. This holds that world wide there is a general 'reactionary evolution' connected with 'the counter-revolution' in the former USSR. In France itself, it has claimed (in an article dated 31 October and published in January, after the strike wave), 'the present period is dominated by a demoralisation of the working class'.[81]

Lutte Ouvrière interpreted the spread of the strikes in the last week of November as simply a manoeuvre by the union bureaucracies. Their paper said, in an article headed 'After Two Weeks', that 'the strike is the product of a process launched from above only. It is in fact because the will of the trade union centres, the FO and the CGT, that the movement broke out, hardened and spread'.[82]

Such an analysis led *Lutte Ouvrière* to take a very passive attitude to the movement until its third week. And even then they did not agitate either for a general strike or for political demands like the overthrow of the Juppé government. Their paper talked about raising the question of qualifying for pensions in the public sector after 37.5 years, but never campaigned for the demands. And there was no sense in the paper that militants should be preparing to counter the union leaders' attempts to sell the movement out. The first direct criticism of the CGT leadership over its role in the strike did not appear in *Lutte Ouvrière*'s paper until after the return to work by the rail workers! And even then, its press could, on occasion, *justify* the union leaders' call for the return to work, claiming 'the climate was shifting towards a return to work and the CGT leaders were kept informed almost by the hour of the mood among the strikers...'[83] The approach recalls nothing so much as the attitude the British Communist Party took in the 1926 General Strike when, despite its intense political disagreements with the union leaders, it issued the call, 'All power to the general council!'[84]

What is more, *Lutte Ouvrière* made no attempt to turn its paper and its meetings into a focus for drawing together those who wanted the strike to go further and to turn it into a total challenge to the politics of the government.

The LCR was just as incapable as *Lutte Ouvrière* of beginning to provide any leadership in the struggle. In formal terms it had a better grasp of what the movement was about. It could recognise the massive, spontaneous rebuff to the political establishment. Its paper attempted to relate to the upsurge of the movement. It did raise the question of the general strike and spreading the movement to the private sector. And its activists in certain unions—for instance the SUD union, composed of people expelled from the CFDT—and localities clearly played a role in spreading the struggle. But in reality it was just as invisible as a political organisation trying to pose a political alternative as *Lutte Ouvrière*. And it suffered the further fault of having less influence among workers. As one revolutionary socialist tells, 'The paper may seem to relate to the movement, but the language it is written in is remote and abstract'.[85] In fact, many years ago, the paper gave up any attempt to be a vehicle for political organisation and instead turned into a collection of articles on different social movements and intellectual currents. It could not transform itself into a fighting organ in December just because some of its writers recognised the scale of what was happening. The members of the LCR put as little effort into selling the paper on demonstrations or at meetings and general assemblies as the members of *Lutte Ouvrière*— being content to come across as good student activists or trade unionists rather than as revolutionary socialists. And so they were unlikely to turn into a magnet for workers or students newly politicised by the movement.

As with *Lutte Ouvrière*, the fault lies in the organisation's theoretical and practical traditions. Historically the LCR leadership held that the regimes of the USSR, Eastern Europe, China, Vietnam and Cuba were degenerated or deformed workers' states which, despite their bureaucratic leaders, played a progressive role in 'the class struggle on a world scale'. This lead to deep demoralisation when the reality of what life was really like in 'workers' state' came to light—and then the regimes themselves collapsed in 1989-91.

At the same time, the belief that there could be possible substitutes for the working class in the struggle for socialism led, in France itself, to an enormous softness on Mitterrand and the Socialist Party in the early 1980s. Instead of warning of what Mitterrand had in store for workers, the LCR gave the impression that with a little shoving from below the Mitterrand government could open the door to fundamental social change. It was hardly surprising that the LCR lost a considerable number of members to the Socialist Party and then suffered from the general demoralisation of the left as the true nature of the Mitterrand government became apparent. In fact it survived as an organisation only by dropping in practice the notion of building a centralised party around a coherent set of politics and instead degenerated into a federation of rival, warring factions, each with its own analysis of events and each doing what it wanted in its own area of struggle. Such an organisation was quite incapable of playing a genuinely independent role in the December movement and of attracting to it the many thousands of workers who began to see the need for a politics that went beyond that of the Socialist Party and the Communist Party.

Between them Lutte Ouvrière and the LCR had won over many of the best activists from struggles going right back to 1968. But their politics demoralised some in the 1970s and 1980s and left those that remained unable to act as a focus for those looking for leadership in December 1995. There could hardly be better proof of the need for French revolutionary socialists to create a new organisation.

Socialisme International has been attempting to do just this. Its problem is that, born in the 1980s when the old organisations still dominated the field, it finds itself still very small as it faces the struggles of the late 1990s. With barely 200 members it could not even begin to give leadership to a movement of 2 million workers. The best it could do was to ensure its members were active in their own workplaces and colleges, attempting to provide a focus for people who were looking for a new sort of leadership by openly selling their paper. The fact that they were as visible when it came to selling their paper on some demonstrations as organisations five or ten times their size and often the only people in meetings prepared to announce their own politics openly is testimony to the scale of the vacuum on the left during the December strikes.

Aftermath

There was much debate in the days immediately after the return to work about whether the outcome of the movement was a victory or a defeat. On the one hand, the government had made considerable concessions. On the other, it remained in office, able to prepare new offensives for the future, replacing its disastrous 'all at once' strategy with a piecemeal approach of divide and rule.

In the weeks since, it has become clear that the government made many more concessions than it wanted to, clearly frightened by the degree of support for continuing the strike among the rail workers in particular, and further pushed into a corner by the way groups like the Caen postal workers and the Marseilles transport workers held out over Christmas until their demands were met. Faced with such a level of resilience it was terrified of provoking any sort of new movement.

But the workers' victory over the immediate issues still raises the question as to the long term significance of the struggle.

One of the major arguments within the left internationally over the last two decades, since the post-1968 left began to go into decline after the defeat of the Portugese Revolution at the end of the 1975 and the Italian revolutionary left began to disintegrate a few months later, has been over whether the working class can once against play an active role as the agent of history. Many of the 1968-1975 generation concluded it could not. This led them, typically, to a political trajectory through feminism and left social democracy to right wing social democracy. Intellectually they moved on from Marxism to structuralism and from structuralism to postmodernism.

Predictably, there have already been attempts by such people to explain away the French events as, at best, a merely defensive protest by members of a relatively privileged social stratum.

For instance, the sociologists Pascal Perrineau and Michel Wiviorla have argued it would be 'a mistake' to see the movement as involving 'politicisation and generalisation'. The movement involved 'sectional conflict', confined to 'the defence of the acquired interests of public sector employees. At no point, except in a sloganising way, did it seek to take up and articulate the demands of the excluded, the unemployed, the students, or those in rundown estates.' It lacked a 'globalising dimension'. 'It would be a mistake to fall back into leftism', into the belief that the state functionaries or the personel of the big public enterprises are 'the salt of the earth', 'and that their struggle represents a resurgence of class struggle'. It would even be wrong to see the struggle as a 'constructive response after 12 years of the most liberal [ie free market] capitalism'. For, 'the strike has hardly involved looking to the future, but has been defensive'. The key slogans have been 'maintain', 'reaffirm', 'defend'. The strikes fell away 'the moment their immediate demands were met'. They 'counterposed social justice to modernisation, rather than seeking to combine the two.'

The conclusion of this line of argument was that, in reality, the strikes were backward looking, and to have been otherwise they would have had to embrace a 'modernising', social democratic perspective, of the sort allegedly put forward by Nicole Notat, the CFDT union leader who opposed the movement.[86]

But it is not only on the social democratic right that you find a tendency to dismiss struggles like that in France as of only transitory importance. There is a left version in 'downturn determinism'—the belief that the impact of past defeats has produced a situation in which defensive struggles can never lead to victory and to a revival of class confidence and consciousness. It is a view that all too easily ends in apologetics for sections of the trade union bureaucracy, with claims that they have pushed the struggle as far as it was possible to go. It is also a gospel of sheer despair, since it implies that there can be no real revival of working class struggle until some magical return to full employment alters the balance of forces in the everyday economic struggle.

In fact, the French movement was a living refutation of such an approach. Of course, it began as a defensive struggle and bore within it the imprint of two decades of defeat. But as it gathered momentum it became more than defensive and began to challenge the whole way society is run. It was a prime example of how sudden leaps can take place in confidence and consciousness.

For very few of those involved was the strike simply about their pensions or their social security payments. It was about what they felt had been happening to them for some 20 years. The *Sécu* attack was simply the last straw. Only this can explain the level of activism in the strikes, the way in which it only required a small lead from a couple of activists for hundreds to go from one workplace to another, to gather daily to organise activities, to reach back to all but forgotten memories of class struggle, of the Commune and the *Internationale*. Only that can explain the way in which rail and postal workers lined up to applaud students and went out to meet with civil servants and teachers, car workers and nurses. Only that, too, can explain the welcome on the demonstrations given to the groups of the unemployed and homeless who joined in.

It was as if anger that had been simmering for 20 years suddenly boiled over and then rejected attempts to confine it within narrow channels. But the pressure which led it to boil over—the 'last straw'—was not just some accidental mistake by the government. It was an integral part of the attempt to allow French capitalism to maintain its competitiveness in the face of recurrent world economic crises. Eight years ago, in my book *The Fire Last Time* I argued that the economic instability of the world system necessarily leads to sudden changes in the political situation:

We cannot take for granted the political stability that the Western countries have known for the last 10 years. Even the strongest political structures can

*be like castles built on ice of unknown thickness. Economic pressures can
lead rulers or ruled suddenly to break, at least partially, with the framework
within which their relations with each other have previously been organised.*[87]

Since this was written, the long recession of the first half of the 1990s
has everywhere served on the one hand to increase the pressure on governments and employing classes to attack conditions which workers have
taken for granted in the past, and on the other to intensify the feelings of
bitterness at the base of society, among both the traditional working class
and increasingly proletarianised groups who used to regard themselves
as 'middle class'.

The French strikes show how, under such conditions, immense social
struggle can suddenly erupt—and how, when they do so, previously
'non-political' workers can begin to organise themselves and to generalise politically. They also show how such a general upsurge in struggle
can produce a sudden shift in the balance of class forces despite the willingness of the trade union bureaucracy to halt the movement at the first
hint of concessions. There seems little doubt that the December 1995
strikes have dented the French government's confidence in its ability to
proceed with its offensive against workers' conditions. There also seems
little doubt that the new confidence felt by many sections of workers will
find expression in new struggles in the months ahead.

That, however, is not the end of the story. The international competitive pressures on French capitalism which produced the Juppé plan will
not go away. It may have made concessions to end the strikes, just as De
Gaulle did in 1968 or Denmark's government did in 1985, but the overall
context in which it operates is different. The French events of 1968
occurred while the great boom of the 1950s and 1960s still had some life
left in it and ruling classes could afford, when pushed, to grant long
terms reforms. The Danish strike took place just as ruling classes were
beginning to convince themselves the nightmare recession of the early
1980s was giving way to a new period of unstoppable boom. The French
ruling class certainly do not believe that today. They feel the only way
they can guarantee future profitability is by clamping down hard on
workers' conditions. That, in itself, ensures that the concessions will not
be followed by a new period of class peace. Rather we can expect a desperate ruling class to return to the offensive and a rejuvenated working
class to fight back.

But more will be involved in the period ahead than just economic
pressures on both sides. Two decades of economic crisis have not just led
to workplace struggles. They have also torn apart many of the certainties
by which millions of people used to lead their lives, leaving bitterness
and frustration that expresses itself in many different ways: protests by
sections of the petty bourgeoisie that recall the 'Poujade' movement of

1950s; a wave of mini-riots on suburban housing estates originally built to house the burgeoning industrial labour force of the 1960s and plagued by 40 or 50 percent levels of unemployment; a growth of popular racism among some layers of the population; a willingness of some sections of the government and the police to exploit this with an increased level of harassment of ethnic minorities; a tendency for some ethnic minority youth to react by an enhanced identification with Islam; the growth of the fascist National Front until it regularly achieves around 15 percent of votes and enters into the political calculations of all the main parties.

The December strikes temporarily overshadowed all these other expressions of the crisis by acting as a focus for the bitterness of huge numbers of people besides those directly involved in the stoppages and demonstrations. Thus the strikes posed considerable difficulties for the National Front leadership. Its position was that it was hostile to the strikes and believed that there should be no right to strike in the public sector. But it was also aware than many of the people who voted for it in the spring were now enthusiastic supporters of the strikes. So in a radio interview, 'Le Pen was involved in a difficult exercise, which consisted in expressing his hostility to the unions, his animosity to the civil servants, his opposition to the Juppé plan and his understanding as to why some sympathisers of the National Front supported the strikes'.[88] But this does not mean that the strike movement will have destroyed the National Front's influence or any other forms by which the deeper social crisis expresses itself. They can re-emerge in the aftermath of the strikes just as a wreck rises above the water as the tide falls. And the French ruling class will take them into consideration, seeking to manipulate them for its own ends, as it prepares to the next round of confrontation.

Sections of the governing majority will step up their efforts to build up the forces behind them by combining anti-Maastricht rhetoric with encouragement of police attacks on ethnic minorities and calls for ever more stringent action against 'illegal' immigrants. The Socialist Party will continue to make concessions to them. The Communist Party will still be torn between sharing a common anti-European language with them and disliking their racism. The National Front can still have leeway, not merely to hold on to its votes but also to build a cadre as it attempts to turn the 'soft racism' of its sympathisers into the hardened Nazi ideology of activists.

This means the question of politics will become ever more important. The lack of a revolutionary alternative to the misleadership of the CGT, FO, CFDT, Communist Party and Socialist Party meant, in December, that the movement did not achieve the great victory that was open to it. It could, nevertheless, make gains. The next time it probably will not be so easy. The government will try to be more prepared and will seek to divide as a precondition for ruling. Beating it will be difficult without a network of revolutionary socialists with a presence in the workplace, capable not only of taking up the easy arguments about cuts in pension rights or wages, but also 'difficult' ones over immigration, the awful record of the Socialist Party governments or the behaviour of the trade union bureaucracies.

Notes

1   Quoted in *Le Monde*, 11 November 1995.
2   *Financial Times* editorial, 6 January 1995.
3   Ibid.
4   For discussions on this, see, for example, E Ball, 'Lurking Threat of First World Debt Crisis', *Financial Times*, 27 October 1993; M Wolf, 'The Looming Crisis of Industrial Country Public Debt', *Financial Times*, 12 July 1993; editorial, *Financial Times*, 3 January 1995.
5   *Financial Times* editorial, 6 January 1996.
6   Figures from *Institut der Deutschen Wirtschaft*, reproduced in *Le Monde*, 21 December 1995.
7   *Le Monde*, 21 December 1995.
8   Opinion poll figures given in *Le Monde*, 21 October 1995.
9   Quoted, *Le Monde*, 28 October 1995.
10   *Le Monde*, 17 November 1995.
11   *Le Monde*, 21 December 1995.
12   Quoted in *Le Monde*, 21 December 1995.
13   *Le Parti des Traveilleurs*, formerly the Parti Communiste Internationale, of Pierre Lambert, which controls the leadership of a couple of federations within *Force Ouvrière*.
14 See the lengthy report on Blondel's somersaults in *Le Monde*, 23 November 1995.
15   Quoted in *Le Monde*, 21 December 1995.
16   Quoted in *Le Monde*, 18 November 1995.
17   The CFDT is a little smaller in terms of membership than the CGT, sometimes doing better sometimes worse than it in elections for works councils. But historically it has been less important when it comes to beginning—and ending—struggles.
18   Account of protests in *Le Monde*, 26 November 1995, see also *Socialist Worker*, 2 December 1995.
19   For accounts of this incident, see *Le Monde*, 26 November 1995 and 21 December 1995.
20   *Le Monde*, 21 December 1995.
21   Quoted in *Le Monde*, 29 November 1995.
22   *Le Monde*, 30 November 1995.
23   Le Monde, 30 November 1995.
24   Ibid.
25   Report in *Lutte Ouvrière*, 8 December 1995.
26   An analysis in *Le Monde* suggested that only in the east of the country was the movement relatively weak, and that in the provinces it grew in magnitude until it surpassed that in Paris. *Le Monde*, 8 December 1995 and 27 December 1995.
27   Report in *Lutte Ouvrière*, 8 December 1995.
28   Ibid.
29   Ibid.

30   Main front page story, *Le Monde*, 2 December 1995, and the report inside on the same day of the meeting of 500 RPR supporters held in Saint-Jean-de-Luz to create such committees.

31   See T Cliff, 'The Belgian General Strike', *International Socialism* (old series) No.4, Spring 1961.

32   T Cliff and D Gluckstein, *Marxism and Trade Union Struggle, the General Strike of 1926* (London 1986), p189.

33   C Harman, *The Fire Last Time: 1968 and After* (London 1988), p36.

34   Ibid, p369. The reports of the Danish strike are from *Socialist Worker Review*, May 1985, and from *Socialist Worker*, 13 April 1985.

35   The Communist Party, the Socialist Party, and the Lutte Ouvrière candidate, Arlette Laguiller.

36   According to *Le Monde*, 3 December 1995.

37   *Le Monde*, 3 December 1995.

38   Report by Paul McGarr in *Socialist Worker*, 2 December 1995.

39   Report in *Lutte Ouvrière*, 8 December 1995.

40   *Le Monde*, 21 December 1995.

41   Interviews with workers in *Le Monde*, 21 December 1995.

42   Quoted in *Le Monde*, 3 December 1995.

43   Report in *Lutte Ouvrière*, 8 December 1995.

44   Interview with J Perez, in *International Viewpoint*, January 1966.

45   Account contained in *Rouge*, 4 January 1996.

46   This is the term used by the former Socialist Party mayor of the town in her interesting study of the rise of the Nazis. See F Gaspard, *A Small City in France* (Harvard, 1995).

47   *Le Monde*, 4 December 1995.

48   Interview in *Le Monde*, 19 December 1995.

49   *Le Monde*, 6 December 1995.

50   Interview with Denis Godard 3 January 1995.

51   See the reports in *Le Monde*, 5 and 6 December 1995

52   *Le Monde*, 7 December 1995

53   'Postal workers hesitate to strike', *Le Monde*, 3 December 1995

54   Interview, as above. Another report tells very much the same story, see 'A la Poste', *Lutte Ouvrière*, 8 December 1995

55   Interview, as above, fn50.

56   *Le Monde*, 17 December 1995.

57   *Le Monde*, 3 December 1995.

58   *Le Monde*'s expression.

59   Quoted in *Le Monde*, 17 December 1995.

60   *Socialisme International*, 20 December 1995.

61   See the description of mobilisations in *Le Monde*, 2 December 1995

62   Interview, as above, fn50.

63   *Socialisme Internationale*, 20 December 1995

64   *Le Monde*, 24 December 1995.

65   Report in *Le Monde*, 9 December 1995.

66   *Le Monde*, 12 December 1995.

67   'The Union Machines in the Strike', *Class Struggle*, January 1996, p13.

68   Account of meeting in *Le Monde*, 17 December 1995.

69   Reports in *Lutte Ouvrière*, 22 December 1995.

70   See the account in my book *The Fire Last Time*, op cit, pp101 and 108.

71   Quoted in *Le Monde*, 17 December 1995.

72   Report of speech of a member of the party secretariat, Jean-Claude Gayssot, opening a debate at the party's national committee, in *Le Monde*, 8 December 1995.

73   *L'Humanité*, 7 December 1995, quoted in *International Viewpoint*, January 1996.

74   *Le Monde*, 8 December 1995.

75   Report of Hue's views in *Le Monde*, 6 December 1995 and *Rouge*, 14 December 1995.

76   *Le Monde*, 8 December 1995.

77   Ibid.

78   Report in *Le Monde*, 26 November 1995.

79   According to exit polls for the first round of last spring's presidential election.

80   For more details about *Lutte Ouvrière*'s politics, see, '*Lutte Ouvrière* and SWP Debate the French Railway Workers' Strike', in *International Socialism* 26, April 1987.

81   'La situation interieure', *Lutte de Classe*, No.17, January-February 1996.

82   Roger Girardot, *Lutte Ouvrière*, 8 December 1995. This argument is repeated in article, 'The Union Machines in the Strike'—much of which is simply a translation of Girardot's piece—in *Lutte Ouvrière*'s English language publication, *Class Struggle*, January/February 1996. But the other article on the strikes, 'The Class Struggle with a Vengeance', provides a quite different account, in which the initial push from above by the union bureaucracies gave rise below, to 'workers' democracy in practice, something very few workers had ever experienced before.'

83   'The Union Machines in the Strike', op cit.

84   See the account in Cliff and Gluckstein, op cit.

85   Interview, as above, fn 50.

86   *Le Monde*, 20 December 1995.

87   C Harman, *The Fire Last Time*, op cit, p367.

88   Report in *Le Monde*, 22 December 1995 .

The making of a revolutionary

A review of Huey Newton, **Revolutionary Suicide** *(New York, 1995), £9.99*

BRIAN RICHARDSON

> *By surrendering my life to the revolution,*
> *I found eternal life.*
> *Revolutionary Suicide.*[1]

Revolutionary Suicide, the autobiography of Huey P Newton, is a fitting testament to the Black Panther Party for Self Defence, the revolutionary black nationalist organisation founded by Newton and Bobby Seale, which rocked America in the late 1960s. The title refers to the burning commitment with which the Black Panthers fought back against the police harassment and the oppression which dominated the lives of black people in America's ghettos. Newton developed the concept of revolutionary suicide after studying French sociologist Emile Durkheim's text *Suicide* which argues that social rather than personal factors are the principal cause of suicidal behaviour. This struck a chord with a young black man living at a time when suicides among his contemporaries had doubled. In addition Newton observed amongst blacks a hopelessness, demoralisation and apparent acceptance of their oppression which he termed 'reactionary suicide'.

By contrast, the Black Panthers were determined to resist, whilst remaining acutely aware of the consequences of challenging the police, racism and the American state. Hence, their strategy was both revolutionary and suicidal. However, as Newton eloquently points out:

The concept of revolutionary suicide is not defeatist or fatalistic. On the con-
trary, it conveys an awareness of reality in combination with the possibility of
hope—reality because the revolutionary must always be prepared to face
death, and hope because it symbolises a resolute determination to bring
about change.[2]

Newton's revolutionary commitment was forged by a childhood and
youth during which the pervasiveness of racism was burned into his consciousness. Born the youngest of seven children in Monroe, Louisiana,
in 1942, he records that one of his earliest childhood memories was of
black families so poor that they could not afford store bought toys for the
children. Instead, the playthings for Newton and his friends were sym-
bolic of their poverty: dirt, rats and stray cats.

Newton, like other black children, went to school believing that it
would provide the passport to fulfilment of the American dream. Instead,
what they found was that the few references to black people were in
books such as *Little Black Sambo*, which reinforced feelings of humilia-
tion and inferiority. Consequently, Newton could summon little
enthusiasm for formal education and soon found himself having count-
less confrontations with teachers. He was suspended from school on
numerous occasions and found himself out on the streets where he
drifted into petty crime, burglary and pimping. Extraordinary though this
may seem, Newton's formative years were by no means exceptional. The
biographies of other activists—Malcolm X, Bobby Seale and George
Jackson—bear witness to the fact that institutionalised racism made this
the common experience for generations of blacks.

However, two interlinked factors did make this particular group stand
out. Firstly, theirs was an experience rooted in the northern US cities
where, in contrast to the southern states, blacks supposedly enjoyed the
same equality before the law as whites. The everyday reality of racism,
therefore, taught them that overcoming their oppression would require
much more than the passage of civil rights laws. Newton remarks that:

There were enough laws on the books to permit black people to deal with all
their problems, but the laws were not enforced. Therefore, trying to get more
laws was only a meaningless diversion from the real issues.[3]

This clearly set them apart from the leaders of the civil rights movement, such as Martin Luther King, who pursued that particular goal in
the hope that new legislation would put an end to discrimination and
provide a springboard for black advancement.

The second significant point about these northern activists was that
they acted upon their conclusions. They took inspiration from the civil

rights movement, but recognised its shortcomings and began to develop a more militant strategy to carry the struggle into the north.

By the mid-1960s Malcolm X was beginning to seriously challenge King as the leading black anti-racist activist. He split from the conservative Nation of Islam, which denounced racism but did nothing to build the real struggles that were occurring in the streets. Instead, Malcolm predicted that those struggles would soon hit the north and he encouraged blacks to fight racism 'by any means necessary'.

Malcolm never lived to see the outcome of those struggles and the organisations he established were in their infancy when he was assassinated in March 1965. However, within months of his death, the very explosions he had foreseen shook many northern cities. Watts, in Los Angeles, witnessed the first of those rebellions, and over the next few years similar uprisings rocked Chicago, Cleveland, Detroit and Washington. It was out of these uprisings that the Black Panther Party was formed by Newton and Bobby Seale, a fellow student at Oakland City College in the bay of California in October 1966. Newton acknowledged that the party was born and existed 'out of the spirit Malcolm X' and that it was 'a living testament to his life work'.[4]

The party's name reflected the principal activity of the organisation. A panther is a defensive animal, but one which fights ferociously when it is attacked. Newton and Seale were inspired to set up the party to defend the black community from police harassment and brutality. This the Panthers did in the most spectacular manner, by asserting the constitutional right of blacks to bear arms and to monitor police activities. Hence, the party's full name was the Black Panther Party for Self Defence.

Melvin and Mario Van Peebles' 1995 film *Panther* brilliantly portrays how the party 'patrolled the pigs' as they termed it, driving the police at gunpoint out of the ghettos. Newton also records how the Panthers marched, guns at hand, into San Francisco airport to escort Malcolm X's widow Betty Shabazz and how, in similar fashion, they stormed into the state legislative building in Sacramento to protest against legislation aimed at banning their use of guns. It was this courage and combativity in the face of the authorities that was the central appeal of the Panthers for millions of black people.

The Panthers experienced spectacular growth in the first couple of years after their formation. By the summer of 1968 the party had recruited thousands of members, could claim to sell 100,000 copies of its newspaper and to have the support of 25 percent of the black population. Among the under-25s this figure rose to 43 percent. Federal Bureau of Investigation (FBI) chief J Edgar Hoover certainly believed this, confessing as much to President Lyndon Baines Johnson. Indeed, so frightened was the FBI, that they declared the Panthers 'Public Enemy Number One'.

It is not difficult to see why the Panthers proved so attractive to blacks. Slavery may have long since been abolished, but millions still shared the experience of police harassment, the petty racism, the contemptuous treatment they received in shops, schools, workplaces and on public transport. They were supposed to turn the other cheek, carefully ensuring that their eyes did not meet their oppressors.

However, Newton's book clearly shows that there was far more to the leaders of the Panthers than their extraordinary bravery. Newton and Bobby Seale were proud to call themselves socialists. Although Newton confessed that he was 'never convinced that destroying capitalism would automatically destroy racism...', he goes on to say that 'I felt, however, that we could not destroy racism without wiping out its economic foundation.'[5] Indeed, it was their analysis of the need to confront and challenge the system which made the Panthers so critical of cultural nationalists who believed that oppression could be overcome by establishing a lifestyle based upon 'libations' and traditional African dress and behaviour.

In addition, the Panthers set out a ten point programme which was intended as a manifesto of the party's immediate objectives for the black community. They established a programme of practical activities in the ghettos. These included a free food programme for poor blacks, a sickle cell testing scheme and education for black children. Newton described these measures as a 'raft' which kept black people afloat whilst the ground was being prepared for the final struggle against racism and capitalism.

Consequently, the Panthers enjoyed a meteoric rise and influenced the consciousness of millions of people. Yet their history and success was short lived. The weakest point of the Van Peebles' otherwise excellent film is the notion that the FBI sponsored flood of drugs released into the ghettos was responsible for the sudden and rapid decline of the Panthers in the early 1970s. This is not to dismiss the debilitating effect that drugs have had upon the inner cities. Nor is it to deny the sheer ruthlessness with which the state hunted down, imprisoned and killed leading members of the organisation. However, the demise of the Panthers also flowed from weaknesses in their own strategy and politics. For example, their main thrust, the armed self defence of the ghettos, whilst courageous, could not ultimately contend with a much larger, more highly trained and more powerfully armed enemy, the US authorities. Patrolling the pigs could not possibly be anything other than defensive.

The leaders of the Panthers spent enormous amounts of time in prison, on trumped up charges, and vast amounts of time, energy and resources were ploughed into securing their release. Inevitably, this detracted from their ability to operate and to pursue community projects, not least because Newton and Seale were not able to meet and discuss things. Newton concedes that when he came out of prison in August 1970 'the party was in a shambles [because] Bobby and I had been off the streets and in jail for a long time, and it had been difficult to direct the party on a day-to-day basis from prison cells'.[6]

This might not have been such an obstacle to the Panthers had they seriously set out to develop a cadre that could encourage, recruit and educate the young blacks who looked to them for inspiration and leadership. Newton admits that the Panthers were slow to recognise the importance of educating their members and says that 'some of our leading comrades lacked the comprehensive ideology needed to analyse events and phenomena in a creative and dynamic way'.[7] By the time they established an Ideological Institute to develop cadres, the Panthers' popularity was already on the wane.

More fundamentally, although they called themselves socialists, there was a basic flaw in the Panthers' analysis of racism and capitalism. The Panthers owed their greatest political debts to Franz Fanon, Che Guevara and Mao Zedong. It was the anti-colonial struggles in Algeria, Cuba and China with which these figures were respectively associated, that provided the main inspiration for the Panthers. Newton clearly drew very heavily from Fanon, Guevara and Mao's commitment to revolutionary violence:

Mao, Fanon and Guevara all saw clearly that the people had been stripped of their birthright and their dignity, not by any philosophy or mere words, but at gunpoint. They had suffered a hold up by gangsters, and rape; for them the only way to win freedom was to meet force with force. At bottom this was a form of self-defence. Although that defence might at times take on the characteristics of aggression, in the final analysis the people do not initiate; they simply respond to what has been inflicted upon them. People respect the expression of strength and dignity displayed by men who refuse to bow to the weapons of oppression. Though it may mean death, these men will fight, because death with dignity is preferable to ignominy.[8]

Newton's illusions in post-revolutionary China were immense. He dedicates one of the final chapters of *Revolutionary Suicide* to describing his feelings about the visit he made at the invitation of the Chinese government in 1971. He claimed to have achieved a 'psychological liberation' which made him feel 'at home in China' . He believed that the Chinese police and military were there to protect and serve rather than oppress people. At the end of his trip, he concluded:

Everything I saw in China demonstrated that the People's Republic is a free and liberated territory with a socialist government. The way is open for the people to gain their freedom and to determine their own destiny. It was an amazing experience to see a revolution that is going forward at such a rapid rate. To see a classless society in operation is unforgettable. Here, Marx's dictum—from each according to his abilities, to each according to his needs—is in operation.[9]

The Panthers knew that they could not directly replicate the experiences of Algeria, Cuba and China. Nevertheless, they sought to adapt the ideas, principles and strategies of those struggles to their own situation. A key concept, clearly influenced by those struggles, was the Panthers' belief that blacks made up an oppressed internal colony within the United States. Consequently, the tenth and final point of their programme stated, 'We want...as our major political objective, a United Nations-supervised plebiscite to be held throughout the black colony in which only black colonial subjects will be allowed to participate for the purpose of determining the will of the black people as to their national identity.'[10] The key fighting force that would be mobilised to challenge the authorities and push the UN into holding this plebiscite was to be the 'brothers on the block', the lumpen proletariat of young unemployed men from the ghettos.

There are a number of problems with this analysis and the strategies that flowed from it. In reality, the 'brothers on the block' lacked the necessary discipline and real power frequently found among organised workers. The leadership experienced severe difficulties in organising young men who, precisely because of racism, were often forced into petty crime in order to scrape a living. Ultimately, the Panthers were forced to expel hundreds of so called 'jackanapes' from the organisation.

The Panthers were also profoundly mistaken in their assessment of the United Nations. Any serious examination of the UN would reveal that the organisation was, at best, impotent in the face of the aggressive self serving foreign policies of the world's major powers. More often than not its dominant members—Britain, France, China, the USSR and the United States—simply ignored the UN or used it as a figleaf to cover their imperialist aims. One particular example from 1960 might have served as a warning to the Panthers. The American CIA was determined to discipline the government of the newly independent Congo, which they feared was under threat of Communist domination. The CIA therefore ensured that the nationalist leader, Patrice Lumumba was kidnapped and killed. This action was carried out by United Nations forces. It may be open to question how much of this was public knowledge at the time. However, given the centrality of the tenth point within the Panthers' programme, it is reasonable to suggest that they should have monitored the

UN very carefully and that, had they done so, they would have soon discovered the deep hostility that they could expect to receive.[11]

Furthermore, the Panthers' characterisation of blacks as an internal colony within the United States was fundamentally wrong. It was certainly the case that there existed enormous segregation in respect of jobs and neighbourhoods. Nevertheless, blacks still made up a significant proportion of the United States working class. Most blacks held down a job for the majority of their working lives. With that came the interaction with other workers, both black and white, and the possibility of collective struggle at the point of production. Indeed, in the late 1960s, when the Panthers were at their zenith there were some 2.5 million black workers organised in trade unions across the United States.

The Panthers did give formal recognition to the need for collective working class action. They openly stated:

> *The Black Panther Party stands for revolutionary solidarity with all the people fighting against the forces of imperialism, capitalism, racism and fascism. Our solidarity is extended to those people who are fighting those evils at home and abroad ...we will not fight capitalism with black capitalism; we will not fight imperialism with black imperialism; we will not fight racism with black racism. Rather we take a stand against these evils with a solidarity derived from a proletarian internationalism born of socialist realism.[12]*

They were also prepared to work with white organisations. For example, an alliance was formed with the anti-Vietnam War Progressive Freedom Party and they sought a united front with Communists against fascism, declaring: 'We want unity of action by the working class, so that the proletariat may grow strong in its struggle against the bourgeoisie, in order that while defending today its current interests against attacking capital, against fascism, the proletariat may be in a position tomorrow to create the preliminary conditions for its final emancipation.'[13]

However, the Panthers never fully grasped that the key division in society was that of social class and not race. Consequently, they never sought to build a permanent unity of the most powerful section of society, organised black and white workers. The potential to build such unity was certainly there. The campaigns to free Huey Newton and Bobby Seale from prison terms, and the funeral procession for George Jackson, an honorary Panther field marshal murdered in prison, showed that they enjoyed significant support amongst layers of the white population. More significantly, there were strikes in mixed workplaces such as the car plants of Detroit in 1968. These were precisely the kind of struggles in which socialists should intervene. Unfortunately, the Panthers never had an orientation towards the workplaces. Far from being encouraged to agitate on the shop floor, members were often pressed into giving up their jobs in order to become full time members and community activists.

There were black socialists in the Dodge Revolutionary Union Movement (DRUM) that did attempt to build these struggles. DRUM spawned a number of groups which came together to form the League of Revolutionary Black Workers. Based in the car plants, they were inspired by the Panthers, but went much further. They campaigned both against general grievances such as speed-ups and specific discrimination against blacks in terms of the allocation of skilled jobs and promotion. However, the League concentrated its efforts on organising only the black workers, often taking an extremely hostile position towards whites. They therefore repeated the Panthers' failure to tap the potential for black and white unity. Again, lack of political clarity was the major handicap. Nevertheless, the League with its focus on organised workers came closer than the Panthers to the classical Marxist tradition's stress on the centrality of working class struggle to the achievement of socialism.

The reprinting of *Revolutionary Suicide* and the release of the film *Panther* should help to stimulate a much needed debate about the Black Panther Party and its legacy. Nearly a quarter of a century after the demise of the Black Power movement, the social conditions that it fought against are still very much with us. Most vividly, the savage beating of black motorist Rodney Glen King, the initial acquittal of the police officers who administered that beating, and the murder trial of former football star O J Simpson in 1995 have exposed the depths of racism that still exist amongst the police. Further, there is enormous frustration and anger at the redistribution of wealth from poor to rich and the attacks on welfare and affirmative action that have dominated government policy over the last 15 years.

This anger has been met with repression which has led to a situation in which one third of all black men are caught within the criminal justice system. These men are either in prison, on parole or awaiting trial. It is a fact of life for black men that they can more readily expect to go to prison than to university. For those blacks who are able to escape prison, the unemployment rate at 14.1 percent is more than twice the 6.5 percent figure for whites, and the average annual income is 56 percent of that of white households. This grim picture raises the obvious question as to how so great a struggle in the 1960s led to so few positive gains.

It should first be acknowledged that the militancy of the Black Power movement did force major political and economic concessions out of the American ruling class. It was precisely these struggles which led to the introduction of affirmative action in employment, the opening up of colleges to black students and the introduction of black studies courses. It was the movement of the 1960s which created opportunities for blacks to enter the political arena and to establish new businesses. A sizeable number of blacks rode to positions of influence on the back of the Black Power movement. Notable among them was Clarence Thomas, the man George Bush appointed as an associate justice in the Supreme Court. Manning Marable observes:

> *A quarter of a century ago, as a college student in the late 1960s, Thomas proclaimed himself a devoted disciple of Malcolm X. Thomas wore the black beret of the Black Panther Party and signed his letters 'Power to the People'. He secured his position at Yale Law School due to its aggressive affirmative action program, which had set aside roughly 10 percent of all places in each class to racial minorities.*[14]

Subsequently, Thomas's success has been based upon a complete rejection of the measures from which he benefited. Previously as head of the Equal Employment Opportunity Commission and now as a Supreme Court judge, he has consistently denounced and attacked affirmative action, welfare provision and the entire civil rights programme he once not only embraced, but believed was too conservative.

The case of Clarence Thomas is the most striking betrayal, but he is not alone. More broadly, Marable records that some 15 percent of black households have annual incomes in excess of $50,000 and that the black middle class has increased by 400 percent since the late 1960s. Further, there are now over 8,000 black elected officials as against 103 in 1964. Despite this, the predicament of the majority of blacks has worsened over the past generation. Having climbed the social ladder, those blacks who have prospered have been quick to snatch that ladder away to prevent others from joining them.[15]

There is an understandable anger at the social conditions in the ghettos coupled with an alienation from the 'role models' and political leaders who have betrayed working class blacks. It was that anger that erupted in the Los Angeles riot of 1992. But the alienation has created a vacuum in the leadership of the black liberation movement. One of the great ironies of the 1990s is that it is Nation of Islam leader Louis Farrakhan who has been most successful in trying to fill this space. Farrakhan had denounced Malcolm X and his followers as 'worthy of death' after the latter's assassination. In sharp contrast to the Panthers, his sexist, anti-Semitic, pro-capitalist agenda is deeply reactionary. The great tragedy of the Black Power movement is that it was the courage and combativity of its followers who smashed down the barriers through which the renegades of today have stampeded. Overcoming these weaknesses of the Panthers is crucial if we are to prevent another generation in revolt from merely achieving the 'liberation' of a middle class elite.

The urgency of a renewed debate about the struggles of the 1960s is not restricted to the United States, and the lessons apply equally elsewhere. As 1995 drew to a close Brixton in south London, the capital of black Britain, was the scene of a small riot. The immediate catalyst for the protest was the death of a young black man in police custody, the second such death in the area in seven months. Underlying the discontent were a number of factors. Amongst black men aged under 24 the unemployment rate in London was some 62 percent.[16] Huge cutbacks in council services meant there were few amenities for these youngsters. Most of the much touted money that was promised to these areas after previous disturbances never arrived. The little money that was spent was allocated to prestigious projects which looked impressive but created a mere handful of jobs and when completed provided facilities that few of the poor could afford to enjoy. Thus excluded, many youngsters are faced with the choice either to stay at home or roam the streets, where the Metropolitan Police's introduction of Operation Eagle Eye means they encounter constant harassment. Such conditions make further deaths in police custody an inevitability.

With repression, however, there also comes resistance. Within that resistance lies the potential to overthrow the oppression and exploitation that blights people's lives. A striking feature of the Los Angeles riots of 1992 and the Brixton protests in 1995 was that they were mixed rebellions of black and white people. This phenomenon was no accident: blacks have been the worst affected, but the working classes as a whole have suffered as a consequence of the cuts in jobs and attacks upon welfare and social provisions of the last 20 years. The most pressing requirement is an organisation that can take the energy and anger of those protests into every workplace and channel it into a united fight by black and white workers against the bosses who have divided and ruled us for so long. Such a movement will draw inspiration from groups such as the Black Panthers. Crucially, however, it will have the real power that, once and for all, can bury racism and the society that breeds it.

Notes

Thanks to Teresa Brennan and Liz Wheatley for their advice and assistance.

1   H P Newton, *Revolutionary Suicide* (New York, 1995), pix.
2   Ibid, p7.
3   Ibid, p106.
4   Ibid, p113.
5   Ibid, p70.

6   Ibid, p328.
7   Ibid, p298.
8   Ibid, p111-112.
9   Ibid, p326.
10   Ibid, p118.
11   For a fuller analysis of the history of the United Nations, see D Blackie, 'The United Nations and the Politics of Imperialism', *International Socialism* 63 (Summer, 1994).
12   Statement especially written by the national office of the Black Panther Party for *The Guardian*, February 1970, quoted in PS Foner (ed), *The Black Panthers Speak* (New York, 1995), p220.
13   From *The Black Panther*, 17 July 1969 quoted in PS Foner (ed), *The Black Panthers Speak* (New York, 1995),. p223. This declaration prefaced a conference sponsored by the Black Panther Party to establish a united front against fascism. The conference was attended by over 4,000 people from a number of different organisations. The Panthers tended to refer to the police and the entire US political system as 'fascist', a mistake which also retarded the possibility of building a united black and white party rather than temporary alliances.
14   M Marable, *Beyond Black and White* (London, 1995), p93.
15   Ibid. Chapter 17 contains a detailed analysis of the sharp social division that has occurred in black America.
16   This figure is taken from a three part study entitled, 'Black in Britain', printed by *The Guardian* newspaper (March 20-22, 1995) which drew attention to the continued pervasive effects of institutionalised racism in British society.

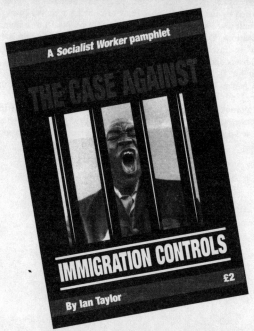

'Why Lucky Jim turned right'—an obituary of Kingsley Amis

GARETH JENKINS

When Kingsley Amis died last year at the age of 73, the general verdict was that he had been the greatest comic novelist of his generation. After making his mark with *Lucky Jim* (1954) he never looked back, as one comic novel after the other flowed from his pen. Such was the continued acclaim for his work that in 1986 he won the Booker prize for *The Old Devils*. As a contributor to *The Spectator* put it, 'He was above all quick-minded, verbally agile, terribly funny, a vigorous persecutor of bores, pseuds and wankers and a most tremendous mimic.'[1]

Yet many have wondered just how funny and critical Amis, particularly the Amis of the later novels, really was. After all Amis became notoriously hostile to progressive causes and a political supporter of Margaret Thatcher. He was rewarded with a CBE in 1981 and knighted in 1990. Far from being a vigorous persecutor he seemed to have joined the ranks of bores, pseuds and wankers. The heroes of his novels appeared more and more to be the mouthpiece for Amis's pet hates, uttering a never ending stream of extremely unfunny and narrow- (rather than quick-) minded attacks on gays, nuclear disarmers, women's libbers, and so on. What, it might be said, is the point of reading these novels when a visit to the local pub and an interview with the bar bore would yield the same reactionary rant? Perhaps, though, this is too simplistic a dismissal, one which stems from confusing creator and character. Shouldn't we instead put aside what we know about Amis's personal opinions and value the novels for holding up a mirror to the unpleasant realities of our society? This is the view of the liberal minded literary critic Malcolm Bradbury:

> In later works, like **Jake's Thing** (1978) and **Stanley and the Women** (1984), he examined the growing gender conflicts between men and women and their impact on the family and on male psychology. And his prize-winning **The Old Devils** (1986) showed his cantankerously mortal sensibility, still sustaining what was now the long dark comedy of life into later years, in which the once angry young man had turned into a yet more angry and mortal old one.[2]

So, a justification for Amis's novels can be to detach them from the ideology of their author and to read them against the grain—in much the same way as the novels of (say) Evelyn Waugh can serve as critical commentary on what they describe, despite their author's intentions. Where Waugh can expose the limitations of upper class society (particularly, for example, the behaviour of top army brass in his war trilogy), Amis can expose sexist limitations in the drunken self indulgent middle class section of society he chooses to focus on as it advances into middle age.

Can this justification be sustained? Clearly it is possible to benefit from reactionary novelists and there is a long Marxist tradition which refuses to see good literature as simply the expression of a 'correct' political viewpoint. But in Kingsley Amis's case the justification cannot be sustained. The case against Amis rests less on his manifestly reactionary views than on the limitations of the fiction itself.

Kingsley Amis was born in 1922 in south London, the only son of lower middle class parents. The *Memoirs* give some sense of his family and background—ordinary, suburban, with all the minor class and political prejudices one would expect. Though Amis recalls conflict over taste in music, there is little sense that this conflict challenged the acceptance of a mild, pervasive philistinism in respect of culture. The only other tension reported in the *Memoirs* is over sex, with young Amis being warned that masturbation would 'thin the blood' and cause insanity. Later, when he had left home and was in the army, his father tried to tell him off for having an affair with a married woman.[3] After a period of school in London and Wiltshire (where he had been evacuated to on the outbreak of war in 1939), Amis won a place at St John's College, Oxford, in 1941. His university education was interrupted by service in the army between 1942 and 1945. The army made quite an impact on him, as it did on many others in that period. His *Memoirs* bring out the bewildering absurdity of it as an institution:

> The British Army has been compared to many other institutions—school, lunatic asylum, prison and so on—but one parallel which has never been

drawn before, I think, is with a society of the kind you read about in some
science-fiction stories, a world much like our own in general appearance but
with some of the rules changed or removed, a logic only partly coinciding
with that of our own world, and some unpredictable areas where logic seems
missing altogether or to point opposite ways at once.[4]

To get some sense of what the army meant to him politically one
needs to look at the few short stories he devoted to the topic.[5] They
provide graphic illustrations of the arbitrary power senior officers exer-
cised and the pressure to conform at the expense of betraying one's
peers. The best of these stories is 'I Spy Strangers'. It focuses on a mock
parliament, in which soldiers play the political roles of Tory versus
Labour (the soldiers representing Labour are real left wingers and on the
whole sympathetically presented). This becomes real for a moment when
the procedure used to clear parliament of unauthorised persons (I Spy
Strangers) is used to expel the unpleasant, bullying major, who thinks he
has a right to interfere when the argument doesn't go his way. The story
ends with a reference to the shock he and fellow Tories, believing they
were born to rule, experience with the reality of Labour's electoral land-
slide in 1945. This seems to be the extent of Amis's radicalisation,
though the sense of the army as some kind of science fiction conspiracy
to puzzle and confound individuals could be said to have a wider resonance in Amis's fiction. It is present in his two fantasy novels, *The
Alteration* (1976), in which Amis imagines a situation in which the
Reformation never happened in Europe and the Vatican rules the conti-
nent in a way strangely reminiscent of Stalinist Russia,[6] and *Russian
Hide and Seek* (1980), in which Amis imagines a future Britain under
Russian occupation.[7]

Amis resumed his studies when peace came in 1945 and left Oxford,
already married and with a family, in 1949. For the next 12 years he
taught English at Swansea. Amis evidently disliked both the snobbishly
aristocratic cultural ambiance at Oxford and the antiquated English syl-
labus he was forced to study (it is clear from the *Memoirs* that he did not
much like teaching English either). Army experience—and age—gave
him the confidence to stick two fingers up to the sacred traditions of high
culture. He shared his dislikes, together with his love for jazz, with a
fellow student and close friend, the poet Philip Larkin. But his rejection
of what he saw as an effete Bohemian culture did not go much beyond
swapping obscene verses with friends and mocking poets like Dylan
Thomas, whom he met at Swansea. It was not particularly political.[8]
There was, however, a more serious artistic side to this protest. Amis
made his literary reputation initially, not as a novelist, but as a poet. He
was part of the post-war revolt against Modernism, the movement which
had dominated poetry in the earlier part of the century. The 'New

Movement' in poetry (as it was called) rejected the internationalism and artistic experimentation of Modernism in favour of modest and ironic exploration of ordinary situations. Amis and Larkin were much the leaders in this. In *Poets of the 1950s,* edited by D J Enright, Amis claimed that '...nobody wants any more poems about philosophers or paintings or novelists or art galleries or mythology or foreign cities or other poems'; and Larkin, who was the acknowledged leader of the Movement, asserted that he had 'no belief in "tradition" or a common myth-kitty or casual allusions in poems to other poems or poets'.[9]

The targets here are Auden and T S Eliot, as well as Dylan Thomas, whose densely surreal, oratorical and metaphor packed style was the dominant presence in post-war English poetry. The desire to move on was understandable—no artist can continue to repeat the old formulae—but the radicalism of this attack is debatable. It is one thing to want to puncture reputations (particularly Dylan Thomas's); but rehabilitating the ordinary, the provincial and the commonplace (which is what the Movement was attempting to do) can quickly become philistinism, pure and simple. We now know, thanks to Andrew Motion's recent biography of Philip Larkin, just how reactionary that philistinism was capable of being: Larkin emerges as a nasty little racist bigot.

A similar process can be seen in the way the early fiction of Amis developed. His first novel, *Lucky Jim,* which was dedicated to Philip Larkin, came as a breath of fresh air in the stale world of 1950s fiction, much as two years later John Osborne's *Look Back in Anger* did the same for the staid world of genteel drama. It identified Amis as one of the 'Angry Young Men' of the period—irreverent and iconoclastic, in revolt against the establishment and its culture. Just as he rejected Modernist experimentation in poetry, so too did he in respect of fiction.[10] The determination to avoid experimental oddity shows in the lean and unpoetic 'realism' of Amis's first novel, as well as his choice of central character, the anti-hero, Jim Dixon, who is a lecturer in mediaeval history at a provincial university. Jim is presented as an ordinary bloke with ordinary tastes, up against the snobbish, Bloomsbury style culture of his academic superior, Professor Welch. Jim is more at home in the pub than at the ridiculous musical soirées given by the Welches. He also competes for the favours of the girlfriend of the ghastly son of the Welches, the pseudo-artist Bertrand, whose affected speech provides much of the comedy of the novel. *Lucky Jim* is a satire on the aesthetic and artistic establishment of the day, its metropolitan entrenchment and contempt for anything provincial (at one point Jim is accused of being a 'shabby little provincial bore').[11] Down to earth reaction against pretentiousness, dilletantism and toadyism is seen as a good thing, whether that involves playing practical jokes on creeps, giving one's opponent in love a good hiding, or confessing (as Christine, the girl Jim has set his heart on, does) to a liking for brown sauce—a liking at odds with the breakfast arrangements at the Welches.

In the end Jim gets the better of the twisters, snobs, bullies and fools by whom he is surrounded. He wins out in two ways. First, there is the public lecture he has been forced to give by Professor Welch, the subject of which is Merrie England. As a mediaeval historian Jim is expected to provide a eulogy for the past—in line with Welch's contempt for the vulgar culture of the present ('sham architecture'...'the Light Programme'...'the Yellow Press'...'the best-seller'...'the theatre-organ').[12] Instead of this he ends his disastrously drunken lecture with the exact opposite message: Merrie England was 'the most un-Merrie period in our history' contrary to what 'the home-made pottery crowd, the organic husbandry crowd, the recorder-playing crowd, the Esperanto'[13] crowd believe. Secondly, although he loses his lecturing job he gets Christine and a job with the girl's uncle, Gore-Urquhart, in London into the bargain.

Jim's triumph is meant to be the triumph of the ordinary and basically decent person over the pretentious hypocrites who occupy positions of social, moral or sexual authority. Even so, the novel's praise for ordinariness and decency raise a number of problems. First, there is the question of the reaction against artistic pretentiousness: Jim's notorious comment about 'filthy Mozart'[14] might be excused in the context but points to a strand of philistinism which remains unchallenged from within the novel. Secondly, there is what one might call Jim's view of the world. He counters Bertrand's right wing attacks on soak the rich policies with the comment, 'If one man's got ten buns and another's got two, and a bun has got to be given up by one of them, then surely you take it from the man with ten buns'.[15] This redistributionism remains politically vague. Jim's anti-Welchness never becomes a pro-Labour or socialist argument. What Jim finds objectionable about Bertrand is not so much his attitudes as Bertrand himself, his way of talking or behaving. It is almost as if Jim reaches for any argument that will get under Bertrand's skin simply because he, Bertrand, represents the Establishment blocking Jim's social and sexual advancement. Jim's philosophy is summed up in his theory that 'nice things are nicer than nasty ones'.[16] This is certainly undeniably true; but it is crushingly banal. It is also completely abstract. Individuals are always social individuals, for whom 'nice' and 'nasty' vary according to class position. As a world view it does not help decide what side one is on in the pursuit of the 'nice' in preference to the 'nasty', given that they mean different things to different classes. Anyone holding to such a position could easily swing—as Amis did—from left to right.

In the 1950s, this individualist philosophy of common sense might pass muster.[17] The enemy was the old effete political and cultural establishment, identifiable by its style rather than its content. But style says little about the forces involved. A provincial accent, such as Jim is said to have, is not necessarily more radical than an upper class drawl and the modernity which Jim valued above Merrie England is not necessarily at odds with the long term interests of the Establishment, or, to be more precise, the ruling class.[18] *Lucky Jim*'s radicalism can work just so long as the Establishment itself doesn't shift. The ambiguities can be passed off as acceptable. So, for example, Jim's getting the job with Gore-Urquhart that Bertrand thought his by right can be viewed as his triumph over the Establishment, a triumph for the common man over privilege and snobbery, of the provincial over the metropolitan. On the other hand—and in a sense truer to the developments in the period—it could be seen as his entry into it: he does, after all, gain a place in the despised metropolis. Gore-Urquhart has a nicer attitude towards Jim but the novel leaves untouched the question of whether he will be a better employer than Welch.

The novel which followed *Lucky Jim*, *That Uncertain Feeling* (1955) was recognisably the same terrain: the target this time was the Welsh establishment and their pet bard (a parody of Dylan Thomas).[19] The next novel, *I Like It Here* (1958), represented the beginning of a shift. The target is still cultural pretension (the novel features an expatriate novelist, Wulfstan Strether, who writes in the exaggeratedly complex style of the early Modernist novelist, Henry James). But the tone—as suggested by the title—shades into being anti-foreign. Has the champion of ordinariness, of provincial life turned into a little Englander? Perhaps not quite: the hero of the novel likes the cheapness of Portuguese booze, but on the whole thinks the country would be improved if it were closer to somewhere like Eastbourne. The final novel in the 'filthy abroad' mode was *One Fat Englishman* (1963), where the target is America, in particular American as opposed to British linguistic forms. Arguably, none of these novels' heroes represent Amis,[20] but rather the prejudices of a certain kind of Englishman—particularly, insecure Englishmen by virtue of their sexual weaknesses and (in the case of *One Fat Englishman*) physical unpleasantness. Amis might be said to have played up the philistinism, the better to criticise the limitations of the central characters' responses. In short, authorial comment which would guide the reader is deliberately missing, the better to get the reader him- or herself to react to the limitations of the central characters. The reader who takes the lack of authorial guidance for endorsement is therefore missing the point. The argument is not convincing, partly because there is so much gusto put into the philistinism that any disclaimer that it is not being endorsed is suspect (one is reminded of the comedian who insists that the racist or sexist jokes he tells do not amount to belief in racism or sexism). More importantly the argument is not convincing because the novels themselves are not structured in a way which 'place' or act as a counterweight to the central characters' reactions. The structure of Amis's novels, for all their 'realism', is seldom objective. It is the central character's subjectivity which colours and shapes the material despite the fact that the novels are told in the third person. The effect of this is to allow subjective reaction (ie philistine prejudice) to pass itself off, by and large, as objective comment (ie as analysis of how things really are).

The limitations in Amis's revolt, then, begin to become clear. The philistinism of sticking up for ordinariness and the philosophy of individual common sense (nice things are nicer than nasty things) became an accommodation to right wing ideas.[21] With Labour in office for the last six years of the 1960s and with the rise of progressive ideas (particularly in education), superficially it looked as if a new, lefty Establishment had replaced the old one. Where cocking a snook, taking the mickey, insults and name calling had once got up the noses of the right-wing establishment, now the target was progressivism in all its forms. The Angry Young Man turned into the angry young reactionary. 'Why Lucky Jim Turned Right' was the title of his own 1967 essay.

Nowhere was this truer than in the field of education, where Amis was a key figure at the centre of the notorious Black Papers which appeared at the end of the 1960s. The authors' argument was that the advent of the comprehensives under Labour in the mid-1960s had brought about a dramatic decline in standards of literacy and numeracy. They were concerned not just to reverse the process but to conduct a campaign to save liberal values from the totalitarian threat of revolutionary ideas (the late 1960s had seen a mass student movement challenging authority in the universities and many of the contributors to the Black Papers clearly saw that as the beginning of the end of civilisation as we know it). They weren't just anti-Labour: they were also against what they saw as the softness of the Tories' response. To them the capitulation to fashionable cant about 'progressive' methods had affected even the Tories. Theirs was a crusade to stop what they saw as betrayal on a grand scale. Much of the argument was Cold War rhetoric about the threat from the Soviets, who in any case, as the Black Paper authors pointed out, did not themselves practise the dangerous egalitarianism which had so infiltrated British thinking on education.

By the late 1960s, when the Black Papers appeared, Amis was associated with Cold War politics. He had become a close friend of Robert Conquest, who wrote three books on Stalin's reign of terror from an anti-Marxist viewpoint, and collaborated with him on a novel called *The*

Egyptologists (1965) and on editing science fiction anthologies. Amis's *Memoirs* suggest that they shared a similar taste for smutty limericks and practical jokes. In those days, Amis claimed, 'I was some sort of man of the Left' while Conquest belonged to the libertarian right.

> *Some time later he was to point out that, while very 'progressive' on the subject of colonialism and other matters I was ignorant of, I was a sound reactionary about education, of which I had some understanding and experience.*[22]

Amis's claim to have been progressive on the issue of colonialism needs to be taken with a very large pinch of salt but his boast about his attitude towards (but not his understanding of) education is true enough. Even in *Lucky Jim*, one of the sympathetic characters complains about the 'outside pressure to chuck Firsts around like teaching diplomas and push every bugger who can write his name through the Pass courses'.[23] In 1961 Amis notoriously claimed that 'more will mean worse', by which he meant that expansion of numbers going into higher education would entail an increase in cultural illiteracy—or what H J Eysenck, mocking the idea of meritocracy, termed the 'rise of the mediocracy'. By 1969, when he and Conquest contributed to the second Black Paper, the argument about the expansion of higher education was tied to horror at student revolt (they refer to the London School of Economics, but without further explanation, presumably because right wing lecturers being prevented from speaking by student militants was too obviously the result of expansion to require further comment) and the growth of sociology courses ('not a suitable undergraduate subject'),[24] an objection which now looks quaint to us but which at the time seemed self evident to the right: wasn't sociology part of the student demand for 'relevance' and wasn't it partisan propaganda for Marxist change thinly disguised as an academic subject?

The strongest feeling that comes across from their contribution to the debate is the sense that they are part of a beleaguered group of people, smeared as fascists for wanting to uphold standards in the face of a new, authoritarian establishment of 'progressives' who are leading us to disaster. So, if there is a move on Amis's part from being a 'man of the left' to 'a sound reactionary', there is also an element of continuity: he is against what he takes to be the Establishment. In the 1950s it is the cultural establishment of pompous old bores, with their aristocratic manners; in the 1960s, 1970s and 1980s it is the trendies, the lefties, the politically correct, psychiatrists, women's libbers, and so on. No wonder, then, that Amis came to be a political supporter of Margaret Thatcher. Characteristically his *Memoirs* dwell on her appearance and manner ('never forget she's a bloody woman with the rest of them'[25]) rather than her politics, about which he claims to know little more than any other newspaper reader or bar chatterer, except in the field of education where he is disappointed that her government has undermined education as education, 'the free pursuit of knowledge and truth for their own sake.[26]'

Amis's philistinism could be considered a fairly minor sin compared with his attitude towards women. The generally reactionary mood of his later novels extends to his presentation of the relationship between the sexes. The male characters are unremittingly chauvinist in the way they view women. The question we have already raised in connection with the philistinism of his major characters needs to be raised in this context: is the chauvinism simply an unpleasant side of characters who are meant to be unpleasant? We can approach this by looking at the justification sometimes advanced, namely that his view of women was the product of the unenlightened times in which Amis started his writing career and that it continued to mark his fiction as a consequence. It is true that in 1950s and 1960s culture one pervasive theme is the 'woman problem'. It is all the more jarring in that the tolerance of backward views about women often coexists with a refusal to accept the status quo in respect of other values. The reason for this was that one element of revolt was a revulsion against being tied to home, marriage and domesticity. Given women's traditional identification with this area of life, antagonism (by men) towards the social order often tended to involve a more or less conscious element of antagonism towards women. Social conflict became expressed as a battle between the sexes.[27] Of course, real political understanding would have resolved this antagonism and shown that women's identification with the family was a sign not of their being on 'the wrong side' but of their victimisation at the hands of society. But in the less political 1950s such insights were rare. Not surprisingly, therefore, given the generally unpolitical nature of Amis's revolt against the Establishment, the perception of women is ambiguous from the start.

On the one hand, there is the rejection of the (hypocritical) sexual codes preached by the Establishment. Jim's pursuit of Christine in *Lucky Jim* is part of his fight against the world of the Welches. She is won from being 'dignant': a condition which is a product of consorting with the enemy and one which distorts her 'natural' feelings. Though this is presented as being liberatory for her, given the perspective is Jim's, it is very much liberation on his terms: she seldom rises above the stereotypical blonde. But the other woman in Jim's life is treated much more harshly. She is shabbily treated, first courted, then shunned by Jim as he pursues Christine. This could have made for a fairly complex picture of tangled emotions. But instead Margaret's neurosis is revealed as self-created. Her previous boyfriend, Catchpole, appears at the end of the novel to prove to Jim that her suicide attempt at the beginning of the novel was a total fake. Catchpole states:

> ...*Quite soon I realised that she was one of these people—they're usually women—who feed on emotional tension. We began to have rows about nothing, and I mean that literally. I was much too wary, of course, to start any kind of sexual relationship with her, but she soon started behaving as if I had. I was perpetually being accused of hurting her, ignoring her, trying to humiliate her in front of other women, and all that sort of thing.*[28]

Absolved of all responsibility, Jim is reassured by Catchpole that not only is it too dangerous to help her any more but that she doesn't need any help either. His pursuit of Christine is therefore totally justified. What is objectionable is not so much the situation itself—sexual treachery has been the staple of the novel virtually from its inception—as the way in which Amis rigs the fiction to get the result. Catchpole is a character solely designed to give the desired outcome without its in any sense arising from the objective structure of the novel itself. Margaret is manipulated authorially into becoming a monster, an enemy—part of the conspiracy to stand in the way of Jim and the realisation of his desires. Catchpole's comment, quoted above, is delivered as an unchallengeable truth.

The only thing to be said in mitigation is that the earlier depiction of Margaret in the novel is much less manipulative—even sensitive (within limits). Any such restraints disappear in Amis's later novels: the women are much more crudely portrayed, tending to be divided into sex objects or manipulators—or both. Men may be predators, in the sense that they take every opportunity to pursue women, and that may be the source of tension and unhappiness for their long suffering wives or girlfriends, and indeed for the men themselves. But the message is that this is the nature of male desire, a frailty that in the end can be resisted but not conquered, forgiven but likely to be repeated. That, at any rate, is the message that comes across in *Take a Girl Like You* (1960) and its sequel, *Difficulties with Girls* (1988). The long suffering girlfriend is Jenny Bunn who marries handsome womaniser Patrick Standish, and the two novels feature his infidelities and adulteries and his attempts to atone. It could be argued that by making Jenny Bunn one of the central characters Amis was at least trying to understand from a woman's point of view what being the object of sexual pursuit is like (the perspective in most of Amis's work is overwhelmingly male). But Jenny comes across as a woman hopelessly unable to cope with the sexual attention she receives and irrationally fond of a man she knows to be a shit. In other words, she conforms to a fairly typical male chauvinist stereotype of what 'normal' women want. She is contrasted with Anna, the independent, strong woman—who turns out to be a pathological liar and manipulator: even her lesbianism is a fraudulent attempt to gain attention.

The crudeness of the portrayal of women goes with another kind of crudeness—that of social setting. This is sketchy, more a parade of social prejudice than anything else. Jenny Bunn herself is meant to be a northerner, from a working class background, down to earth but a bit unaware of the devious ways of the big city. But Amis hardly bothers to establish this except in the most perfunctory way. Her father, down with his wife to visit Jenny and Patrick, is 'proved' to be genuine working class because he is against 'chaps with beards and silk scarves marching to and fro with their banners and petitions' (having Aldermaston protesters wear inherently unlikely silk scarves is presumably a way of insinuating they are all middle class trendies) and forces Jenny's penny pinching but Labour supporting landlord to buy his round of drinks.[29] In effect, in this and others of Amis's later novels, we seldom move out of a world constructed out of reactionary fantasy. The most extraordinary example comes from *Stanley and the Women*, in which progressive psychiatry is 'disproved' by having its practitioner, Dr Trish Collings, pursue Stanley in a manipulatively sexual manner. The novel has a strong element of paranoia about it. Stanley seems to believe that there is a plot to get him and that women really are mad.[30]

The final element to consider in Amis's view of sex is homosexuality. For a writer so committed to red blooded male heterosexuality, there's an awful lot of 'it' around. No novel is complete without its 'pansy' or 'queer'. The final image in *Lucky Jim* of Welch and son is of Gide and Strachey, ie posing effeminates. It is as if Jim's masculine right to Christine has to be confirmed by what is perceived to be a lack of masculinity. In *Difficulties with Girls* Patrick's marriage to Jenny is paralleled by his neighbours' homosexual 'marriage' (complete with traditional roles and 'feminine' tantrums by the 'wife'—always called 'she'). Although there is never any attempt to see male homosexuality as other than deviant, there is nevertheless a peculiar kind of tolerance for it (as of some different species).[31] Indeed, perhaps the justification for its tolerance in the novel is that it can absolve the 'deviancy' of Patrick's philandering ways. If 'queers' can't help their deviancy, neither can 'real' men. At a key moment in the novel, Eric, the 'husband', who has had problems of jealousy with Stevie, tells the other husband, Patrick, who is in trouble with Jenny because of his infidelities:

...you and I are by nature, by our respective natures, males who are irresistibly attracted by a non-male principle. In your case, straightforward, women; in my case not straightforward, not women—but, non-male, except

anatomically. And it's the clash between male and non-male that causes all the trouble. They're different from us. More like children. Crying when things go wrong. Making difficulties just so as to be a person.[32]

Like Catchpole's comment in *Lucky Jim,* this is delivered as truth and the basis for the acceptance and forgiveness which marks the reconciliation between Jenny and Patrick at the end of the novel: men can't help themselves and women can't help being emotional. Stripped to its basics, this amounts to no more than reactionary conventional wisdom about the relationship between the sexes. The only intriguing aspect is the way in which the attempt to create a male definition of individuality (women are 'non-male'; like children they are not real persons) is perpetually undermined by the question as to whether some men are really men at all. Ironically, masculinity has to include its destabilising opposite, the male homosexual. What one might call the exclusive male club view of the world is plagued by the suspicion that there may be traitors within.[33]

Whatever this may reveal psychologically about Amis's depiction of male-female relationships,[34] it does not make for satisfactory literature. The deep vein of misogyny in his writing is not compensated for by fictional subtlety. On the contrary, as we noted earlier, the subjectivity masquerading as objective analysis produces artistic crudeness. The novels increasingly become a vehicle for reactionary prejudice.

How can we sum up Amis's career? One explanation is that he is a product of his period. The revolt against the Establishment never got much beyond a repudiation of high culture. Without any positive pole of attraction the revolt remained essentially negative. If we compare him with George Orwell, there are, of course, differences of background. But there are certain similarities. Orwell's dislike of upper class life and espousal of common decency are shown in his pre-war novels, *Keep the Aspidistra Flying* and *Coming Up for Air.* There is also a tendency to philistinism: the sweeping rhetoric against cranky radicalism, for example, in *The Road to Wigan Pier,* which mars his personal commitment to change for ordinary people. What essentially saves Orwell is both the keenness of his exposure to the misery created by the depths of the slump and, more importantly, the searing experience of revolution in Spain (though by the end of the Second World War the confidence that things can be changed has given way to a pessimism that allowed his work to be co-opted by the enemies of socialism, despite his own continuing personal commitment to change). No comparably radicalising events were available to Amis. He was too young for the 1930s to have any real effect and the long boom of the 1950s and 1960s—the period of his maturity—were mostly bereft of any historically significant upheavals (in the West, that is). That left only his experience of the army to have any impact on him—enough to make him look at the post-war world with a jaundiced eye and poke fun at its shibboleths, but little more. Hence his revolt is largely individual and personal: a fight for the right to do what one wants. There was nothing to take that revolt in a left wing direction. The movement was to the right—partly because an increasingly successful career left less to be cynical about, partly because the left wing politics he espoused (vague at the best of times, but useful as a stick to beat the cultural establishment with) became less meaningful—or so it appeared—in the context of the 'affluent society' and the Cold War characterisation of Stalinism.

Another consequence was that there was less to explore. His ear for voices, for mimicry of a certain type of speech, gave his early fiction—particularly *Lucky Jim*—real energy. But even here, with Amis at his best, there is not much sense of an objective social dimension to the novel. Of course, one doesn't necessarily read a novel for its ability to tell us something about the world in which it is set. But there are limits to the number of ways in which the form can be fruitful if its prime virtue is the ability to impersonate a certain kind of consciousness, however brilliantly that is done. The social world of his novels becomes increasingly stuck in a narrow realm of pubs and parties. The outside world is no more than a distant echo, an understanding of it no more than a parade of unthinking and reactionary reflexes. Not surprisingly, perhaps, the world is reduced to a sexual battleground, with little concrete sense of the social determinations of sexual conflict.

Is the force of this argument that Amis was necessarily going to be limited because of the period in which he lived? That would be grossly reductionist. The 1950s may not have been a fantastically productive period as far as the novel was concerned. But one should not conclude that only an Amis was possible. Other novelists in the period give the lie to such determinism. Take, for example, Angus Wilson, a novelist who also had an acute ear for dialogue, who moved in a similar social world, whose career spans much the same period and whose fiction was as resolutely unexperimental and as satirically funny as Amis's. There is an objectivity in his writing, quite at odds with Amis's subjectivity: a breadth of interest in the social world of his period, and an attempt to understand its impact on individual destinies in the modern world. Sadly, all this is missing in Amis. His undeniable skill was harnessed to an increasingly reactionary and limited view of the world. The talent that had the power to satirise the pretensions and foibles of official culture became a talent to offend only the victims. Comedy became comedy in the service of reaction—and so ultimately of that world he had started his career by mocking.

Notes

1   Eric Jacobs in *The Spectator*, 28 October 1995, p28.

2   Malcolm Bradbury, *The Modern British Novel* (Secker and Warburg, 1993), p324.

3   One suspects that a somewhat idealised version of his suburban existence—particularly its musical interests and sexual activities—is recreated in his 1973 novel, *The Riverside Villas Murder*. Even the form of the novel itself, a detective thriller, is a kind of homage to 1930s middle class culture and the novel is saturated, obsessively so, with detail designed to locate it in its period. There is never simply dance band music on the wireless, always an exact enumeration of a band and its members. No one ever simply smokes a cigarette—it is a Turban or a Weights or a Woodbine. The cereal is never simply cereal, but Farmer's Glory wheat flakes. The effect is one not so much of nostalgia—there isn't enough emotion for that—but of pastiche. There is no analysis of this world: it is background, faithfully realised, to the main character, the adolescent hero with a precocious capacity to solve the murder clues who is also initiated by an older married woman (an idealisation of the young Amis himself?).

4   Kingsley Amis, *Memoirs* (Penguin, 1992), p78.

5   'My Enemy's Enemy' (1955), 'Court of Enquiry' (1956), 'I Spy Strangers' (1962), all to be found in the *Collected Short Stories* (Penguin, 1980).

6   There are two minor figures, police agents called Foot and Redgrave who do the system's particularly dirty work. Amis was never one to stint on paranoid slurs about the revolutionary left.

7   Amis tried to get his hero, Margaret Thatcher, to accept an inscribed copy at a party he attended at Number 10. On being told by the humble adorer what the novel was about, she crushed him with the comment: 'Can't you do any better than that? Get yourself another crystal ball!). See *Memoirs*, p318.

8   The *Memoirs* claim that when he returned to Oxford after the army he refused to rejoin the Communist Party he had briefly belonged to during his first stay at the University (p37).

9   Quoted in Charles Tomlinson, 'Poetry Today', in *The Modern Age, Volume 7 of the Pelican Guide to English Literature*, ed Boris Ford (Penguin, 1961), p458.

10   See Rubin Rabinowitz, *The Reaction Against Experiment in the English Novel, 1950-1960* (New York, 1967), for a useful account of this.

11   Kingsley Amis, *Lucky Jim* (Penguin, 1992), with introduction by David Lodge, p158.

12   Ibid, pp204-5.

13   Ibid, p227.

14   Ibid, p63.

15   Ibid, p51.

16   Ibid, p140.

17   David Lodge points out that Amis's style 'owes something to the "ordinary language" philosophy that dominated Oxford when Amis was a student there' (*Lucky Jim*, pvi). Such a philosophy presupposes that there is nothing very important to talk about except the way we talk about the world. Such a view is only possible on the assumption that as things have been so they will remain—except for some tinkering at the edges.

18   Harold Wilson skilfully exploited this ambiguity in his pre-1964 campaigning against Lord Home in the name of a technological revolution. Culturally, the satire of *Private Eye* and the BBC's *That Was the Week That Was* also rested on an ambiguous response to the way in which the Establishment marginalised talent. Many satirists had a genuine desire to attack privilege; but some used it as a road to advancement (David Frost, Bernard Levin...).

19   Dylan Thomas is also the target, under the name of Brydan, in *The Old Devils*. This much later novel has a broader aim. Brydan/Thomas represents the temptation to literary bullshit and more general dishonesty (including sexual dishonesty) which besets the central character, Alun Weaver. Weaver is a London based TV pundit who has made a career out of being a professional Welshman (as Dylan Thomas could have been accused of being) and who has now retired to his native country (the better to go on dishonestly bullshitting and in the process messing up the lives of his former friends). Arguably, this is one of Amis's better late novels, perhaps because it represents a revisitation of earlier material, though the offensiveness quota remains high.

20   Amis always protested that given his political support for the US he could hardly be accused of being anti-American.

21   Where individualism in the 1950s could be anti the Tory establishment, Mrs Thatcher (and the monetarist right) used it as an ideological assault on corporatism, welfarism and the rest. Giving back to the individual what the state had taken from them was her rallying cry. Needless to say, only a certain number of individuals benefited. But clearly Amis happily adapted to this right wing individualism. The shift is shown by comparing Jim's commonsense reaction against Establishment codes with the praise poured on by the stolid and sensible policeman in *Stanley and the Women*: 'Misprize common sense at your peril is my motto,' he says, having rescued Stanley's schizophrenic son from a spot of bother with a Middle Eastern embassy (mad Arabs, this time, rather than mad women)— *Stanley and the Women* (Penguin, 1985), p247.

22   Kingsley Amis, *Memoirs* (Penguin, 1992), p146.

23   *Lucky Jim*, p169. If, of course, the complaint is correct, then those who make the same criticism in the 1990s, and look back to the 1950s as the era after which standards fell, have some explaining to do.

24   *Black Paper Two*, ed C B Cox and A E Dyson (Hull), p157.

25   *Memoirs*, p317.

26   Ibid, p319.

27   To give just a few examples from the culture of the period. Alan Sillitoe's *Saturday Night and Sunday Morning* (1958) has its hero resist being forced to marry because he fears losing the freedom which the relatively good pay from his mindless factory job allows him to enjoy (the film version brings out the suffocating respectability of his girlfriend's mother). *Look Back in Anger*'s Jimmy Porter rails against his upper class wife, whose perpetual ironing and silence he takes to be part of what's wrong with the world. Stan Barstow's *A Kind of Loving* (1960) manages (just about) to reconcile his hero to being trapped into marriage by his girlfriend's pregnancy.

28   *Lucky Jim*, pp235-236.

29   *Take a Girl Like You* (Penguin, 1962), p178. He is also anti-semitic, imagining Patrick's real name is Schtundisch. He warms to Patrick, however, because Patrick is prepared to stand his round and shows he is not a 'Jew' with his money. Amis's depiction of Jenny's father is so caricatural, so Alf Garnett like in seeing workers as patriotic bigots, as to be laughable.

30   The novel features Stanley's son's violent schizophrenia, so Stanley's paranoia could be said to reflect the theme of the book. Significantly, though, the only sane and sensible psychiatrist is a man, who despises his radical female colleague, Dr Collings.

31   Part of the subplot revolves round a friend who is experiencing sexual difficulties in his marriage. He has been told by his psychiatrist that he must be subconsciously homosexual and so is determined to be 'queer' though he doesn't feel any desire for a man. He simply isn't the type: you either are or aren't 'queer' and that's the end of it. This is yet another appeal to common sense. (Fear of not

performing sexually with a woman and so fear of not being a real man suggests a side to Amis that only a Freudian would dare explore.)

32   *Difficulties with Girls* (Penguin, 1989), p256.

33   The preference for all male company—and a paranoid fear that there may be a plot to infiltrate and undermine the institution—is an abiding element in Amis's work (perhaps derived ultimately from his experience of those very male institutions, his Oxford college and the army). See *The Egyptologists* for a fantasy version of this theme. An obsession with plots could also be said to be a Cold War theme. Paranoia for Freud was linked with fear of homosexuality; whether that applies to Amis is beyond the scope of this writer.

34   It may be that that idealised version of Amis's childhood suburban existence, *The Riverside Villa Murders*, says more about Amis than he would have cared to reveal. It contains a psychologically intriguing triangle. Young Peter, the hero of the tale, is the subject of the sexual interest of both a married woman, who seduces him, and an avuncular ex-military homosexual, who self denyingly does not. He is flattered by the attentions of both, since both confirm his sense of self: the woman is proof, so to speak, that although he enjoys mutual masturbation with a school friend, his orientation is not towards men; the homosexual colonel is proof that he is an adult (the colonel treats him as an equal by making him a co-partner in solving the crime). Peter's real object of desire, however, is Daphne, the girl next door. She baffles his every move to get her to go out with him, trapping him in adolescent uncertainty. Seduction by the married woman gives him confidence but is implicitly problematic (the need for secrecy, the threat of scandal—to say nothing of the Oedipal implications). The threat is eliminated when she is unmasked as a neurotic and sexually predatory murderess by the colonel and again when she is persuaded to do the decent thing and commit suicide. He, Peter, is now free to impose on Daphne, the implication being that he knows her true feelings better than she does. We have here a pattern which often emerges in more veiled form in his fiction: the idea that the hero becomes a real person by release from helplessness induced by involvement with a sexually manipulative woman. The suspicion that this rejection of things feminine involves being uninterested in women can be countered by giving space to the homosexual (that embodiment of lack of sexual interest in women) as something one most definitely is not—or as we saw Patrick doing, in *Difficulties with Women*, making the homosexual a chaser after 'women' of the non-anatomical variety—in other words, an honorary man.

The bloody birth of capitalism

A review of J L Hammond and B Hammond, **The Labourer 1760-1832**
(Alan Sutton, 1995), £16.99

MARK O'BRIEN

The Labourer 1760-1832 is in fact a collection of three books that were published separately as *The Village Labourer* (1911), *The Town Labourer* (1917) and *The Skilled Labourer* (1919). They were to become classics in the flowering of working class history writing which marked the post-war years, as the impact of workers' revolution reverberated around the world. They set a standard of scholarship and tilled the ground that E P Thompson was to re-work in the early 1960s.

The excitement of the Hammonds' work lies not only in its historical detail but in the powerful contemporary resonance of its pages. Understanding the roots of capitalist society illuminates our understanding of the system we struggle against today and reminds us of the barbarism which lies at the core of that system.

The period covered by the Hammonds can be characterised as that in which the social and economic preconditions for the industrial revolution were created. This was not a slow painless process of gradual but inevitable change—a kind of calm before the storm of the massive industrialisation that was to follow. Rather it was a period of cruel and determined intervention by mainly Whig (Liberal) governments against a reluctant population. That force was required to clear the way for the factory system should not surprise us when we look at what the changes meant for the mass of labourers and their families who were to become the new manufacturing proletariat.

Life in the rural areas at the end of the 17th century and for much of the 18th century was based on arduous labour and could be suffocatingly parochial, oppressively landlord dominated and, in times of disease or crop failure, short. On the other hand, however, these were old communities with families and names which went back further than people could remember. At their strongest the old villages could be places of social stability, albeit of a kind that was riven by hierarchical social relationships and petty rivalries. In fair times an artisan or small landholder might prosper. Certainly these communities were not without their comforts. At the very least even the poorest labourer or farmer would have common rights which enabled them to collect firewood or forest fruits or to graze an animal or two on open pasture.

The historically progressive aspect of the industrial system found no intellectual appeal or enthusiasm amongst the mass of the village populations. On the contrary, these communities were resistant to change. It was this resistance that the new industrialists and their political representatives were determined to smash.

The principal instrument used to undermine the old rural communities was land enclosure. By this means common land, to which common rights had become attached by ancient custom allowing even the poorest to have access, was now expropriated into large estates and private hands. Enclosures actually began in the reign of Henry VII at the end of the 15th century. The number of enclosures increased rapidly after the Reformation in the 16th century with the breaking up of the monasteries and the land rights associated with them. But in our period a new systematic approach to enclosure began to develop with the power of the state behind it.

The process by which the soil was transformed into capital became more and more intensive. The agricultural revolution of the earlier part of the 18th century had massively increased food production by the systematic application of more scientific farming principles such as crop rotation, liming and manuring of the soil, and selective breeding, and had provided the basis for an increasing population. The later decades of the 18th century saw the establishment of institutions for scientific research such as the Royal Veterinary Society, Kew Gardens and the Royal Botanical Society. The confidence of the new 'progressives' was secured by a new world view which abhorred the untidiness of the natural landscape and which worshipped above all order, system and symmetry—the celebration of nature found in Wordsworth and Constable came as a later reaction against these rationalists.

The optimism of the age, however, meant absolutely nothing to the labourer. For the mass of the rural population the enclosures were devastating. Whole regions became depopulated. Small farmers now became day labourers and hirelings. Some emigrated to America. Many joined the bands of the destitute who roamed the agricultural districts. Finally they were drawn with a terrible inevitability into the black holes of the growing industrial ghettos.

The ruling class regarded the whole scene with delight. To them the small landholders had been unproductive and wasteful. They sermonised about the fecklessness of the poor and celebrated their plunder with visions of their own advancement and human progress. In fact the ruling class, despite their ideological pretensions, were clear about the benefits of this shift both for the new capitalism they were inaugurating and for their own interests within it. One Mr Bishton wrote the following: 'The use of common land operates upon the mind as a sort of independence.' When the commons are enclosed 'the labourers will work every day in the year, their children will be put out to labour early' and 'that subordination of the lower ranks which in the present times is so much wanted, would be thereby considerably secured'.[1]

Something of what these changes meant to the labourers is captured in this piece from a chronicler of the time:

> Go to an alehouse kitchen of an old enclosed country, and there you will see the origin of poverty and poor rates. For whom are they to be sober? For whom are they to save? For the parish? If I am diligent, shall I have leave to build a cottage? If I am sober, shall I have land for a cow? If I am frugal shall I have an acre of potatoes? You offer no motives; you have nothing but a parish officer and a workhouse! Bring me another pot.[2]

Pauperism was not now an episodic occurrence but rather a defining feature of the landscape of pre-industrial Britain. The pauper for the new ruling class was an object of annoyance and contempt. The Radical pamphleteer William Cobbett commented on how the language of respectable society changed with respect to the poor. The old name of 'the commons of England', for example, gave way to 'the lower orders' or 'the peasantry' and when the poor gathered together to voice their grievances they became 'the mob'. After the French Revolution of 1789, however, a different emotion became mingled in the minds of the rich as they regarded the poor—fear. The poor were now not merely a nuisance. They were a threat and pauperism was a problem which required a solution.

Even as elements within political circles and local magistrates and poor relief officials began to address the problem of mass destitution they betrayed their class hostility to the labourers. Could not the poor, for example, change their diet?

The solution seemed to lie in the simple life. Enthusiasts soon began to feel about this proposal the sort of excitement that Robinson Crusoe enjoyed when discovering new resources on his island: an infinite vista of kitchen reform beckoned to their ingenious imaginations: and many of them began to persuade themselves that the miseries of the poor arose less from the scantiness of their incomes than from their own improvidence and unthriftiness.[3]

These reformers boasted of their own thrift by cutting the edges off pastry dishes and reducing the subsistence of their servants. Surely labourers in the south did not really have to eat wheaten bread. Was not oatmeal just as good? The drinking of tea by the poor was seen as downright scandalous. In fact the diet of the labourers already crudely reflected the realities of life and work in their different regions. Where fatty meat was unavailable, for example, good bread was essential as a source of energy. Breads of mixed grain and oatmeal were only consumed in regions where the availabilty of milk had not been eliminated by enclosures. And tea was consumed as a stimulant against fatigue. The labourer, who in the imagination of the well to do was something akin to a roughly built and sturdy animal, proved infuriatingly impervious to the wisdom of the dieticians.

Another option briefly considered and rejected, although favoured by the labourers themselves, was that of the minimum wage. There was a notion that wage levels might be pegged to the prices of staple foods. Indeed a table of wages and prices was actually drawn up. The plan was soon dropped, however. As prices rose, an increase in wages would have become a working class demand and even an issue of dispute between labourers and employers. As prices fell, however, it dawned on the magistrates that reducing wages might be easier said than done!

Finally a new form of poor relief carried the day in the form of the Speenhamland system of 1795. What distinguished the new system from the old, somewhat ramshackle and regionally based parish relief which dated back to the reign of Elizabeth I, was both its near national spread and the way in which it was to become a structural element in the accelerating development of capitalist society. The Speenhamland system was not a mere safety net designed to save the poorest from starvation in times of economic collapse. It was a system which actually institutionalised pauperism and which locked poverty into capitalist social relations on the employer's terms. Under Speenhamland an employer might reduce wages to below subsistence level in the knowledge that the poor rates would make up the difference. The immediate effect was to depress wages and to impose universal pauperism even amongst the working population. Those without work suffered even greater abuse. They were now in the hands of the Speenhamland overseers. These local officers would hire out the unemployed who were forced to go from house to house seeking work. Any wages would be paid to the overseer to finance relief. Despite respectable society's preachings on the subject of frugality, if a labourer had indeed worked hard to put a little aside for himself and his family he was now punished by the Speenhamland system. Only paupers could obtain relief. It was dangerous even to look neat and tidy lest this arouse suspicion of hidden savings.

It needs to be borne in mind that agriculture by the 1790s was a vast and specialised capitalist industry which was enjoying fabulous profits. The high prices of farming produce were the result partly of enclosure, partly of the application of scientific methods and partly of the French war. The labourer enjoyed no share in this:

> *The village population whose condition...was compared by supporters of the slave trade with that of the negroes in the West Indies, to its disadvantage, might have been rehoused on its share of this tremendous revenue. In fact, the revenue went solely to increase rent, tithes and to some extent profits. The labourers alone had made no advance when the halcyon days of the industry clouded over and prices fell. The rent receiver received more rent than was needed to induce him to let his land, the farmer made larger profits than were necessary to induce him to apply his capital and ability to farming, but the labourer received less than was necessary to maintain him, the balance being made up out of the rates. Thus not only did the labourer receive no share of the surplus; he did not even get his subsistence directly from the product of his labour... The landlord therefore made no sacrifice in introducing the Speenhamland system...*[4]

Just as poverty and ruling class attitudes towards the poor were becoming systematically redefined, so too was the meaning of crime. Punishments meted out for stealing began to assume a new ferocity. Transportations to Australia and Van Diemen's Land (Tasmania) became commonplace. Hangings too became common and even expected for theft accompanied by any form of violence or for repeated offence. In many magistrates courts it was normal practice to hand out a sentence of death only to commute it to one of transportation on the basis of a character witness or of a plea from grief stricken relatives or a sympathetic parson. Frequently the rich of an area would express their disgust at commutations of the death sentence, regarding transportation as a soft option. Magistrates who were seen as lenient were usually removed. One Suffolk magistrate, Capel Lofft, was struck off the Commission of the Peace for trying to argue for clemency in the case of a girl who had been sentenced to death for stealing. Indeed youth was no defence. *The Annual Register* for 1791 records the execution of two boys for stealing at Newport, one aged 14 and the other 15. Children were committed to

Houses of Correction in their hundreds in some districts. The transportation of children was not uncommon. One diarist gives us the following
entry in 1813:

> *Oct 13—I was attending to give evidence against a man. Afterwards two*
> *boys, John and Thomas Clough, aged 12 and 10 years, were tried and found*
> *guilty of stealing some Irish linen out of Joseph Thorley's warehouse during*
> *the dinner hour. The Chairman sentenced them to seven years transportation.*
> *On its being announced the mother of these unfortunate boys came to the Bar*
> *to her children, and with them was in great agony, imploring mercy of the*
> *bench. With difficulty the children were removed. The scene was so horrifying*
> *I could remain no longer in court.*[5]

Some of the cruellest punishments were handed out under the new
game code against poaching. With such high levels of poverty, poached
game was an indispensable supplement on the table of many a home:

> *The close relation of this great increase of crime to the general distress was*
> *universally recognised. Cobbett tells us that a gentleman in Surrey asked a*
> *young man, who was cracking stones on the roadside, how he could live upon*
> *half a crown a week. 'I don't live on it,' said he. 'How do you live then?'*
> *'Why,' said he, 'I poach: it is better to be hanged than to be starved to*
> *death.'*[6]

We have already followed the Hammonds' description of the process
of enclosure and its significance. The question of land ownership was
precious to the ruling class. Poaching was seen as an intolerable infringe-
ment. More than this, however, it was outside any system. It was in a
sense an unregulated form of poor relief. The point here is that for the
new system poverty was essential. It was the whip of poverty which
drove the rural populations into the towns. It was poverty too which was
a weapon in determining wage levels. It was poverty and distress which
were to keep the wheels of industry turning faster and faster. Anything
which undermined this, which softened the sting of poverty, including
such working class entertainments as the public fairs—hated by the rich
as events of excess and ribaldry—was seen as detrimental to the new
capitalism. The conviction rate for poaching increased along with industrialisation. Between 1827 and 1830 one in seven of all convictions came
under the game laws.

There were those within the ranks of the wealthy who rationalised
such repression in terms of a higher aesthetic sense. There were some,
for example, who prided themselves on their love of nature and of
animals. They were appalled at such barbarous sports of the working

class as bull baiting and cock fighting and campaigned for their suppression by parliament. That such sports reflected the brutalisation and cruelty of the lives of workers of the time would never have occurred to them.

It was in the towns, at the heart of the new industry, that these depths of disregard for human life and the quality of life for the working class were found at their most systematic and mechanised. The towns of the early decades of the 19th century were growing too fast to assume any aspect that we might call 'character' or 'colour'. They were not evolving in the way that the medieval conurbations had evolved. Rather they were expanding in a frenzied drive for profit. The only buildings built with any real thought or planning at all were the factories themselves. The homes of the workers, if indeed they warranted such a title, were built without regard for ventilation or sanitation. The supplies of clean water were minimal if they existed at all. Landlords crammed in tenant families on top of one another. Beds were shared between families, rotating according to shifts. It was commonly said that a bed in a Manchester working class tenement was never cold:

> They were not so much towns as barracks: not the refuge of a civilisation but the barracks of an industry. This character was stamped on their form and life of government. The medieval town had reflected the minds of centuries and the subtle associations of a living society with a history; these towns reflected the violent enterprise of an hour, the single passion that had thrown street on street in a frantic monotony of disorder.[7]

Inside the factories a regime existed designed to crush any spirit of independence out of the working class. Even the slightest infringements of factory discipline were punished with penalties and fines. During a spinners' strike in Manchester the strikers published a pamphlet listing the fines to which they were subjected:

	s.	d.
Any spinner found with his window open	1	0
Any spinner found dirty at his work	1	0
Any spinner found washing himself	1	0
Any spinner leaving his oil can out of its place	1	0
Any spinner repairing his drum banding with his gas lighted	2	0
Any spinner slipping with his gas lighted	2	0
Any spinner putting his gas out too soon	1	0
Any spinner spinning with gaslight too long in the morning	2	0

The list contains 19 separate infringements.[8]

Conditions in these factories were not only oppressive—they were dangerous. Reports of accidents were regularly suppressed. The most shocking abuse perpetrated by the factory system both to the modern mind and to observers and workers of the time was the exploitation of children. Child labour had always been a feature of working life in pre-industrial Britain. Generally, however, it had tended to be within the family sphere of the artisan's home or workshop. What was different now was the scale and form of the phenomenon. The factories, mills and mines now pulled in literally thousands upon thousands of child labourers, sometimes as young as five or six. They worked the fastest spindles and dug into the narrowest and most dangerous seams. They worked the ventilation shafts, they trimmed the oil lamps, they fetched and carried for the skilled labourers, they swept the factory floors. It is not too much of an exaggeration to say that in some industries child labour formed the basis of production. The length of the working day for children at that time is almost hard to imagine:

> The 14 or 15 hours' confinement for six days a week were the 'regular' hours: in busy times hours were elastic and sometimes stretched to a length that seems almost incredible. Work from 3am to 10pm was not unknown... At the mill aptly called 'Hell Bay,' for two months at a time, they not only worked regularly from 5am to 9pm, but for two nights each week worked all through the night as well. The more humane employers contented themselves when busy with a spell of 16 hours (5am to 9pm).[9]

Such a system could not be physically maintained without a regime of terror. In many mills the sound of beatings and screams of pain were heard by the hour. Some children were indentured into the factories by parents who were themselves brutalised by the savagery of early capitalism. In other cases agonised parents would drag their crying children to the gates each day and beat them themselves to save them from even worse beatings which they knew would be dealt out inside. In many areas poor relief would not be given to families who refused to put their children out to work.

Child labour came into the homes of the well to do and of the middle class reformers in the form of the chimney sweeps. Young children, usually boys, would be forced, almost naked and almost paralysed by fear, up the chimneys. Sometimes an older boy might be sent up after them to force them to keep moving. Sometimes a fire might be lit beneath them to help their passage. The 'invention' of the sweep actually encouraged the building of narrower and narrower flues. Stories of children becoming trapped and dying in these sooty tombs were commonplace.

The Hammonds expose brilliantly the mentality and attitude of the rich towards these horrors. That attempts were made to justify the exploitation of children, is amazing in itself. The 'justifications' themselves, moreover, can only be described as perverse. It was said, for example, that the rapid and intricate movements of the spindle frames caught the fancy of lively little minds. The factory children were attributed a kind of cheerful elvish quality. Their work then was a kind of amusement. A factory commissioner in 1832 even produced the following ingenious argument to the effect that the work of children at the 'mules'—devices which moved up and down the spinning machines—was light. After all, he reasoned, whilst the mule was moving away from the child, or had not yet reached them, they were doing no actual work. This led to the triumphant conclusion that 'if a child is normally working 12 hours a day,' for nine hours he performs no actual labour !¹⁰

Against this background the ability of the ruling class to cocoon themselves in a soft focused rationalisation of the world which they had created arouses disgust. The age of the factory children is also the age when a new romantic myth of childhood was being created in literature and art. Books such as *Poetry for Children* and *Tales from Shakespeare* by Charles and Mary Lamb were a must in the children's bedrooms of any fashionable middle class home. Painters such as Sir Joshua Reynolds created an image of childhood which dripped with sentimentality. Childhood was an age of innocence and fancy, of chasing dandelion clocks and playing with puppies. Even the urchins were painted with cheeky faces, glowing at play. The poor wretches pulling coal wagons on their hands and knees in the darkness would never see these images. Many would never see sunlight.

In all that we have seen so far—the mass impoverishment of the working class, the treatment of crime, the exploitation of children—there was an underlying logic. This barbarism had a point. The way to be cleared for the industrial system had nothing whatever to offer the working class of the time. The main means by which to force workers from the fields and into the furnaces of the early industrial towns was by violence and the threat of starvation. The social experience of the working class in our period, however, was not simply one of oppression. Our story is also one of resistance.

The entire period of the second half of the 18th century and the opening decades of the 19th century was shaped, not only by the depredations of an increasingly vicious and avaricious ruling class, but also by disturbances, rioting, strikes and working class organisation. The enclosures, for example, provoked rioting again and again. Widespread food riots, in which women played a conspicuous part, took place in 1795. The rioters were actually highly organised. Once they had mastered an area, they did not simply plunder what they could. Rather they seized grain, for example, and then forced storekeepers to sell it to them for what they considered to be a reasonable price. They then set about distributing it fairly.

In 1816 large scale rioting occurred in the counties of Norfolk, Suffolk, Huntingdon and Cambridgeshire. Nightly assemblies were held, threatening letters sent to local landowners and houses, ricks and barns were fired. The rioters marched under a banner inscribed with the words 'Bread or Blood' and there were several clashes with yeomanry and dragoons. In 1830 the 'Swing' riots took place against the threshing machine which had been used to replace agricultural workers whilst many of them were away fighting or being killed in the continental wars.

As the working class grew in size and cohesion increasingly strikes came into prominence as the focus of the social contradictions of the new society shifted to the industrial regions. Significant strikes occurred amongst the miners in 1795, 1810, 1816, 1831 and 1832; the cotton spinners in 1810, 1818, 1829 and 1830; the cotton weavers in 1808 and 1818; the woollen spinners in 1819; the woollen weavers in 1819, 1823, 1825, 1827 and 1828-9; the shearmen in 1802; the woolcombers and worsted weavers in 1825; the framework knitters in 1814, 1817, 1819, 1821 and 1824.

Frequently strike waves would occur as the result of disillusionment following the shattering of false hopes placed in the system itself. The weavers, for example, looked to the Arbitration Act of 1803 to redress their grievances. The act, however, worked entirely and systematically in favour of the masters. Other groups of workers petitioned parliament for better wages or placed hope in legislation for a minimum wage. In every case their illusions were shattered. Often it took such an experience for workers to turn towards ideas of political reform. The great 1819 gathering at St Peter's Field, for example, at which the Peterloo Massacre took place, and which was to mark a high point of the movement for parliamentary reform, took place against the background of the largest strike wave ever up to that point.

One problem for the authorities facing this new phenomenon of increasingly organised action by workers was the unreliability of the men at their command. Sometimes their forces were simply intimidated. In the cotton spinners' strike of 1830 special constables refused to act against strikers who were parading the streets with pistols and bludgeons. But often there was genuine sympathy with workers when they took action. In the Tyne and Wear seamen's strike of 1815 a 20 gun ship was sent to Shields. The officers, however, reported that they seriously doubted whether the bluejackets aboard would act against the strikers, so strong was their sentiment in support of the seamen. There are frequent reports of locally raised militias either standing aside or even actually taking sides with rioters and strikers.

It was for this reason that the first attempts were made to establish a permanent body whose sole role it would be to police the urban centres. William Pitt's volunteers were an early attempt to institute such a body. These proved just as unreliable, however. In most of the northern towns the volunteers acted with the rioters in the cases of food riots and strikes at one time or another. When the volunteers were finally disbanded in 1813, the one force that was retained was the yeomanry. They were essentially the well to do of the area, in uniform, on horseback and armed with cutlasses. Their hostility towards the working class ran deep and they became known for their arrogance and ferocity. It was the yeomanry who were responsible for the slaughter at St Peter's Field in 1819 which triggered a wave of protests and strikes. The government was briefly forced to ponder the possibility of a revolutionary response. It was after this episode that the ruling class moved more and more towards the notion of a domestic, demilitarised body, able to use less than lethal force to quell working class unrest. Robert Peel's Metropolitan Police Bill and the Special Constables Act came at the very end of our period.

The Hammonds end their work with an extended discussion of the Luddite movement. This is appropriate. In many senses, although there were other strands within the working class in which we can see the seeds of the movement that was to follow—the reform movement and general unionism, for example—the Luddites represent a defining moment in the period about which the Hammonds have written. Although Nedd Ludd and his friends were at large in the hard months between 1811 and 1812, in terms of the evolution of working class consciousness they mark, not so much the birth of the modern working class, but the end of its gestation.

The background to the Luddite movement was the destruction of small scale production in the cottages and workshops of pre-industrial England. A new spirit of commercial innovation began to make itself felt from the early decades of the 18th century. By 1760 the flying shuttle, which halved the labour of yarn production, was in general application. The spinning jenny, patented in 1770, made it possible to drive at first eight and later as many as 100 spindles with one spinning wheel. The mule, invented in 1779, mechanised the production of fine high quality muslins. The gig mill, in general application by the turn of the century, reduced the time required to raise and shear the nap on textiles, again saving on labour. Watt's steam engine made possible the shift of production from the rural areas, where water power had been used, to the towns. This revolution of techniques in industry was to have

a devastating effect on those whose livelihoods had depended upon the
highly skilled processes of the old artisan craft industries. Many thousands of labourers, and many of the masters, now found themselves in
reduced circumstances or even destitute. Some, such as the Spitalfields
silk weavers, had once regarded themselves as a sort of aristocracy
within, or perhaps slightly above, the working class. By the 1820s they
were facing ruin.

It is against this background that the breaking of machines, particularly the knitting frames, began:

> *The frame breakers called themselves Luddites, and signed their proclama-*
> *tions Ned Ludd, sometimes adding Sherwood Forest. The original Ned Ludd,*
> *according to the **Nottingham Review**, was a boy apprenticed to learn frame-*
> *work knitting at Anstey, near Leicester. Being averse to confinement or work,*
> *he refused to exert himself, whereupon his master complained to a magis-*
> *trate, who ordered a whipping. Ned in answer took a hammer and demolished*
> *the hated frame. His later fortunes history does not relate.*[11]

The Luddites have become known to history as a movement which
opposed the introduction of new machinery. Although it is true that it
was technical innovation that destroyed the old cottage industries, the
Luddites did not see themselves as opponents of new technology as such.
Claiming the authority of a charter given to the trade by Charles II they
targeted those manufacturers who were producing cheap, inferior gar-
ments, or 'cut ups', or who were paying low wages. It made no
difference whether they were using new or old machinery. The real spirit
of Luddism is captured in a song of the time with the title *General
Ludd's Triumph*:

> *The guilty may fear, but no vengeance he aims*
> *At the honest man's life or estate*
> *His wrath is entirely confined to wide frames*
> *And to those that old prices abate.*
> *These Engines of mischief were sentenced to die*
> *By unanimous vote of the Trade;*
> *And Ludd who can all opposition defy*
> *Was the grand Executioner made.*
>
> *Let the wise and the great lend their aid and advice*
> *Nor e'er their assistance withdraw*
> *Till full fashioned work at the old fashioned price*
> *Is established by Custom and Law.*
> *Then the Trade when this arduous contest is o'er*

Shall raise in full splendour its head,
And colting and cutting and squaring no more
Shall deprive honest workmen of bread.

Squaring referred to all forms of what was considered unfair practice by the masters.[12]

These lines also give the lie to the historical image given to the Luddites as driven by blind opposition to the new machines. What they wanted was legislation for their industries and protection under the law. Neither is it true to say that Luddism was a movement of spontaneous outbursts of anger. Machine breaking had not in fact begun with Luddism. Cases of such attacks were occurring in the 1790s. What was new about the Luddite movement was both its scale—thousands of frames were smashed in these months—and its highly organised nature. They were organised through 'Secret Committees' and planned their attacks in quasi-military style. To disguise their identities they adopted false names such as Oliver Cromwell, Sir Francis Burdett, Lord Grey and Lord Grenville. The following description is given of the preparations for an attack at a heavily fortified mill at Liversedge:

> *The attack was carefully organised. Contingents from Halifax, Huddersfield, Liversedge, Heckmondwike, Gomersal, Birstall, Cleckheaton, and other places, numbering about 150, met in a field belonging to Sir George Armytage near the 'Dumb Steeple' or obelisk, some three miles from the mill, between 10 and 11 o'clock. They were armed with guns, pistols, stakes, hammers, or whatever weapon came to hand, and after being mustered by numbers into companies of musket men or pistol men or hatchet men they marched to the mill, which they reached rather more than half an hour after midnight.*[13]

The result on this occasion was a gunfight in which two of the assailants were killed.

Women too were involved. One Manchester woman, Hannah Smith, won notoriety after leading the seizing of potatoes from local merchants and selling them at a lower price. She was condemned to death for jumping on a butter cart at Ardwick and selling 20 pounds of butter, worth 36 shillings, at one shilling a pound.

In the end the Luddites, despite their individual courage, were not a movement which could take the working class forward. The conspiratorial nature of their organisation meant that only handfuls of workers could be actively involved. The great leaps forward in terms of class consciousness and socialist ideas would have to wait until the mass politics of the Chartist movement which falls outside of our period. It is in this sense that Luddism marks the end of that stage in the history of the working class in which the model of the underground conspiracy and secretive organisation still held sway.

In *The Labourer* the Hammonds chronicle that era in the history of capitalism in which the process of industrialisation quickened until it culminated in the industrial revolution of the 1820s and 1830s. In this period too the social contradictions by which we characterise capitalism were intensified and forged into the foundations of the new system. At the same time a new historical class, that of the industrial worker, was undergoing its painful growth and development and, in faltering steps, discovering its strength. In all of this the Hammonds remind us of the barbarity of the historical roots of the system we fight today and of the violent logic at heart of that system. The most fitting tribute to their contribution comes in their own words:

> *In their terror of the French Revolution they* [the ruling class] *treated the sovereign hope that has inspired its best minds throughout the long pilgrimage of the race as an overwhelming illusion: in their confidence in the unchecked rule of capital they made law, order, and justice the sentinels of a new and more terrible inequality between man and man. The life of a society in which violence so deliberate as this is done to the instincts and the passions of mankind turns inevitably into civil war.* [14]

Notes

1   J L and B Hammond, *The Village Labourer* (Alan Sutton, 1995), p33.
2   Ibid, p105.
3   Ibid, p123.
4   Ibid, p167.
5   Ibid, p102.
6   Ibid, p191.
7   J L and B Hammond, *The Town Labourer* (Alan Sutton, 1995), p39.
8   Ibid, pp20-21.
9   Ibid, p159.
10   Ibid, p159.
11   J L and B Hammond, *The Skilled Labourer* (Alan Sutton, 1995), p259.
12   Ibid, pp259-260.
13   Ibid, p304.
14   Ibid, p381.

Studies in revolution

A review of **Religion, Culture and Society in Early Modern Britain**
edited by Anthony Fletcher and Peter Roberts (Cambridge UP) £40

LEE HUMBER

This collection of essays centres on the English Revolution and brings together nearly all of the people currently setting the pace in the study of the subject. It has been compiled to celebrate historian Patrick Collinson's contribution to the area and contains some absolutely fascinating material.

There are all sorts of ways to learn from these articles. Some are just very interesting, like Peter Roberts's piece on the developing state's first attacks on vagabonds and wandering minstrels in the 16th century, or Peter Lake's excellent piece on Puritanism and popular pamphlet literature in the 17th century. The articles by Conrad Russell and John Morrill are of particular relevance since these were two of the leading proponents of the anti-Marxist revisionism which marked the study of the English Revolution in the 1980s. But we should start with Keith Thomas on 'Cleanliness and Godliness in Early Modern England', since his short piece is a wonderful historical study.

Thomas is president of Corpus Christi college, Oxford and president of the British Academy, but don't let that put you off his books, *Religion and the Decline of Magic* and *Man and the Natural World*. One of his strengths is his ability to link ideological issues with the material circumstances in which they occur. For example, his short piece in this collection considers the issue of personal and social hygiene throughout the 17th century as peasants thrown off common owned land thronged to increasingly overcrowded towns and cities looking for work. He traces the religious arguments used to encourage cleanliness, arguments for and against cleanliness from the medical profession, how cleanliness was used as a mark of social distinction and how ideological offensives to promote personal hygiene were used to help preserve social order. On this last point Thomas quotes, among others, the social reformer Bishop Berkeley writing in the 1750s on Irish immigrant workers:

> A little washing, scrubbing, and rubbing, bestowed on their persons and houses would introduce a sort of industry, and industry in any one kind is apt to beget it in another... You shall not find a clean house inhabited by clean people, and yet wanting necessaries; the same spirit of industry that keeps folk clean being sufficient to keep them also in food and raiment.[1]

The information Thomas amasses tells us a lot about the very practical political reasons behind the do gooding of the middle classes of this period.

Equally illuminating is what Thomas tells us of the medical profession in the 1640s. In 1648, one year before the king was beheaded, as progressive ideas flourished and London authorities proposed to erect public baths for the first time, the Royal College of Doctors argued that too much bathing was morally and physically harmful, 'effeminating bodies, and procuring infirmities, and...debauching the manners of the people'.[2] It is a small point but it does tell us that ideological ferment even reached this seemingly obscure corner of social life. It also gives us an interesting insight into the standards of medical science before the English Republic was proclaimed. It is Thomas's ability to weave these disparate strands together into a coherent whole which gives his work its power, even though his last paragraph conclusion to this particular piece does peter out disappointingly.

The meat of the book for Marxists is undoubtedly the two middle pieces by the terrible twins of revisionist history, John Morrill and Conrad Russell. Morrill is Reader in Early Modern History at Cambridge and author and editor of 15 books. His most recent, *The Nature of the English Revolution*, contains 20 of his most influential essays, some of which would have been read by any student studying history over the last decade or so. The fun for socialists reading Morrill is in sharpening a Marxist analysis of the English Revolution through arguing against him.

Morrill's article is entitled 'A British Patriarchy? Ecclesiastical Imperialism Under the Early Stuarts', in which he attempts to discuss why the English church became more interventionist in Scotland and Ireland from Elizabeth I in the late 16th century through to the 1630s and the rule of Charles I. Early on Morrill explains Elizabeth's relative lack of enthusiasm for imposing the English church's will over the borders in this way:

> *The reluctance of Elizabeth or her bishops to get drawn into the internal affairs of the kirk* [Scottish church] *was based in part on English indifference to developing closer cultural and institutional links with Scotland; in part on English fears that once broad strategic objectives in Scotland had been secured, there was a danger for the English in being felt to be interfering... and in part on the queen's instinctive dislike of active policies anywhere.*[3]

This is fairly typical Morrill fare in that it begs far more questions than it answers. For example, were the English simply indifferent to developing closer links with Scotland, or incapable of doing so for all sorts of economic and political reasons? Was it really the case that Elizabeth shied away from 'active policies' (a term which itself needs justification) because she was instinctively against it? If we try to shade in a little of the economic and political realities of Elizabeth's reign, answers begin to suggest themselves.

The period to which Morrill refers comes at the end of the 16th century in which huge amounts of land and property had changed hands as Henry VIII led his crusade against the Catholic church and its great wealth. Estates with a capital value (in today's money) of £15 million to £20 million found new owners.[4] New class forces and class interests arose, with new ideas to justify their influence and power. Confusion reigned as medieval certainty and rigid social stratification were slowly nudged aside by the practice and values of a new kind of society. As R H Tawney puts it:

> *In practice, since new class interests and novel ideas had arisen, but had not yet wholly submerged those which preceded them, every shade of opinion, from that of the pious burgess, who protested indignantly against being saddled with a vicar who took a penny in the shilling, to the latitudinarianism of the cosmopolitan financier, to whom the confusion of business with morals was a vulgar delusion, was represented in the economic ethics of Elizabethan England.*[5]

This wide range of opinion and the political consequences of it are reflected in the infighting around Elizabeth at court throughout the late 15th century. For example, in 1587 Sir Christopher Hatton was appointed Lord Chancellor of England after steadily courting the Queen's favour throughout the 1570s. A crypto-Catholic throughout this period, he was instrumental in getting John Whitgift appointed Archbishop of

Canterbury. Whitgift was not a Catholic himself but he was keen to defend the existing structures of the church, largely established by Catholicism, and hold back the tide of Puritanism which had gathered pace up until his appointment. The Earl of Leicester, formerly the queen's favourite and throughout an advocate of Protestantism, found himself on the defensive over these events. He tried to reassert his influence at court by arguing for an aggressive foreign policy in defence of Protestantism across Europe, in particular to defend the Dutch rebels then fighting against the rule of the Catholic King of Spain. But these ideas brought him into conflict at court with Lord Burghley who, though an enthusiastic supporter of Protestantism, was worried about the diplomatic and financial implications of English armies trooping off to northern Europe.[6]

This great political instability at court, which reflected that in the country generally, did not allow for decisive policies. If you cannot be sure whether your own religion is crypto-Catholic or fully Protestant what sort of religion do you try to impose on your neighbour? Elizabeth wasn't instinctively indecisive—after all, with the Poor Law of 1572, strengthened in 1576 and again with the Vagrancy Act of 1598, she was certainly decisive when it came to attacking the landless. Her indecision was caused by the fine balance of competing political forces around her at court.

By the time Charles came to the throne in 1621 the political and economic uncertainty of Elizabeth's time was fast becoming a crisis. But we look in vain to Morrill for any sense of this. In comparing James I of England with his son Charles, Morrill writes:

> *James was attempting to…arrogate to himself and a clique of bishops the power to change the liturgy of the church. But faced by a storm of criticism, James backed off… Charles was not to move far from his father's intentions, nor from his preferred means. But whereas James backed off in the face of a fiercer resistance than he had anticipated, Charles was to blunder on to catastrophe.*[7]

The question left unanswered is why did Charles feel the need to reassert his rule so aggressively? To answer this we must move out of the realm of religion and look at the economic and political world in which the battle of religions took place.

By the time Charles came to power, all sorts of social forces had begun to develop whose economic interests did not coincide with those of the king or the members of the ruling class he favoured. This is particularly true of that layer of society which Brian Manning has described as the 'middle sort of people'—small land owners, craftsmen, shopkeepers, traders and others. This layer was deeply influenced by Puritanism. From their ranks came Oliver Cromwell and the dynamic core of the parliamentary party during the English Revolution.[8]

In his recent book, *Merchants and Revolution*, Robert Brenner reflects the extent to which the economic aspirations of the 'middle sort of people' were being denied when he explains that the aim of the chartered companies (those merchants with royal permission to trade overseas):

> *was not merely to keep out poorer, badly connected traders so as to restrict the numbers participating in the trade; it was especially to prevent entry into overseas commerce by the city's shopkeepers, small producers and ship captains, whatever their wealth... Moreover, many of them were by no means poor, and an important minority...undoubtedly possessed sufficient wealth to pursue overseas trade.[9]*

The aspirations of the 'middle sort of people' to break out of the constraints the king and his supporters forced on them are vividly reflected in the Petition of Right of 1628. The bill, moved by a Puritan dominated House of Commons, bluntly puts the case for parliament controlling the finances of England, including those of the king. It was a direct challenge to the old order. As the petition states:

> *It is declared and enacted, that from thenceforth no person shall be compelled to make any loans to the king against his will, because such loans were against reason and the franchise of the land; and by other laws of this realm it is provided, that none should be charged by any charge or imposition, called a Benevolence, or by such like charge, by which the statutes beforementioned, and other the good laws and statutes of the realm, your subjects have inherited this freedom, that they should not be compelled to contribute to any tax, tallage, aid or other like charge, not set by common consent in parliament.[10]*

For Charles to have accepted such a bill would have meant putting himself under the financial, and therefore political, control of parliament. Already independent royal income was flagging. Sales of royal lands by James I had reduced income from this source by a quarter. Charles's right to raise revenue by charging customs on overseas trade was in dispute, parliament refused to grant him the traditional tonnage and poundage taxes and he was forced to introduce a hated Ship Money tax which only added fuel to the growing fire of class hatred.[11] Rather than accept the Petition of Right, Charles chose to dissolve parliament in 1628. This was not the act of a blundering buffoon but a conscious attack by the king on his economic and political rivals in the Commons. It is in this context of class conflict and hardening class positions that we must understand Charles' future actions—from raising Ship Money as a source of income to attempting to impose his ideological rule through dictating codes of religion in England and Scotland and attacking Puritanism in all its forms.

Conrad Russell, Professor of History at Kings College London, is a more enigmatic character. His books include *Parliaments and English Politics* and *The Causes of The English Civil War*, written at opposite ends of the 1980s. His article in this collection discusses the union between England and Scotland from 1603-43. It is an interesting piece with some interesting detail. But what it lacks entirely is any sense of the economic relationship between the two kingdoms or how the relationship changed according to the rhythms of political struggle. For example, the Scots' economic situation is summed up in a passing remark on the 'comparative poverty of the Scottish nobility'.[12] Nor is there any reference to the deepening of class divisions in England during this time and how this might have affected Scottish nobles and merchants. Yet these issues are key to understanding why the Anglo-Scottish alliance was fundamentally strengthened in 1643 when Scottish forces joined parliament's side in the English Civil War.

In 1643 the House of Commons promised money and religious and political influence throughout the realm to religious progressives in Scotland. In September that year the Solemn League and Covenant was enacted by parliament promising to 'sincerely, really and constantly... endeavour in our several places and callings the preservation of the reformed religion in the Church of Scotland...against our common enemies; the reformation of religion in the kingdoms of England and Ireland'[13]—a declaration of support for parliament and against the king. A few months later a combined force of English parliamentary and Scottish Covenantor armies scored the first decisive victory of the Civil War, defeating the Royalists at Marston Moor. The promise of religious influence very quickly turned out to be a dead letter. But the allegiance had served its purpose, tipping the military/political balance in parliament's favour. This was the decisive factor pulling the two countries together. The union between the English and Scots was not a gradual coming together of two cultures, as Russell suggests. It took a great leap forward in the 1640s directly because of the English Revolution.

You are almost certain to come across the opinions of Morrill and Russell if you delve into the history of the English Revolution. They were both involved in the so called 'History Debate' of the late 1980s and early 1990s which, as you may remember, was a Thatcherite project to further the 'British' content of teaching of history in schools and colleges. Both spent large parts of the Thatcher years attempting to dismiss the notion that Marxist analysis had anything useful to offer the study of history. Interestingly both have reappraised their anti-Marxist position in the years since Thatcher's political demise. Indeed, after the onslaught against Marxist techniques of historical study throughout the 1980s, in the early 1990s many historians began to rediscover at least some of the great strengths of historical materialism.

Another of the featured writers in this volume is Peter Lake. Dodge Professor of History at Princeton University, his work is more difficult to get hold of but is well worth the effort. His books include *Moderate Puritans and the Elizabethan Church* and *Anglicans and Puritans? Presbyterianism and English Conformist Thought from Whitgift to Hooker*. They might sound a bit dry but they are in fact fascinating studies of the inter-relationship between ideological and material forces in the 16th and 17th centuries, valuable for their detail and insight.

His piece here is 'Popular Form, Puritan Content?' It reflects on the seemingly incongruous coming together of two distinct forms of publications of the mid-17th century—the Puritan conversion narrative—written to build the ranks of the Puritan faithful—and the popular murder pamphlet—written purely for entertainment and profit. Lake focuses on two examples of this alliance, the stories of the hangings for murder of Nathaniel Butler and Thomas Savage. Lake argues that these two represent the:

> *logical outcome of that process of glossing murder narratives, a commercial literary form, whose saleability almost certainly resided in its most titillating, even pornographic aspects, in terms of certain central Protestant or Puritan doctrines and attitudes.*[14]

Furthermore Lake explains that:

> *For all the Puritan credentials of the authors—respectable Presbyterian divines in the case of the Butler narrative, notable nonconformists in the case of the Savage pamphlet—both accounts retained many of the central characteristics of the average murder pamphlet. Both seemed designed to exploit the buzz of notoriety and rumour surrounding peculiarly unpleasant murders.*[15]

That Puritan ministers—those stuffy, aloof people in the black capes and black hats—could be sufficiently socially aware to tap in to the popular consciousness in this way is quite a revelation and helps bring them and their movement to life. Lake maps out in fascinating detail the involvement of the Puritans in the trials of the two murderers, sketching out what the murderers and the Puritan movement gained from the alliance. Puritan ministers visited both Savage and Butler in the condemned cells in the run up to their hangings. Their aim was to bring the felons to a full realisation of the extent of their sins, and to offer them redemption through accepting Christ. The Puritans left full accounts of the conversations and emotional interactions between the felons and their clerical mentors so we learn that, though Savage thought a simple repentance would be enough to save his soul, the Puritan ministers had other ideas. As Lake explains:

> It became clear that he needed first to be brought 'to a sight and sense of the corruption of his nature and of the sinfulness of his heart'. Confronted with the depth of his own sin he would have to acknowledge that his own puny tears and sighs of repentance counted for nothing.[16]

According to the Puritan ministers Savage required the full treatment. This of course put the ministers in control of Savage's spiritual welfare—he would be ready for eternity when they said so. The gallows work of the Puritan ministers helped further the Puritan cause in many ways. It also clearly helped the felons come to terms with the barbarity of their punishment. According to the numerous and varied sources which Lake quotes, both Savage and Butler went to their deaths calmly, in the certain knowledge that they were at one with Christ and therefore assured of salvation. This of course was also marvellous propaganda for Puritanism. As the felons made their way through the crowds to the scaffold, the gathered masses could not but marvel at how at peace with themselves the condemned men were. And of course, as Lake points out:

> If God could save such unregenerated and desperate sinners he could save anyone... Such cases were, therefore, a powerful corrective against hopelessness for all Christians languishing in despair at the enormity of their own sins.[17]

Lake's great strength is the way in which he connects up the ideological aspects of the religious battles being fought out throughout this period with the social and political aspects. His summation of the motives behind the Puritan murder/conversion pamphlets is wonderfully succinct and dialectical:

> As ever with Puritan piety, the internal was inextricably connected to the external, the private, interior world of spiritual introspection, linked to the external world of public policy and godly reformation.[18]

In my opinion Lake's piece is the highlight of this useful collection. For anyone just starting to get to grips with the period the book maps out some of the main areas of importance and contention. Those with a wider knowledge of the period will find it stimulating and useful. There is no definite political agenda mapped out in the book, which is refreshing coming after a period which has seen numerous collections of essays with a particular, invariably right wing, axe to grind. In this sense the collection reflects the more open climate of debate in historical study today. True, none of the demons of the left, like Brian Manning or Christopher Hill, were asked to contribute. But at least a number of the authors displayed a more than passing knowledge of the Marxist techniques of historical study. And that, after a decade which has seen Marxism driven on the defensive, is to be welcomed.

Notes

1   G Berekeley, 'A Word to the Wise', *The Querist* (1750), quoted by Thomas, p80.
2   P Chamberlen, 'A Paper Delivered...for Bathes and Bath-Stoves' (1648), as quoted by Thomas, op cit, p74.
3   A Fletcher and P Roberts (ed), *Religion, Culture and Society in Early Modern Britain* (London, 1995), p211.
4   R H Tawney, *Religion and the Rise of Capitalism* (London, 1987), p168.
5   Ibid, p172.
6   D MacCulloch, *The Later Reformation in England 1547-1603* (London, 1990), p45.
7   *Religion, Culture and Society,* op cit, p221.
8   B Manning, *English People and the English Revolution* (London, 1991).
9   *Merchants and Revolution: Commercial Change, Political Conflict and London's Overseas Traders, 1550-1653* (London, 1993), p83.
10   Ed S R Gardiner, *The Constitutional Documents of the Puritan Revolution 1625-1660* (London, 1979), p66.
11   C Hill, *The Century of Revolution 1603-1714* (London, 1986), pp41-42.
12   *Religion, Culture and Society,* op cit, p241.
13   S R Gardiner, op cit (London, 1979), p267.
14   *Religion, Culture and Society,* op cit, p318.
15   Ibid, p318.
16   Ibid, p319.
17   Ibid, p330.
18   Ibid, p332.

A new life for Lenin

A review of Paul Le Blanc, **Lenin and the Revolutionary Party** *(New Jersey, 1993), £16.99, and George Fyson (ed),* **Lenin's Final Fight. Speeches and Writings, 1922-23** *(New York, 1995), £12.95*

ADRIAN BUDD

Erich Fromm once wrote that 'the successful revolutionary is a statesman, the unsuccessful one a criminal'.[1] Lenin's political genius only ensured that he survived criminalisation to become a 'statesman' because his energy and genius were directed towards fashioning and building a tool, the Bolshevik Party. So Lenin was able, in 1917, to lead the world's first successful socialist revolution. Lenin the 'statesman' was a product of Lenin the party builder.

Le Blanc's book focuses on Lenin the party builder, on Lenin's organisational thought. He reclaims and restates what he calls 'authentic Leninism—qualitatively different from the grotesque distortions of Leninism that are so widely circulated'.[2] He is no ivory tower historian but a Trotskyist and supporter of the Fourth International, and as such sympathetic towards, but not uncritical of, Lenin's ideas. This contemporary engagement in socialist politics elevates Le Blanc's book to a position alongside a small number of classic studies of Lenin, notably Tony Cliff's three volume *Lenin,* Marcel Liebman's *Leninism Under Lenin*, and Neil Harding's two volume *Lenin's Political Thought.*[3] While these explore Lenin's politics as a whole, Le Blanc's narrower focus on Lenin's most important contribution to Marxism underlines both the centrality of the revolutionary party to the socialist revolution of 1917 and the abiding necessity of building similar parties today in preparation for the revolutionary possibilities of tomorrow.

From the late 1890s Lenin's whole activity was directed towards understanding European and, more specifically Russian, society. But the world was not just to be understood: it was to be changed, and in a very specific way—namely, by linking the elementary struggles of the newly awakened Russian workers to wider political questions and, most importantly, the task of taking state power. It was a commonplace amongst both Russian and other socialists that some form of organisation was required to wage the class struggle. But, Lenin argued, to turn the workers' 'spontaneous struggle against their oppressors into the struggle for definite political and socialist ideals' required a break with localised organisation and the federal framework of the Russian social democracy and with organisation around purely economic goals (economism). The parts of the class struggle, immensely important as spontaneous opposition to capitalism was, had to be fused together, via a Russia wide party, into something that would be greater than the sum of the parts.

Hence the attacks on localism and economism were not designed to centre control over the working class in the hands of the party, as Lenin's critics at the time and since have claimed, but to further the activity of that class and raise the general level of working class consciousness. To achieve this the party could not simply exist alongside workers' struggles, preaching the need to generalise and posing the question of state power, but had to be part of the lived experience of the working class.

Using the account of a Bolshevik committee member in Baku, Cecilia Bobrovskaya, Le Blanc highlights the dangers of counterposing the general to the particular. In a strike in the Baku oilfields a Menshevik agitator 'was never tired at mass meetings of discussing minor questions like the provision of aprons, mitts, etc, by the employers without touching upon the real significance of the strike'. The Bolsheviks' academic and rather abstract approach to the strike meant, however, that they 'were often interrupted by uncomplimentary shouts about the Bolsheviks who instead of demanding mitts and aprons demanded the overthrow of the autocracy'. Simply expounding upon wider political questions does not automatically connect immediate struggles to these questions. Running them in parallel rather than together meant that when, in 1905, the overthrow of autocracy assumed real importance, 'the Bolsheviks were, to a large extent, not in a position to provide real leadership'.[4]

If that lived experience was to inform the nationwide party's practice then inner party democracy, including at times intense polemical battles, was crucial. Local initiative and critical thinking were not to be abandoned in the new centralised party, as Lenin's critics suggested.

They were indispensable, both for the class struggle, which never conforms to any national plan, and for the party's intervention within it. But
they lose their significance if they are not integrated into a party wide
understanding of the possibilities and processes of development that
they reveal. There was thus a reciprocal relationship between the party's
base and centre in which both engaged in a process of collective
learning and development. This development meant that Lenin's conception of the party was not timeless and fixed. Once the party's
revolutionary principles had been established, and the members had self
selected themselves on the basis of adherence to them, flexibility was
essential and Lenin frequently criticised members for continually refer-
ring practical questions to higher bodies.

None of this flowed directly from Lenin's pen into the activity of
members. It had to be fought and argued for and the experience of the
party and the class constantly reassessed in the light of changing circumstances. This is only possible, Le Blanc argues, where the party has
'a deeply ingrained democratic sensibility that manifests itself even
when unusual conditions preclude the formal observance of democratic
procedures', for example under state repression.[5] If, as Trotsky later
argued, the revolutionary party must always look reality in the face,
there must be democratic means to assess that reality, and the tasks and
perspectives most appropriate to it, using all the material available.

There is thus an intimate connection between the tasks of the party,
which exists in the present state of the class struggle, is informed by and
remembers the past, and prepares itself and the class for the future, and
its internal organisation. Lenin's great achievement was to combine the
twin necessities of democracy and centralism. But democratic centralism is no fixed set of rules. If the party is immersed in a changing
social context then the Central Committee, elected at Congress to
ensure party cohesion and coordination, cannot simply read off a list of
prescribed organisational formulae. The precise balance between
democracy and centralism is subordinate to the political tasks confronting the party at the time. Thus, in his battles with Menshevism,
Lenin emphasised different elements at different times. In 1906 he
wrote that 'the principle of democratic centralism and autonomy for
local party organisations implies universal and full *freedom to criticise*
so long as this does not disturb the unity *of a definite action*; it rules out
all criticism which disrupts or makes difficult the *unity* of an action
decided on by the party'. He adds that 'criticism within the limits of the
principles of the Party Programme must be quite free...not only at party
meetings, but also at public meetings'.[6] So in 1906 there is an exagger-
ated emphasis on democracy. By 1912, however, the coexistence of the
two factions in the Russian Social Democratic and Labour Party had

become a hindrance to the Bolsheviks, as the Mensheviks increasingly sought to liquidate the revolutionary workers' party into reformist organisations. The Bolsheviks called a party conference, organised it in their own favour (such that the Mensheviks refused to recognise it) and declared the bulk of their opponents to be outside the party.

Formalists have a field day criticising such activities. But formalism fails to see that the party must be located within definite historical circumstances and that it is not an organisation that perfectly prefigures the future socialist society, with its flourishing of creativity and democracy on a mass basis, but is simply a tool for ushering in that new society. Attachment to procedures that fit one period but which hinder the party's effectiveness in another limits flexibility and, ultimately, postpones the arrival of that new society.

Whether they be openly bourgeois, or social democrats who prefer to work within bourgeois democratic procedures and have given up on the socialist transformation of society (arguing, like Bernstein, that the movement is everything and the goal nothing), opponents of Lenin tie themselves in knots over this tactical flexibility. They argue that for Leninists the end justifies the means, as if any connection between the two were unacceptable and any and every means were available to Leninists. The real problem is that Lenin's opponents camouflage their opposition to the end, socialism, under attacks on Lenin's means. But if the end is socialism, whereby the emancipation of the working class is the act of the working class, then certain actions, for example the plotting of coups or political assassinations, are not means towards it at all and must be rejected.

With socialism as the goal, then, as we have seen, the party must maintain a deep democratic sensibility to ensure the most intimate possible connection with advanced workers and thereby enable appropriate tactical shifts to be made. And Lenin himself, far from having an iron grip over his party, was also subject to that democracy. Thus he sometimes had articles rejected by editors of party publications. Before 1917 Lenin's party experienced a series of often bitter arguments, for example in April 1917 over the nature of the coming revolution, and in the autumn of 1917 over the insurrection, in which Lenin had to fight to turn his minority into a majority. These continued after the revolution, for example over the peace of Brest-Litovsk, and, as we shall see, right through to the end of Lenin's life, albeit in increasingly difficult circumstances. Usually Lenin eventually won his line, but not because of any personal dictatorship, but because the party was conditioned to internal debate and, equally importantly, because its connections to the advanced layers of the working class enabled Lenin to appeal to them over the heads of the leadership. This relationship between party and class, built over two decades, was the cornerstone of the Bolsheviks' success. Its absence on any significant scale in all subsequent radicalisations and pre-revolutionary situations has ensured the defeat of the working class.

This account of Lenin and the revolutionary party is inevitably sketchy. Le Blanc's book, however, is an excellent single volume analysis of how Lenin the revolutionary became Lenin the statesman which provides a wealth of historical background and situates the Bolshevik Party within its historical context. It also explores alternative thinking of the time on the questions addressed by Lenin and, very usefully, assesses Lenin's thought and practice against the criticisms of latter day detractors. But Le Blanc's book has one significant weakness: it condenses his work after the seizure of power into a single chapter. Yet this period, especially 1922-1924, is crucial to Lenin's work as a whole and provides some of Lenin's most brilliant applications of Marxist theory to concrete circumstances.[7]

The Russian Revolution was the high point of a massive radicalisation that shook world capitalism at the end of the First World War. This period promised the realisation of Marxism's vision of liberation after four years of carnage and showed that the hopes Bolsheviks had placed on revolutions in at least some of the advanced capitalist countries were not misplaced. But the period also shows that Lenin's theory of the party had a relevance beyond Russia. Elsewhere there were no parties of the Bolshevik type, schooled over two decades in preparation for the revolution. Gradually, as capitalism hesitantly stabilised itself, revolutionary Russia was left to fight the invading imperialist armies and White counter-revolutionaries in isolation. War raged for a further three years and the party and state that emerged from the ultimate victory in 1921 were very different from those of 1917. The whole context of Lenin's work had changed. The heyday of Bolshevism in 1917 had become the crisis of Bolshevism by 1921. As Rosa Luxemburg put it, 'even the greatest energy and the greatest sacrifices of the proletariat in a single country must inevitably become tangled in a maze of contradictions and blunders'.[8]

Much had been achieved, against enormous odds but at great cost, particularly to the working class, the base of the revolution in the towns. By the end of the civil war the economy of the new Soviet state was devastated. Since, for Lenin, the 'elementary truth of Marxism, that the victory of socialism requires the joint efforts of workers in a number of advanced countries',[9] was just as true now as it had been in 1917, the regime needed a breathing space, needed to hold on until reinforcements arrived.

There was now no question of building socialism but of honestly assessing the grave danger of the revolution being crushed by the gigantic forces of imperialism. With the threat of counter-revolution defeated in the short term the link between the two revolutionary processes—workers' power in the cities and peasant revolts in the countryside—was broken. The Kronstadt rising of March 1921, and peasant uprisings, which had begun to infect the industrial centres, revealed a deep bitterness towards War Communism, and particularly the forced requisitioning of food surpluses. If the peasants were to be reconciled to the regime, coercion had to give way to the reintroduction of private commodity production in the countryside, under the New Economic Policy (NEP). But there could be no simple coexistence between peasant capitalism and the state economy. The state industries 'must win the competition against the ordinary shop assistant, the ordinary capitalist, the merchant, who will go to the peasant without arguing about communism'.[10]

To fail this test would see the workers' state crushed both economically and politically. To pass it and win peasant acceptance of, if not identification with, the regime, the state sector's own functioning had to be exemplary, even if that meant in the short term that it had to practise capitalist management techniques. But these techniques were not purely a matter of administration but also of politics and the balance of class forces. Lenin insisted on the need for independent and democratic trade unions to defend workers against the workers' state. However, this was an increasingly bureaucratised workers' state in which officials outnumbered industrial workers five to one by the end of 1920. The problem was not simply numerical but also political. The bulk of the bureaucratic machine had been recruited from Tsarism, to the extent that Lenin asked whether the Communists were directing or being directed, especially given the low cultural level of the workers and Communists. As the party and regime that he had helped create were being swamped in red tape and, worse still, adapting to the swamp, Lenin went on to the attack.

It was in Lenin's battle to save his life work against bureaucratic strangulation that the tragic consequences of the civil war and Russia's isolation became fully apparent. In past crises Lenin had frequently appealed over the heads of the leadership to the advanced workers, but by 1922 the bulk of these had either perished at the front defending the revolution, returned to the countryside to find food, or joined the ranks of the state apparatus, albeit for the best of motives. Furthermore, in the moment of danger when the partial retreat of the NEP was launched, the Bolsheviks had taken the temporary emergency measure of banning factions, in order that retreat should not degenerate into chaos. But this ban, although not an attempt to silence all dissent within the party, unwittingly played into the hands of the bureaucracy whose administrative methods increasingly prevailed over debate.

This situation was difficult enough but from mid-1922 Lenin's health deteriorated dramatically. He suffered a stroke in May, recovered briefly in the summer, but suffered relapses in December and early in 1923. A severe stroke in March 1923 effectively brought his political life to a close and he died in January 1924. Worse still, Stalin, who feared a campaign against his growing power, was chosen by the CC ostensibly to ensure that the doctors' orders were carried out, but in practice he sought to protect and enhance his own position. Not surprisingly, Fotieva, one of Lenin's secretaries, wrote that 'Lenin got the impression that it was not the doctors who gave the orders to the CC, but the CC to the doctors'.[11] Lenin was fighting an increasingly powerful bureaucracy from his sickbed, without an army to call on and under the surveillance of that very bureaucracy.

Yet such was Lenin's determination that this period of illness coincided with some of the most important political work of his life. And, united in a bloc with Trotsky, small victories were possible, especially while Stalin's position was not yet secure. One such was over the defence of the state monopoly of foreign trade. Without it 'there is the political risk of letting through not foreign merchants by name, which we check, but the entire petty bourgeoisie in general'.[12] Stalin, himself in favour of relaxation of the monopoly, conceded but Lenin, increasingly aware of bureaucratic degeneration, wrote to Trotsky that they 'should not stop but continue the attack'.[13]

The next attack concerned one of the fundamentals of Marxism and Bolshevism, internationalism. In September 1922 Stalin published his 'autonomisation' plan for the reorganisation of relations between the Russian Soviet state (RSFSR) and the five smaller independent Soviet states on its borders. These were to be incorporated into the RSFSR as 'autonomous' republics and the government of Russia would form the government of the whole. Lenin's response was to insist that there should be no incorporation and that all the Soviet republics should form a union of Soviet republics of Europe and Asia with the federal all union executive institutions separate from those of the RSFSR. Lenin's sensitivity to the national feelings of republics long under the Tsarist yoke was passed off as 'national liberalism' by Stalin who, nevertheless, conceded at this point. Lenin had declared 'war to the death on dominant nation chauvinism', but it was a war that he was soon forced to wage earlier than expected.

Stalin and his emissary in Georgia, Ordzhonikidze, continued to use Great Russian chauvinist tactics in their dealings with the Georgian Communist Party and Central Committee. Ordzhonikidze appointed a docile and incompetent CC when the old CC, resistant to Stalin's plans for a Transcaucasian Federation, resigned, and also struck a Georgian supporter of the old CC.

For Lenin the question of the national minorities had to be solved politically, not suppressed administratively. He argued that internationalism on the part of oppressor nations 'must consist not only in the observance of the formal equality of nations but even in an inequality, through which the oppressor nation, the great nation, would compensate for the inequality which obtains in real life' and for the wrongs to which the oppressed nation had been subjected in the past. This was nothing to do with any national liberalism but because 'nothing holds up the development and strengthening of proletarian class solidarity so much as national injustice'.[14] This overriding concern for international class unity meant that Lenin was prepared to accept that the USSR might only operate in military and diplomatic affairs, with full independence in all other matters restored to the individual republics. The harm of administrative disunity was tiny relative to the political necessity of taking the Georgians, and millions of others in Asia, along with the new Soviet power, rather than leaving them prey to the nationalism of counter-revolutionaries.

Stalin, who, along with Dzerzhinsky, head of the Cheka, Lenin held responsible for the Russian chauvinism against Georgia, rejected all this. He formally accepted Lenin's position at the Twelfth Party Congress in April 1923 but implicitly rejected its substance when he spoke against 'bowing and scraping before the representatives' of minority nationalities.[15]

With Lenin's continuing ill health, Trotsky had agreed to fight for Lenin's line over Georgia within the leadership, but at the congress he absented himself from the crucial debates and Stalin won the day. Certainly the USSR was created according to Lenin's plan, but institutions do not float above society. They are instruments that reflect the interests of the dominant force in society and the USSR fell into Stalin's hands just as the RSFSR did. The consequences of this episode and the whole of the subsequent nationalities policy of Stalinism reverberate to this day.

Lenin's notes on the national question were part of a wider fight conducted from his sickbed against the bureaucracy and to shape the future of the regime. The dictations he made between 23 December 1922 and 4 January 1923 became known as his 'Letter to the Congress'.[16] It was here that Lenin proposed concrete steps to thwart bureaucratisation and restore the party's relationship to the working class.

He proposed the expansion of the CC, with the new members drawn from the working class, 'people closer to being rank and file workers and peasants'.[17] He also proposed the expansion of the Central Control Commission, again with workers and peasants, to oversee the rooting out of bureaucracy. The Workers' and Peasants' Inspectorate (WPI) which had been established as a super-commissariat to fight encroaching bureaucratism was also enlarged. The hope was that the transfusion of new working class blood would reinvigorate the body of the state and party institutions. But, although Lenin was the first to realise the danger of bureaucratisation and to take up the fight against it, he was already too late. Stalin had been head of WPI from March 1919 to April 1922 and it had already been transformed into Stalin's private office and private police force within the state. In May 1922 he was appointed party general secretary.

More importantly, Lenin was arguing in a social void. The working class was demoralised and atomised, while within the party workers made up an increasingly small proportion of the membership compared with officials and managers. Recognising this, Lenin was forced to rely on personal changes in the leadership of the party and state where in the past he would have turned to the rank and file. Thus, it is in the 'Letter' that he famously draws his character descriptions. At first he does not come out in favour of Trotsky against Stalin but simply highlights the danger of Stalin having concentrated excessive power in his own hands. Only after the full details of the Georgia affair became known to him at the very end of 1923 did Lenin suggest that the party consider ways to remove Stalin from the post of general secretary.

The tragedy was that Lenin could not see his attack through to a successful conclusion. The fate of his testament, part of the 'Letter', highlights this. It was not distributed to the whole congress for debate, but read out to each delegation in turn. No notes were allowed and no discussion of its contents was permitted. Meanwhile, Stalin, growing in confidence but still overshadowed by Lenin's authority, took up Lenin's proposals for the expansion of the state and party institutions and over relations with the smaller republics. But, while acting in apparent conformity with Lenin's wishes, he systematically subverted the substance of his proposals such that there is an 'enormous gulf between the subsequent course of events and the direction Lenin wished them to take'.[18]

The apparatus that Lenin helped to build had turned against him, stifled him, controlled him and vetted his communications. Ultimately it destroyed Lenin's revolutionary project which had originally motivated the Bolsheviks and the Russian masses, physically destroying those who made the revolution in the process. In its place it erected the Stalinist dictatorship.

None of this was inherent in Bolshevism. Lenin '...was not a dictator in his party, but its leader. His leadership was incontestable and uncon-

tested but it demanded of him a constant effort of thought and organisation; he had to act as if he was reaffirming and reconquering it each
day'.[19] But Lenin was not superhuman and neither he nor the party he
created stood above history and society. The degeneration of the
Bolshevik Party and Soviet state can, in the final analysis, only be
explained by reference to this context. But explanation is not justification. Alternatives were possible, as Lenin's, and later Trotsky's, fight to
redirect the regime onto a path closer to the original one of 1917 shows.
Tragically, despite his political will, courage and honesty, the obstacles
were too great.

Serious studies of Leninism, of which Le Blanc's book is a splendid
example, and of Lenin's political struggles, which Fyson provides for
the last two years of Lenin's life, protect us from the distortions and car-
icatures of the historical record propagated by Stalinists and bourgeois
scholars. They allow us to learn from what happened in history, in particular the history of our class. And the lessons are not just curios for
scholars. Le Blanc's commitment to socialism means that for him, as for
other socialists, 'the primary importance of all this, of course, is not
simply to get the history right, but to orient ourselves in present and
future struggles.'[20]

Across the globe the contradictions and horrors of capitalism are just
as acute as they were in 1917 and the need for socialism is just as
urgent. The recent mass strikes in France offer a glimpse of the possibility of the leap from the realm of necessity into the realm of freedom.
For that leap to be successful, as 1917 revealed in a positive sense and
the failed revolutions negatively, socialists have to recognise another
necessity: that of building revolutionary parties of the type built by
Lenin.

Notes

1   E Fromm, *The Fear of Freedom* (London, 1943), p224.
2   P Le Blanc, *Lenin and the Revolutionary Party* (New Jersey, 1993), p9.
3   Le Blanc's engagement in socialist politics is a strength. But his commitment to
    the Trotskyism of the Fourth International is the source of occasional flaws. He
    insists, for example, on the revolutionary socialist credentials of the Cuban and
    Sandinista leaderships and intermittently forays into minor debates within the US
    section of the Fourth International. But these are minor irritants that detract little
    from his analysis of Bolshevism.
4   P Le Blanc, op cit, p90.
5   Ibid, p54.
6   Ibid, pp130-1.
7   Fyson's book collects this work together but without commentary. Those
    unfamiliar with Lenin's fight against the bureaucracy should read it alongside
    T Cliff, *Lenin: Revolution Besieged* (London, 1987), and M Lewin, *Lenin's Last
    Struggle* (New York, 1968).
8   Quoted in T Cliff, op cit, p177.
9   Quoted in M Lewin, op cit, p4.

10   Quoted in G Fyson, op cit, p36.
11   Quoted in M Lewin, op cit, p93.
12   Quoted in G Fyson, op cit, p91.
13   Quoted in M Lewin, op cit, p40.
14   Quoted in G Fyson, op cit, p197.
15   Quoted in Fyson, op cit, pp300-301, note 6.
16   Y Buranov, *Lenin's Will. Falsified and Forbidden* (New York, 1994). Buranov's access to Kremlin archives enables him to illustrate the lengths that Stalin went to in his struggle with Trotsky during Lenin's illness. He altered Lenin's dictations, for example, in an attempt to cast Trotsky in a less favourable light. But this detective work provides no political reason for Stalin's actions and simply confirms the view that he was a scheming, unscrupulous machine politician. Indeed, Buranov states that his study is not concerned with the economic and social factors which influenced the character of the inner party struggle.
17   Quoted in G Fyson, op cit, p185.
18   M Lewin, op cit, p130.
19   Ibid, p42. In the same vein Hanna Arendt argued in *The Origins of Totalitarianism* that Lenin did not have 'the instincts of a mass leader—he was no orator and had a passion for public admission and analysis of his own errors, which is against the rules of even ordinary demagogy'. Quoted in Le Blanc, op cit, p377.
20   P Le Blanc, op cit, p379.

Bookwatch: The General Strike

MARTIN SMITH

This year sees the 70th anniversary of the 1926 General Strike. The strike began when 1 million miners were locked out by their employers for refusing to take a pay cut. The response of the British working class was magnificent. Over 2.5 million workers responded to the call for action. However, their heroism was not matched by the trade union leaders who, even in the heat of the battle, were plotting to betray their own members. The traditional view of the events of May 1926 has helped to disguise the disgraceful role of the trade union leaders. Enshrined in history books is the idea that the strike was dominated by football matches between police officers and strikers, rather than bitter class conflict. It is a version of history that reinforces the idea that Britain is exceptional, having evolved gradually by democratic and constitutional methods rather than revolts and revolutions. King George V summed this view up perfectly in his diary entry of 12th May 1926 when he said, 'Our old country can well be proud of itself, as during the last nine days there has been a strike in which 4 million people have been affected, not a shot has been fired and no one killed, it shows what a wonderful people we are.'

However, there is an alternative view of the strike, one which shows that at least a minority of workers were willing to play by a different set of rules. For example, in East Fife 700 strikers joined a defence corps which ensured that police did not attack picket lines. More importantly not only were the workers more militant than is remembered, it is now clear that the strike was in fact gaining strength when the TUC's General Council called off the vital solidarity strikes. All union leaders, both on the left and the right of the movement, were involved in leaving the miners isolated.

It is often said by socialists that workers' struggle is 'hidden from history'. This is literally the fact in the case of the General Strike. There was at the time of writing not one book on the subject in any of London's major book shops! However, if you hunt around you will find what you are looking for.

Events leading up to 1926

The great strike was the climax of a series of struggles that began with the strike wave of 1919. This was a time when Lloyd George, the prime minister of the time told the leaders of the TUC, 'In our opinion we are at your mercy'.[1] He was not exaggerating. The working classes of Europe, inspired by the Russian Revolution of 1917, were in revolt and Britain was no exception. The cities of Glasgow and Belfast were paralysed by a general strike. Troops and sailors mutinied and, if that was not bad enough for the government, the police went on strike and organised flying pickets! 'The trade union organisation was the only thing between us and anarchy and, if the trade union organisation was against us the position was helpless', Bonar Law said of the events of 1919.[2] The best account of this movement is Chanie Rosenberg's *1919, Britain on the brink of revolution*. The book not only brings together accounts of all the different strikes, but it also shows how this militancy was dissipated by Lloyd George's clever use of negotiation and intimidation.

Between 1921 and 1922 Britain experienced a number of bitter and protracted sectional struggles. Both the miners and engineers were locked out and forced to take pay cuts. The defeat of the miners was known as Black Friday. However, from 1923 the trade union movement experienced a recovery. There was a halt in the decline of trades union membership and a slight increase in the number of strikes.[3] For an in depth analysis of the changes in the structure of trade unions and disputes of the era, there is no better account than Hugh Armstrong Clegg's *A History of British Trade Unions* (vol 2, 1911-1933). An eventual showdown between the employers and unions was inevitable.

Red Friday

When Tory Stanley Baldwin took office on 29 October 1924, the country faced serious economic problems. The decision of the government to return to the gold standard meant that a major revaluation of sterling had to take place and this put pressure on export industries including coal.

Coal exports fell from 65 million tons a year to 43 million tons and by 1925 the industry was losing £1 million a month. As usual the workers were expected to pay for the crisis. Baldwin summed up the employers' position when he said, 'All workers of this country have got to take a reduction in wages to get this country on its feet'.[4]

The Miners Federation of Great Britain (MFGB) was the largest and strongest union in the country with 800,000 members. Their leader was A J Cook, the most radical trade union leader Britain has produced. The miners were to be the first group of workers to fall under Baldwin's axe. On 30 June 1925 the mine owners announced their intention of ending the National Wages Agreement fixed in 1924. This would have led to the break up of national pay bargaining and to wage cuts. Fearful that the rest of the trade union movement would suffer the same treatment, the TUC responded to massive pressure from ordinary rank and file trade unionists, and agreed to support the miners by placing an embargo on the movement of coal.

Baldwin was forced to back down. He gave a nine month cash subsidy to the mine owners. He also organised a Royal Commission to look into the miners' case (the use of a commission was a tactic adopted by the government again in the 1992 pit crisis). 'It is difficult to express in words the indignation and consternation with which the public has received the government's capitulation to the extreme socialists', *The Daily Mail* worried on Red Friday.[5] Why did Baldwin back down? According to his biography he said, 'We were not ready'.[6] Everybody knew that the 'day of reckoning' had merely been postponed for nine months. The chair of the MFGB, Herbert Smith, said at their annual conference that year, 'We have no need to glorify about a victory. It is only an armistice.'[7] The key to victory was how each side prepared in the coming months.

The General Strike

There are two good accounts of the General Strike itself: *The General Strike 1926* by Christopher Farman and *The General Strike* by Julian Symons. Readers may notice that authors of books on the General Strike do not use much imagination with their titles! Both these books are sympathetic and good factual accounts of the strike. Symons was a novelist and Farman a journalist for the *Sunday Times*. Neither of them have a close connection with the left. However, they both clearly demonstrate the failure of the TUC to prepare for the strike, and how, once it began, the workers rose to the challenge.

The Daily Mail may have believed that the government had rolled over in the face of a united TUC, but in fact Baldwin used his nine months well. He created the Organisation for the Maintenance of Supplies (OMS), a glorified name for a scabbing agency. He enrolled tens of thousands of 'special constables' and imprisoned 12 leading members of the Communist Party of Great Britain. The organisation also put the fear of God into the leaders of the TUC by claiming that the strike would be a threat to the British constitution. The TUC was to spend an inordinate amount of time claiming that it was only a trade dispute. These preparations alone would not have secured victory for the government. United working class action *could* have swept it away, but how did the trade union movement respond?

The following exchange gives some indication. Thomas, leader of the rail workers, asked, 'How are the mine workers going to be saved?' A J Cook replied, 'Working class families, knowing that a strike was inevitable, would be laying secret supplies. My own mother in law has been taking in an extra tin of salmon these past weeks.' Thomas replied, 'Good God, a revolution on a tin of salmon!'[8] It may sound flippant, but for those nine months the TUC did nothing either technically or politically to prepare for the strike. It always hoped that a solution would be found or that it could bluff its way through as it had on Red Friday. The report of the official inquiry decided that miners' wages had to be cut. By 1 May 1926 over 800,000 miners were locked out. Using the pretext of unofficial action by printers on *The Daily Mail* who refused to print an article attacking the miners and calling on the readers of the *Mail* to support 'King and country!'[9] Baldwin ended negotiations with the TUC. The strike began.

The strike begins

A J Cook described workers' reaction to the strike:

> *What a wonderful response! What loyalty!! What solidarity!!! From John O'Groats to Land's End the workers have answered the call to arms to defend us, to defend the brave miner in his fight for a living wage.*[10]

While workers celebrated, the militancy of the response was stronger than the TUC really wanted it to be.[11] The railways were out almost to a man—on the last day of the strike 98.9 percent of engine drivers were out.[12] None of London's tramcars were in operation. There were exceptions to the rule: in places such as Bristol, Grimsby and Chatham an almost normal bus service ran. However, in all the major accounts of the strike, trades council after trades council reported that the strikes in their area were solid. The real problem was not keeping the workers out on strike but keeping those in the second wave in work![13]

Rosa Luxemburg in her pamphlet *The Mass Strike* argues that if vast numbers of workers go into action the movement can become a challenge to both the economic power of capitalism and the political authority of the state. Sadly this did not occur during the General Strike. It was a solid strike but the TUC was able to keep it passive. The TUC encouraged sectionalism by calling groups of workers out in waves. Some key groups, such as post and telecommunication workers, were never going to be called out. This action limited the impact of the strike. Secondly the TUC did nothing to strengthen the strike. It refused to set up workers' defence groups even though picket lines were attacked by police and the government was using the OMS to the best of its ability. It even refused much needed money donated from Russian workers. Finally it tried to depoliticise the strike, as is clearly demonstrated by the instructions given to the strikers in the first edition of the *British Worker*, the TUC's official strike paper:

●*Do all you can to keep everybody smiling—the way to do this is to keep smiling yourself*
●*Do your best to discountenance any ideas of violent or disorderly conduct*
●*Do the thing that is nearest—that will occupy you and will steady your nerves*
●*Do a little to interest and amuse the kiddies now that you have the chance*
●*Do what you can to improve your health, a good walk every day will keep you fit*
●*Do something. Hanging around and swapping rumours is bad in every way.*[14]

However, strikers did not limit themselves to the TUC's instructions. There are two good books that give a real flavour of the activities of the strikers. Firstly there is Robin Page Arnot's *The General Strike May 1926*, an account that chronicles the strike day by day, and includes many relevant contemporary documents. Secondly there is *1926 The General Strike*, edited by Jeffrey Skelley, which contains both regional studies and personal reminiscences of Communist Party of Great Britain (CPGB) activists of the time.

These two accounts smash two important myths: firstly that the strike was passive. Defence committees, such as that in East Fife mentioned above, were set up in many other parts of the country although not on such a large scale as East Fife. Arnot's book describes how each day the number of violent confrontations with the police and scabs increased. Buses were never able to run in Poplar and Bermondsey.[15] In Edinburgh a football pitch was used to impound vehicles that did not have trade union passes[16] and in Leeds a scab bus was halted by strikers who were armed with guns ![17]

The second argument the books demolish is that the strike was being weakened by strikers returning to work. In fact, both government and TUC reports suggest that the strike was getting stronger. A report by the TUC intelligence committee stated, 'There is a small return to work in some outlying areas, this was due to lack of information by the TUC and was easily offset by those joining the strike and industries closed by it'.[18] As the strike entered its second week, key industries were closing down through lack of supplies.

There are, however, real weaknesses with these books. Both authors were members of the CPGB, and although Skelley's book is a collection of essays, the vast majority are written by CP members or fellow travellers. Both give good accounts of the strikes but fail to explain how or why the leaders of the TUC sold out the strike. This is no accident. The CPGB at the time of the General Strike did not want to break politically with the left leaders of the trade union movement.

Most major libraries and many trade union centres have a whole section of pamphlets and handbills dating from the strike which give a valuable insight to events in certain areas. I have seen reports of the General Strike in areas such as Sheffield, St Albans and Southwark. Also worth hunting out are copies of the *British Gazette* (the government's strike paper) and *The British Worker* (the TUC's equivalent). They show clearly who was in control.

The best accounts of the General Strike by far are Tony Cliff and Donny Gluckstein's *Marxism and Trade Union Struggle: The General Strike of 1926* and a short pamphlet by Duncan Hallas and Chris Harman, *Days of Hope—The General Strike of 1926*. Both give a general outline of the events and explain the role of the trade unions and the failure of the left, especially the CPGB, in dealing with the historic events that were occurring. In his collection of essays, 'Where is Britain Going', published under the title *Leon Trotsky on Britain,* Trotsky addresses three arguments. First is the notion that the only political changes in Britain have come through gradual reform. Secondly, he is critical of the role played by both left and right wing trade union leaders, and finally he is critical of the role of both the Russian CP international leadership under Zinoviev and the CPGB. Although Trotsky overestimates the revolutionary situation of Britain at that time and is factually wrong on some aspects (this is due to his lack of information and exaggeration of the situation by revolutionaries in Britain), it is still a brilliant collection of essays that are as relevant today as they were then.

The trade union bureaucracy

For nine days the working class was solidly behind the miners. The strike was not defeated by the strong arm of the state or a lack of determination on the part of the strikers themselves. It was the leaders of the unions who called off the strike without any agreed terms. It was the union leaders who left 800,000 miners to fight on their own for six months and eventually to be starved back to work.

While the mass of workers accepted the leadership of the TUC, the CPGB, instead of challenging this, reinforced the TUC's dominance with their slogan, 'All power to the General Council'. Only one lone voice, that of Leon Trotsky, stood out not only against the right wing of the trade union movement but also against the left wing. Trotsky argued that:

> Both the right wingers and the left wingers, including Purcell and Cook, have the greatest fear of commencing the final action. Even when they verbally admit the inevitability of struggle and revolution they hope in their heart of hearts for some kind of miracle that will deliver them from this prospect. At any rate they will put a brake on the movement, they will evade and wait and see.[19]

Of course revolutionaries would rather see a left wing trade union leader than one from the right, but at the end of the day they *all* behave as a conservative social group scared to unleash the power of the working class. The biggest fear any trade union leader has is that the movement may get out of their control. Charles Dukes of the GMWU explained, 'Every day that the strike proceeded the control and the authority was passing out of the hands of responsible Executives and into the hands of men who had no authority, no control and wrecking the movement from one end to the other'.[20] Although the General Strike did not reach the heights of a revolutionary movement, the mere shadow of revolution was enough to scare them. Ben Turner, a right wing member of the TUC in 1926, wrote to the *Sunday Worker,* a CP influenced paper:

> I don't think you were just to the General Council in dividing us into left and right wingers...the absolute unanimity of the General Council in declaring the General Strike off did not divide us into left wingers and right wingers.[21]

The strike constituted an ultimate test for the left wingers, a test which they all failed—even A J Cook, who was described in a Home Office intelligence report as 'an agitator of the worst kind'.[22] The best introduction to A J Cook is a pamphlet by Paul Foot, named after this comment.[23] The role of A J Cook in the General Strike has reached mythical proportions and he was without doubt the best leader the British trade union movement has had. But the fact remains that throughout the strike, even though he was critical of the leadership of the TUC, he would never go over their heads and argue for rank and file solidarity. Even when the TUC were urging their members to go back to work, leaving the miners isolated, Cook offered no concrete alternative. Cook's brilliant pamphlet *The Nine Days* exposes the role of the General Council in dealing with the government behind the MFGB's back. However, according to P Davis's book, *A J Cook* (part of a series of books on lives of the left), there were at least two occasions when Cook himself had meetings with industrialists without his members' knowledge.

The Nine Days was a time bomb as far as the TUC was concerned. It was published while the miners were still out on strike. The TUC asked Cook to withdraw it for as long as the dispute continued as it would create division in the movement. Cook obliged, giving the TUC the cover they needed. He maintained his illusions in the left wing leaders. His pamphlet ended with the following : 'We hope still that those leaders of the TUC who feel that a mistake has been made will rally to our cause and help us to victory'.[24]

The left parties

There were two main left wing parties during the General Strike. The first was the Labour Party. Although many thousands of its ordinary members threw themselves into the strike, the attitude of its leadership can be summed up by this quote from Beatrice Webb:

> *The General Strike will fail... We have always been against a General Strike ...The failure of the General Strike will be one of the most significant land-marks in the history of the British working class.*[25]

The leader of the Labour Party, Ramsay MacDonald, did everything he could to end the dispute. It was the Labour Party, at the expense of the miners, who benefited when despair of industrial action led workers to look for salvation through the ballot box.

The CPGB was the other main left organisation. Even though the CPGB had only about 5,000 members at the beginning of the strike, its influence far outweighed its size, and, at the time, it was still a revolutionary organisation. No one could deny the bravery of its members. Of the 5,000 workers arrested throughout the strike, 1,200 were members of the CPGB. The problem was not the bravery of its members, but the poor political direction given by their leaders. The CPGB's political weaknesses were twofold. Firstly it was uncritical of the president of the

Communist International, Zinoviev, and slavishly followed his directions (it became even more of a mouthpiece of the Russian leadership when Stalin came to power). Secondly, it failed to provide an alternative to the TUC or at least give a lead to the minority that could challenge the TUC.

There are two books on the role of the CPGB in the General Strike. The first is James Klugmann's *History of the CPGB* (Vol 2, *The General Strike 1925-1926*). This is the official history of the CPGB. It was commissioned in July 1956 and was not produced until 1968.[26] (Readers can draw their own conclusions as to the cause of this delay.) This is a useful book but is uncritical of the role of the party in the strike and gives a crude analysis of the turns it made.[27] These turns were made not in response to the day to day needs of the movement, but at the orders of Russia. The communist parties of the world paid a high price for their unprincipled zig zags at the behest of Russia. It has been said that 'when they were zigging they should have been zagging and when they were zagging they should have been zigging'.

A much more useful book is Brian Pearce and Michael Woodhouse's *A History of Communism in Britain* published by Bookmarks. This gives an accurate picture of Trotsky's criticism of the failure of both the Russian and British communist parties. The introduction by Chris Bambery in the reprinted version is particularly useful.

The end of the strike

The cost of betrayal was immense. A bulletin produced by the Hull strike committee described the situation thus: 'Alarm—Fear—Despair—a victorious army disarmed and handed over to its enemies'.[28] Most employers saw the surrender as a green light to break up union organisation and victimise trade union militants. Yet 24 hours after the strike was called off, 100,000 more workers went on strike, some against management attacks, some believing that the government was lying about the ending of the strike.

Five months after the strike ended, 45,000 rail workers had still not been allowed to return to work. Some unions had to promise not to strike in support of other workers before they were allowed to return to work. The miners paid the highest price; they would be starved back to work six months later. The strike did not have to go down to defeat. *The Daily Herald* summed up the leadership's role when it said, 'We shall never have another revolution for Mr Baldwin has announced that the strike is unconstitutional, and so the TUC packed up and went home.' *The Daily Herald* was wrong on one count. While the actual events of May 1926 will never recur, a situation of social crisis and class struggle will. Understanding the General Strike will help make sure that the movement does not make the same mistakes again.

Notes

1   T Cliff and D Gluckstein, *Marxism and Trade Union Struggle: the General Strike of 1926* (Bookmarks, 1986), p84.
2   C Rosenberg, *1919 Britain on the Brink of Revolution* (Bookmarks, 1987), p36.
3   H A Clegg, *A History of British Trade Unions Since 1889,* Vol 2, 1911-1933 (Clarendon Press, 1985), p568.
4   T Cliff and D Gluckstein, op cit, p129.
5   H A Clegg, op cit, p390.
6   J Symons, *The General Strike* (Cressit Press, 1957), p20.
7   Ibid, p18.
8   C Farman, *The General Strike May 1926* (Rupert Hart Davis, 1972), p50.
9   J Symons, op cit, p34.
10   R Page Arnot, *The General Strike May 1926* (E P Publishing Ltd, 1975), p153.
11   J Symons, op cit, p52.
12   T Cliff and D Gluckstein, op cit, p197.
13   R Page Arnot, op cit, p174.
14   T Cliff and D Gluckstein, op cit, p203.
15   J Symons, op cit, p75.
16   T Cliff and D Gluckstein, op cit, p163.
17   J Symons, op cit, p75.
18   Ibid, p210.
19   TUC General Council Report of Proceedings of a Special Conference of Executives, p58.
20   J Symons, op cit, p211.
21   T Cliff and D Gluckstein, op cit, p246-247.
22   P Davies, *A J Cook* (Lives of the Left) (Manchester University Press, 1987), p260.
23   P Foot, *An Agitator of the Worst Kind* (Bookmarks, 1986).
24   A J Cook, *The Nine Days*, p24.
25   B Webb, *Diaries 1924-1932* (London, 1956) p90.
26   J Klugman, *History of the CPGB,* Vol 2, The General Strike 1925-1926 (Lawrence and Wishart, 1969), p163-164.
27   Ibid, p142.
28   C Farman, op cit, p215.

The following issues of *International Socialism* (second series) are available price £3.00 (including postage) from IS Journal, PO Box 82, London E3 3LH. *International Socialism* 2:58 and 2:65 are available on cassette from the Royal National Institute for the Blind (Peterborough Library Unit), Tel 01733 370777.

International Socialism 2:69 Winter 1995
Lindsey German: The Balkan war: can there be peace? ★ Duncan Blackie: The left and the Balkan war ★ Nicolai Gentchev: The myth of welfare dependency ★ Judy Cox: Wealth , poverty and class in Britain today ★ Peter Morgan: Trade unions and strikes ★ Julie Waterson: The party at its peak ★ Megan Trudell: Living to some purpose ★ Nick Howard: The rise and fall of socialism in one city ★ Andy Durgan: Bookwatch: Civil war and revolution in Spain ★

International Socialism 2:68 Autumn 1995
Ruth Brown: Racism and immigration in Britain ★ John Molyneux: Is Marxism deterministic? ★ Stuart Hood: News from nowhere? ★ Lee Sustar: Communism in the heart of the beast ★ Peter Linebaugh: To the teeth and forehead of our faults ★ George Paizis: Back to the future ★ Phil Marshall: The children of stalinism ★ Paul D'Amato: Bookwatch: 100 years of cinema ★

International Socialism 2:67 Summer 1995
Paul Foot: When will the Blair bubble burst? ★ Chris Harman: From Bernstein to Blair—100 years of revisionism ★ Chris Bambery: Was the Second World War a war for democracy? ★ Chris Nineham: Is the media all powerful? ★ Peter Morgan: How the West was won ★ Charlie Hore: Bookwatch: China since Mao ★

International Socialism 2:66 Spring 1995
Dave Crouch: The crisis in Russia and the rise of the right ★ Phil Gasper: Cruel and unusual punishment: the politics of crime in the United States ★ Alex Callinicos: Backwards to liberalism ★ John Newsinger: Matewan: film and working class struggle ★ John Rees: the light and the dark ★ Judy Cox: how to make the Tories disappear ★ Charlie Hore: Jazz: a reply to the critics ★ Pat Riordan: Bookwatch: Ireland ★

International Socialism 2:65 Special issue
Lindsey German: Frederick Engels: life of a revolutionary ★ John Rees: Engels' Marxism ★ Chris Harman: Engels and the origins of human society ★ Paul McGarr: Engels and natural science ★

International Socialism 2:64 Autumn 1994
Chris Harman: The prophet and the proletariat ★ Kieran Allen: What is changing in Ireland ★ Mike Haynes: The wrong road on Russia ★ Rob Ferguson: Hero and villain ★ Jane Elderton: Suffragette style ★ Chris Nineham: Two faces of modernism ★ Mike Hobart, Dave Harker and Matt Kelly: Three replies to 'Jazz—a people's music?' ★ Charlie Kimber: Bookwatch: South Africa—the struggle continues ★

International Socialism 2:63 Summer 1994
Alex Callinicos: Crisis and class struggle in Europe today ★ Duncan Blackie: The United Nations and the politics of imperialism ★ Brian Manning: The English Revolution and the transition from feudalism to capitalism ★ Lee Sustar: The roots of multi-racial labour unity in the United States ★ Peter Linebaugh: Days of villainy: a reply to two critics ★ Dave Sherry: Trotsky's last, greatest struggle ★ Peter Morgan: Geronimo and the end of the Indian wars ★ Dave Beecham: Ignazio Silone and *Fontamara* ★ Chris Bambery: Bookwatch: understanding fascism ★

International Socialism 2:62 Spring 1994
Sharon Smith: Mistaken identity—or can identity politics liberate the oppressed? ★ Iain Ferguson: Containing the crisis—crime and the Tories ★ John Newsinger: Orwell and the Spanish Revolution ★ Chris Harman: Change at the first millenium ★ Adrian Budd: Nation and empire—Labour's foreign policy 1945-51 ★ Gareth Jenkins: Novel questions ★ Judy Cox: Blake's revolution ★ Derek Howl: Bookwatch: the Russian Revolution ★

International Socialism 2:61 Winter 1994
Lindsey German: Before the flood? ★ John Molyneux: The 'politically correct' controversy ★ David McNally: E P Thompson—class struggle and historical materialism ★ Charlie Hore: Jazz—

a people's music ★ Donny Gluckstein: Revolution and the challenge of labour ★ Charlie Kimber: Bookwatch: the Labour Party in decline ★

International Socialism 2:60 Autumn 1993
Chris Bambery: Euro-fascism: the lessons of the past and present tasks ★ Chris Harman: Where is capitalism going? (part 2) ★ Mike Gonzalez: Chile and the struggle for workers' power ★ Phil Marshall: Bookwatch: Islamic activism in the Middle East ★

International Socialism 2:59 Summer 1993
Ann Rogers: Back to the workhouse ★ Kevin Corr and Andy Brown: The labour aristocracy and the roots of reformism ★ Brian Manning: God, Hill and Marx ★ Henry Maitles: Cutting the wire: a criticial appraisal of Primo Levi ★ Hazel Croft: Bookwatch: women and work ★

International Socialism 2:58 Spring 1993
Chris Harman: Where is capitalism going? (part one) ★ Ruth Brown and Peter Morgan: Politics and the class struggle today: a roundtable discussion ★ Richard Greeman: The return of Comrade Tulayev: Victor Serge and the tragic vision of Stalinism ★ Norah Carlin: A new English revolution ★ John Charlton: Building a new world ★ Colin Barker: A reply to Dave McNally ★

International Socialism 2:57 Winter 1992
Lindsey German: Can there be a revolution in Britain? ★ Mike Haynes: Columbus, the Americas and the rise of capitalism ★ Mike Gonzalez: The myths of Columbus: a history ★ Paul Foot: Poetry and revolution ★ Alex Callinicos: Rhetoric which cannot conceal a bankrupt theory: a reply to Ernest Mandel ★ Charlie Kimber: Capitalism, cruelty and conquest ★ David McNulty: Comments on Colin Barker's review of Thompson's Customs in Common ★

International Socialism 2:56 Autumn 1992
Chris Harman: The Return of the National Question ★ Dave Treece: Why the Earth Summit failed ★ Mike Gonzalez: Can Castro survive? ★ Lee Humber and John Rees: The good old cause—an interview with Christopher Hill ★ Ernest Mandel: The Impasse of Schematic Dogmatism ★

International Socialism 2:55 Summer 1992
Alex Callinicos: Race and class ★ Lee Sustar: Racism and class struggle in the American Civil War era ★ Lindsey German and Peter Morgan: Prospects for socialists—an interview with Tony Cliff ★ Robert Service: Did Lenin lead to Stalin? ★ Samuel Farber: In defence of democratic revolutionary socialism ★ David Finkel: Defending 'October' or sectarian dogmatism? ★ Robin Blackburn: Reply to John Rees ★ John Rees: Dedicated followers of fashion ★ Colin Barker: In praise of custom ★ Sheila McGregor: Revolutionary witness ★

International Socialism 2:54 Spring 1992
Sharon Smith: Twilight of the American dream ★ Mike Haynes: Class and crisis—the transition in eastern Europe ★ Costas Kossis: A miracle without end? Japanese capitalism and the world economy ★ Alex Callinicos: Capitalism and the state system: A reply to Nigel Harris ★ Steven Rose: Do animals have rights? ★ John Charlton: Crime and class in the 18th century ★ John Rees: Revolution, reform and working class culture ★ Chris Harman: Blood simple ★

International Socialism 2:52 Autumn 1991
John Rees: In defence of October ★ Ian Taylor and Julie Waterson: The political crisis in Greece—an interview with Maria Styllou and Panos Garganas ★ Paul McGarr: Mozart, overture to revolution ★ Lee Humber: Class, class consciousness and the English Revolution ★ Derek Howl: The legacy of Hal Draper ★

International Socialism 2:51 Summer 1991
Chris Harman: The state and capitalism today ★ Alex Callinicos: The end of nationalism? ★ Sharon Smith: Feminists for a strong state? ★ Colin Sparks and Sue Cockerill: Goodbye to the Swedish miracle ★ Simon Phillips: The South African Communist Party and the South African working class ★ John Brown: Class conflict and the crisis of feudalism ★

International Socialism 2:49 Winter 1990
Chris Bambery: The decline of the Western Communist Parties ★ Ernest Mandel: A theory which has not withstood the test of time ★ Chris Harman: Criticism which does not withstand the test of logic ★ Derek Howl: The law of value In the USSR ★ Terry Eagleton: Shakespeare and the class struggle ★ Lionel Sims: Rape and pre-state societies ★ Sheila McGregor: A reply to Lionel Sims ★

International Socialism 2:48 Autumn 1990
Lindsey German: The last days of Thatcher ★ John Rees: The new imperialism ★ Neil Davidson and Donny Gluckstein: Nationalism and the class struggle in Scotland ★ Paul McGarr: Order out of chaos ★

International Socialism 2:46 Winter 1989
Chris Harman: The storm breaks ★ Alex Callinicos: Can South Africa be reformed? ★ John Saville: Britain, the Marshall Plan and the Cold War ★ Sue Clegg: Against the stream ★ John Rees: The rising bourgeoisie ★

International Socialism 2:44 Autumn 1989
Charlie Hore: China: Tiananmen Square and after ★ Sue Clegg: Thatcher and the welfare state ★ John Molyneux: *Animal Farm* revisited ★ David Finkel: After Arias, is the revolution over? ★ John Rose: Jews in Poland ★

International Socialism 2:43 Summer 1989 (Reprint—special price £4.50)
Marxism and the Great French Revolution by Paul McGarr and Alex Callinicos

International Socialism 2:42 Spring 1989
Chris Harman: The myth of market socialism ★ Norah Carlin: Roots of gay oppression ★ Duncan Blackie: Revolution in science ★ International Socialism Index ★

International Socialism 2:41 Winter 1988
Polish socialists speak out: Solidarity at the Crossroads ★ Mike Haynes: Nightmares of the market ★ Jack Robertson: Socialists and the unions ★ Andy Strouthous: Are the unions in decline? ★ Richard Bradbury: What is Post-Structuralism? ★ Colin Sparks: George Bernard Shaw ★

International Socialism 2:39 Summer 1988
Chris Harman and Andy Zebrowski: Glasnost, before the storm ★ Chanie Rosenberg: Labour and the fight against fascism ★ Mike Gonzalez: Central America after the Peace Plan ★ Ian Birchall: Raymond Williams ★ Alex Callinicos: Reply to John Rees ★

International Socialism 2:35 Summer 1987
Pete Green: Capitalism and the Thatcher years ★ Alex Callinicos: Imperialism, capitalism and the state today ★ Ian Birchall: Five years of *New Socialist* ★ Callinicos and Wood debate 'Looking for alternatives to reformism' ★ David Widgery replies on 'Beating Time' ★

International Socialism 2:31 Winter 1985
Alex Callinicos: Marxism and revolution In South Africa ★ Tony Cliff: The tragedy of A J Cook ★ Nigel Harris: What to do with London? The strategies of the GLC ★

International Socialism 2:30 Autumn 1985
Gareth Jenkins: Where is the Labour Party heading? ★ David McNally: Debt, inflation and the rate of profit ★ Ian Birchall: The terminal crisis in the British Communist Party ★ replies on Women's oppression and *Marxism Today* ★

International Socialism 2:29 Summer 1985
Special issue on the class struggle and the left in the aftermath of the miners' defeat ★ Tony Cliff: Patterns of mass strike ★ Chris Harman: 1984 and the shape of things to come ★ Alex Callinicos: The politics of *Marxism Today* ★

International Socialism 2:26 Spring 1985
Pete Green: Contradictions of the American boom ★ Colin Sparks: Labour and imperialism ★ Chris Bambery: Marx and Engels and the unions ★ Sue Cockerill: The municipal road to socialism ★ Norah Carlin: Is the family part of the superstructure? ★ Kieran Allen: James Connolly and the 1916 rebellion ★

International Socialism 2:25 Autumn 1984
John Newsinger: Jim Larkin, Syndicalism and the 1913 Dublin Lockout ★ Pete Binns: Revolution and state capitalism in the Third World ★ Colin Sparks: Towards a police state? ★ Dave Lyddon: Demystifying the downturn ★ John Molyneux: Do working class men benefit from women's oppression? ★

International Socialism 2:18 Winter 1983
Donny Gluckstein: Workers' councils in Western Europe ★ Jane Ure Smith: The early Communist press in Britain ★ John Newsinger: The Bolivian Revolution ★ Andy Durgan: Largo Caballero and Spanish socialism ★ M Barker and A Beezer: Scarman and the language of racism ★

International Socialism 2:14 Winter 1981
Chris Harman: The riots of 1981 ★ Dave Beecham: Class struggle under the Tories ★ Tony Cliff: Alexandra Kollontai ★ L James and A Paczuska: Socialism needs feminism ★ reply to Cliff on Zetkin ★ Feminists In the labour movement ★

International Socialism 2:13 Summer 1981
Chris Harman: The crisis last time ★ Tony Cliff: Clara Zetkin ★ Ian Birchall: Left Social Democracy In the French Popular Front ★ Pete Green: Alternative Economic Strategy ★ Tim Potter: The death of Eurocommunism ★

International Socialism 2:12 Spring 1981
Jonathan Neale: The Afghan tragedy ★ Lindsey German: Theories of patriarchy ★ Ray Challinor: McDouall and Physical Force Chartism ★ S Freeman & B Vandesteeg: Unproductive labour ★ Alex Callinicos: Wage labour and capitalism ★ Italian fascism ★ Marx's theory of history ★ Cabral ★

The Socialist Workers Party is one of an international grouping of socialist organisations:

AUSTRALIA: International Socialists, GPO Box 1473N, Melbourne 3001

BELGIUM: Socialisme International, 80 Rue Bois Gotha, 4000 Liège

BRITAIN: Socialist Workers Party, PO Box 82, London E3

CANADA: International Socialists, PO Box 339, Station E, Toronto, Ontario M6H 4E3

CYPRUS: Ergatiki Demokratia, PO Box 7280, Nicosia

DENMARK: Internationale Socialister, Postboks 642, 2200 København N

FRANCE: Socialisme International, BP 189, 75926 Paris Cedex 19

GREECE: Organosi Sosialisliki Epanastasi, c/o Workers Solidarity, PO Box 8161, Athens 100 10

HOLLAND: International Socialists, PO Box 9720, 3506 GR Utrecht

IRELAND: Socialist Workers Party, PO Box 1648, Dublin 8

NEW ZEALAND: International Socialist Organisation, PO Box 6157, Dunedin

NORWAY: Internasjonale Socialisterr, Postboks 5370, Majorstua, 0304 Oslo 3

POLAND: Solidarność Socjalistyczna, PO Box 12, 01-900 Warszawa 118

SOUTH AFRICA: Socialist Workers Organisation, PO Box 18530, Hillbrow 2038, Johannesburg

UNITED STATES: International Socialist Organisation, PO Box 16085, Chicago, Illinois 60616

ZIMBABWE: International Socialists, PO Box 6758, Harare